Interpreting Difficult History at Museums and Historic Sites

T0289471

Julia Rose

ROWMAN & LITTLEFIELD
Lanham • Boulder • New York • London

Published by Rowman & Littlefield
A wholly owned subsidary of The Rowman & Littlefield Publishing Group, Inc.
4501 Forbes Boulevard, Suite 200, Lanham, Maryland 20706
www.rowman.com

Unit A, Whitacre Mews, 26-34 Stannary Street, London SE11 4AB

British Library Cataloguing in Publication Information Available

Library of Congress Cataloging-in-Publication Data
Names: Rose, Julia, author.
Title: Interpreting difficult history at museums and historic sites / By
  Julia Rose.
Description: Lanham, Maryland : Rowman & Littlefield, 2016. | Series:
  Interpreting history | Includes bibliographical references and index.
Identifiers: LCCN 2015049434 (print) | LCCN 2015050358 (ebook) | ISBN
  9780759124363 (cloth : alk. paper) | ISBN 9780759124370 (pbk. : alk.
  paper) | ISBN 9780759124387 (Electronic)
Subjects: LCSH: History—Study and teaching—Psychological aspects. |
  History—Study and teaching—Moral and ethical aspects. | Historical
  museums—Interpretive programs—Moral and ethical aspects. | Historical
  museums—Interpretive programs—Psychological aspects.. | Historic
  sites—Interpretive programs—Moral and ethical aspects. | Historic
  sites—Interpretive programs—Psychological aspects. |
  Museums—Educational aspects.
Classification: LCC D16.25 .R67 2016 (print) | LCC D16.25 (ebook) | DDC
  907.5—dc23
LC record available at http://lccn.loc.gov/2015049434

Printed in the United States of America

In memory of Eric Liban, my father,

who understood the power of kindness and education

Contents

Foreword

What We Risk

Their stories drowned with them when they jumped into the Atlantic Ocean and avoided a life of slavery in the New World. Their stories suffocated with them in gas chambers in Auschwitz-Birkenau. Their stories evaporated with them when a madman in Oklahoma City blew them up. Their stories disintegrated with them when terrorists of a different sort flew planes into the twin towers of the World Trade Center.

These claims of loss might have been made in an earlier era of scholarship, when our leading historians dedicated themselves to producing affirmations of a status quo that said politicians consistently rose above the fray and when the same scholars wrote triumphal narratives that undergird the nation-state averring to the end that the lives of the poor, slaves, women, and the victims of genocide could never be recovered. In the wake of devastating global wars that demonstrated no nation was able to make an unsullied claim to being "civilized," in the wake of international freedom movements that cast a brilliant but unforgiving light on brutalizing representatives of the state, and in the wake of radical transformations of how we interact with technology and thus each other, we find ourselves in a new moment in which we are wrestling with our pasts, our ethics, and our obligations to share our most painful stories with our present and future. This is not easy work. Indeed, it is often profoundly unsettling work.

I am grateful, therefore, that we have this book to help us navigate this uncomfortable space.

In *Interpreting Difficult History at Museums and Historic Sites*, West Baton Rouge Museum director Julia Rose carefully walks us up to, into, and then through the thickets of complications that we encounter when we decide to embrace difficult histories and interpret them for a consuming public. It is daunting, Rose understands, to revisit trauma and to take the incumbent risks that are associated with internment, murder, racism, annihilation, torture, and depraved inequality. Museums exist to tell stories and enlighten, after all. And while they most often are sites of celebration and stand as marvels to humankind's ability to innovate and explore, there is a desperate need to remember that we also possess the ability to do harm.

The simplest of reflections make this much plain:

We celebrate the genteel traditions of the plantation house and the charming cotillions. But who built those houses and crafted those dresses?

We honor those who fought for their motherland or perhaps for an ideology. But what are we to make of those who suffered atrocities or died as a result of the soldiers' patriotism?

We marvel at the technological wonders that provide us comfort or accessibility. But what about the costs of those conveniences?

We treasure symbols of heritage and a noble past. But does one want a heritage that has been secured by the whip, the coffle, or the gallows?

Horrific trauma is not new to the human condition, and a mere glance at today's newspaper headlines makes it safe to assume that large-scale loss, depravity, and tragedy will be familiar to our future selves. But the fact that trauma and pain are familiar to us does not mean that we spend much time thinking critically about these challenging topics. Rose reminds us that we must walk down this stony path, and that the risks of foregoing that journey are real. Here, she joins critical thinkers such as philosopher Avishai Margalit, who, in *The Ethics of Memory*, argued, "The source of the obligation to remember . . . comes from the effort of radical evil forces to undermine morality itself by, among other means, rewriting the past and controlling collective memory."

It is an enormous challenge to be an ethical caretaker of the past and to be responsible in relating all of that past to a public that might not be prepared to learn or, worse, even interested in learning, about a more complicated history. *Interpreting Difficult History at Museums and Historic Sites* identifies the major conceptual and practical hurdles that historians and curators need to cross. Rose does this by relying on the leading thinkers and theorists in many fields—psychoanalysis, literature, history, museum studies, political science—yet her language is never stilted and her ideas are always accessible. She helps us see the critical and moral imperative in cultural critic Walter Benjamin's encouragement to "brush history against the grain," while simultaneously taking us through what she terms "Commemorative Museum Pedagogy." Both the theory (Benjamin's brush) and application (Commemorative Museum Pedagogy) are explained with great lucidity and, with Rose's careful touch, shown to be complementary as they are both committed to the project of helping people understand the ethics of memorialization and memory. Put another way, museum professionals will find here the conceptual rationale to support their desire to interpret difficult histories as well as a practical guide about how to do so.

It is important to understand that committing oneself to interpreting difficult history is, ultimately, a commitment to tell stories of hope and courage, and a determination to engage in a dialog that crosses ideological boundaries. Yes, our pasts are filled with the unfinished stories of those whose lives were cut short for a wide range of horrific reasons, but the human spirit is always buoyed by a powerful faith in the will to remember. Julia Rose encourages us to embrace that faith. I join her.

Jonathan Scott Holloway

Preface

I initially came to the question about how to interpret difficult histories when working in east Tennessee at the Children's Museum of Oak Ridge. In 1992, I curated a commemorative exhibition marking the fiftieth anniversary of the founding of the city of Oak Ridge. Oak Ridge, Tennessee, is one of three secret cities, along with Los Alamos, New Mexico, and Hanford, Washington, where the U.S. government covertly built massive factories and laboratories to develop the first atomic bombs that were eventually used in 1945 to end World War II.

A fundamental challenge to curating the exhibit was aligning the subject matter of World War II atomic weapons with the sensibilities of the museum's young target audience and adults who could remember the events of World War II and those descended from community founders and veterans. The controversy over using atomic weapons, which was initially raised by Albert Einstein and subsequent objectors to nuclear weapons, was another component of the difficult history that the exhibit addressed. The exhibit was called *Difficult Decisions: History of Oak Ridge*.[1]

I felt challenged to develop an interpretation of the difficult history that would both respect the memory of those who sacrificed and served, and also those who suffered. I also needed to address the wide range of anxious responses that I anticipated would come from visitors and also from fellow museum workers. I was beginning to see that I needed to know more about the learning processes that enable us to engage with and learn about histories of violence, suffering, trauma, and loss.

The same issue of understanding how to interpret difficult history arose again during my time as the curator of education at the East Tennessee Historical Society (ETHS) in Knoxville in the mid-1990s. Two well-known traveling exhibits related to the history of American slavery opened in Knoxville. The Smithsonian Institution Traveling Exhibit Service (SITES) exhibit, *Before Freedom Came: African American Life in the Antebellum South, 1790–1865*,[2] opened at ETHS. In the same year, another exhibit, *Back of the Big House: Cultural Landscape of the Plantation*,[3] on loan from the Library of Congress, opened at the University of Tennessee in Knoxville. These exhibits received tremendous visitation, especially from school groups. Then, on the heels of my experience of leading tours for the exhibit *Before Freedom Came* and learning about American slavery while at ETHS, I began to work at a historical plantation called Magnolia Mound Plantation in Baton Rouge, Louisiana.

In my first weeks at Magnolia Mount Plantation in 1999, the director asked me to develop a school tour and program to interpret the recently installed historical slave cabin. Eager to begin work, I asked for the background information and research about the Magnolia Mound Plantation enslaved community that I could use to develop the school tour and program. Ultimately, when I received my director's straightforward response that there was no research about the history of the enslaved people at Magnolia Mound Plantation, I was compelled to better understand the deeper roots of resistance to slavery interpretations from institutions and from individual learners. "How," I wondered, "were museums and workers positioned to fill the demands for interpreting slave life and African American history?" These were among the defining moments on my journey to research how we engage in learning difficult history.

Between 1999 and 2015, I was most fortunate to have access to conduct research at Magnolia Mound Plantation. I am grateful for the administration's support and for the trust and patience extended to me by the Magnolia Mound Plantation volunteer docents and paid tour guides. I was able to document how history workers approached their charge to interpret plantation history, and how they endeavored to learn about the difficult history of slavery. Magnolia Mound Plantation became my laboratory where I was allowed to observe visitors and workers, research and pilot methodologies and historical interpretations, participate in training sessions, and interview staff and volunteers. Over the years, I was a staff member, docent, and board member.

The research at Magnolia Mound Plantation became the basis for Commemorative Museum Pedagogy (CMP), the resulting learning strategy I present in this book for history workers and other museum workers and educators to develop and interpret ethical representations of difficult histories. The strategy includes methods to sensitively engage learners in working through their audiences' anxious moments and resistances to the difficult histories. CMP has also become useful to museum studies students and history workers looking to interpret slavery and other difficult histories and controversial subjects.

On my journey to understanding the pedagogical challenges to teaching and interpreting difficult histories, I have become more aware of how often we are asked to learn traumatic and tough stories. Difficult histories are covered in the news daily, from stories about Nazi looting reparations, genocide in Africa and Asia, wars and the plights of refugees, to civil rights remembrances, slavery's legacy in the United States, to oppressions worldwide. Online blogs and conversations are ongoing as history workers grapple with this question. More often at conferences, workshops, and through publications, I am listening to or reading about the challenges museum workers in multiple disciplines are wrestling with in order to address difficult histories in their work.

Interpreting slave life history continues to dominate my current research. Living in south Louisiana has allowed me to participate in a variety of slave life interpretation and research projects. I documented the enslaved communities from several cotton and sugar plantations for museums and historic sites who were interested in moving beyond the otherwise marginalized and generic representations of the enslaved populations that had been long referred to in their exhibits, historical buildings, and landscapes. Fellow history workers in the region and members of the Louisiana Association of Museums are presently working together to elevate and expand the long marginalized history of slavery, not only from plantation settings. I have had the privilege of volunteering for the American Association for State and Local History, which has afforded me the opportunity of meeting many excellent public historians, museum educators, curators, and students who have shared their ideas and their questions about the risks, benefits, and concerns about interpreting difficult histories.

How "best" to interpret difficult history is a pedagogical question. I have found through my research, while engaged in my doctoral work with faculty and with students while teaching at Louisiana State University and Southern University of New Orleans, that there are even more tools available to the history field that are couched in the field of curriculum theory to better examine historical representations and to better understand the learning processes for difficult histories. I encourage my colleagues in the public history field to also look to curriculum theory to further their work and research about difficult histories.[4]

On my journey, I have been made more and more aware of the breadth of issues and communities that are struggling with discussing and interpreting difficult histories. Through attending and presenting at conferences, leading workshops around the United States and Canada, and teaching courses in museum studies, I can see how important this concern is to history workers who are wrestling with the challenges they face working with difficult histories. The challenge is not restricted to history workers or even to museum workers from other disciplines. Educators and professors in history and science classrooms have discussed with me the controversial, emotional, and resistive responses they face when engaging learners in difficult histories. For example, an American history professor wrote that he will use the methodology in this book in his history classes "because my students often get stuck just where the visitors you describe did (at 'resistance'). Taking them through to reflection and reconsideration is just what I'm supposed to be doing as well."

I have also come to have greater respect for the power of difficult histories. Interpreting difficult histories is far from a benign endeavor. I have received phone calls and letters from worried professional public historians and museum workers who have asked not to be identified in asking for my counsel. They felt their jobs or their reputations were at risk when they were working on difficult history projects for their institutions. They wanted to discuss the pushback and resistance they received from their boards or community stakeholders for developing historical representations of controversial subjects or long-marginalized populations.

We are, indeed, more often facing risks and asking ourselves whose stories do we need to tell and whose stories do our visitors want to learn about. Many history organizations are increasingly recognizing that presenting relevant historical interpretations of difficult histories is one of the "Big Ideas" on the forefront of public history as we continue into the twenty-first century. I believe that public historians' commitment fieldwide is to sensitively address the critics and old guard who find change difficult and the loss of the longstanding meanings hard to let go.

It is my hope that this book can help the public history and museum communities come closer to shaping strategies and tools to take on the hard job of ethically and responsibly telling the tough stories. In the coming chapters, I discuss how difficult histories are commemorative and how they offer learners opportunities to grieve and to make sense of events that can seem unbelievable.

Our efforts are ongoing and will likely take many more decades and many more attempts at crafting representations for interpretations that reach back into the archives to bring forth the stories of afflictions and achievements, of love and hate, of subjugation and of elevation. While difficult histories will never truly be fully written, our understanding of how learners can be guided to engage in learning about the historical oppressions will enable us to more empathetically understand the experiences of the oppressed and suffering today.

What history is not difficult history? I have had the good fortune to be able to work and talk with many professional and volunteer workers, educators, and writers and designers in history, the arts, and sciences who have shared their experiences and thoughts about engaging learners with difficult histories. Many share in the opinion that most histories, if we look at them carefully and critically, contain difficult histories. History is much like peeling an onion. For each layer that we pull away, we find stories that can make us weep, and yet we continue to peel away the layers. In each layer of uncovered history, learners find more and more stories of love and hate. Difficult histories are challenging for learners that include stories and images that are shocking, sad, and reveal wickedness in the world. We can become upset, uncomfortable, and we might weep. Yet we continue to peel away in search of answers, evidence, and stories. We are curious, and we are hungry to better understand the human condition through the process of peeling away at the storied layers, which are filled with meaning and which support how each of us has come to understand the present.

Notes

1. Children's Museum of Oak Ridge, *Difficult Decisions: History of Oak Ridge*, Gallery Guide, Oak Ridge, Tennessee, 1992.
2. Edward D. C. Campbell Jr., ed., with Kym Rice, with essays by Drew Gilpin Faust et al., *Before Freedom Came: African American Life in the Antebellum South, 1790–1865* (Richmond, VA: Museum of the Confederacy and Charlottesville: University of Virginia, 1991).
3. John Michael Vlach, *Back of the Big House: Architecture of the Plantation* (Chapel Hill: University of North Carolina Press, 1993).
4. Julia Rose, "Corroborating Knowledge: Curriculum Theory Can Inform Museum Education Practice," in *From Periphery to Center: Art Museum Education in the 21st Century*, ed. Pat Villeneuve (Reston, VA: National Art Education Association, 2007), 49–57.

Acknowledgments

Interpreting difficult histories will never be easy for me personally, and I sincerely believe that the charge is also hard for my colleagues in museums and history organizations, as well as for teachers in classrooms and for journalists and scholars. Even as parents, we find ourselves grappling with how to explain difficult histories to our children and grandchildren. I thank my husband, Kenny Rose, for encouraging me to pursue my research and to publish my work. Kenny unwearyingly offered advice and served as an editor for all the chapters in this book. His generous commitment of time and his encouragement was what enabled me to drill down into the literature and follow, over many years, practitioners and leaders in the history and education fields in order to assemble a sensitive and workable pedagogy, which became the basis for this book.

I am grateful to my advisors and professors at Louisiana State University for introducing me to the field of curriculum theory during my graduate studies, where I found the resources and ideas to develop the pedagogy I present in this book. In particular, I want to thank Claudia Eppert, Bill Doll, Miles Richardson, Thomas Durant, Tiwanna Simpson, Jay Edwards, Faye Phillips, Michele Masse, and Nina Asher.

I thank the staff and volunteers at the American Association for State and Local History, including Bob Beatty and Russell Lewis, for inviting me to write this book for their history interpretation series. I also thank Bob for the opportunities to initially publish two technical leaflets for *History News* that were the groundwork for two chapters in this book. I thank Charles Harmon at Rowman & Littlefield for his encouragement and advice.

Many colleagues generously gave their time and expertise in shaping the coming chapters, including David Grabitske, Elizabeth Schexnyder, Nancy Gillette, Stephen Small, John House, David Floyd, Kristin Gallas, Gwen Edwards, Sally Yerkovich, Tommy McMorris, Aaron Sheehan-Dean, Brenda Perkins, Caroline Kennedy, and John Sykes. I thank them for their stimulating conversations, reviews of chapter drafts, and for identifying significant historical resources.

I thank John Holloway for writing the foreword, and for critically writing about the Louisiana historical landscape in ways that are helping to bridge the history and public history fields to work on the ethical task of brushing history against the grain in order to rethink how we recall the history of American slavery at historical sites and museums.

I extend my deep gratitude to the staff, volunteers, and board at Magnolia Mound Plantation for opening, for over a decade, their historical site to me for the purpose of researching how learners grapple with difficult history.

Finally, in addition to my husband, I want to acknowledge my children, Ian, Jason, and Diana, and my parents, Felicia and Eric. Throughout my career, they have been my motivation to seek ways to explain difficult histories, often in response to our mutual search for the fragments of our family's stories from World War II and our struggle to tell our stories to younger generations.

CHAPTER 1

Difficult Knowledge

History That Is Too Much to Bear

Introduction: Touched by Difficult Histories

THE TOUR of seventeen third-grade students was going smoothly that morning at Magnolia Mound Plantation in Baton Rouge, Louisiana, in 2000. I had finished leading the tour group through the early nineteenth-century sugar plantation big house, and I had just led the group one hundred yards across the historical plantation grounds to the slave cabin on exhibit. I gathered my group on the front porch, where we stood before entering the two-room cypress cabin. I explained to the group of nine-year-old African American students and their teacher that two families once lived in this small cabin, one family per room. The cabin was brought to this museum from Cherie Quarters in Pointe Coupee Parish, where once cotton and sugarcane were the dominant cash crops cultivated by slaves. The cabin room that we were about to enter was once the home of a family of slaves that likely included a father, mother, two or three children, and possibly a grandmother or another relative. My group was attentive and followed me through the left door. Inside, I gathered the group in front of the open hearth to talk about foodways from the slave quarters in the 1830s. The children were looking at the dimly lit room furnished with a rope bed, a three-legged stool, a work table, a basket with cotton cards, and a cast iron kettle.

The teacher politely asked me if she could have her students' attention. I obliged as she quietly asked her students to gather in a circle in the center of the one-room household. The children wore uniforms. The girls were dressed in gray and maroon plaid jumpers with coordinating cardigans, and the boys wore matching ties with white shirts. The emblem on their uniforms identified the Catholic parochial school in New Orleans that they attended.

The teacher, in a whispered voice, asked the children to join her in prayer. They held hands at first and then knelt in prayer on the bare wood plank floor. The teacher spoke of the importance of this historical space and asked for strength, blessings, understanding, and goodness. The children joined her appropriately as I stood to the side of the room, feeling at once in communion with the group and as a witness to a special moment in the children's lives. As they prayed and listened to their teacher, the children were learning about how to make historical connections to their lives. The teacher was demonstrating to her young students how history was real, personal, and available to them as a tool for living. I was moved. I was enlightened by this moment.

Walking on the grassy courtyard in Vienna in front of an outdoor stage, where Hitler stood seventy years prior to proclaim his leadership of Nazi terror, I felt ill. I began to imagine the sounds of cheering crowds and blaring speeches in German. It was 2008. I was distracted from my tour guide's descriptions of the historical site. I stopped listening. I was lost in my thoughts, recollecting black-and-white photographs of Nazi Germany and the death camps. I was growing emotional, and I needed to express my anger. I wanted to spit on the manicured lawn that tourists stood upon. I wanted to insult the memory of the Third Reich. However, I decided I could not risk insulting my hosts and the tour guide. My timid outburst was a far cry from what I really wanted to do. Instead, I discretely spit into my hand and bent down and wiped the quarter-size saliva droplet onto the grass at my feet and then said a prayer for the forgotten, the murdered, and the survivors of Nazi terror. This was a personal moment that was deeply meaningful to me, and until this writing, it was private. I only share this significant personal demonstration of grief to illustrate to my readers that I felt a connection to this historic space and that I felt compelled to respond. I was moved by the learning experience of being in the historic environment to condemn the horror that the space represented to me.

The curator at the National Hansen's Disease Museum in Carville, Louisiana, explained that the museum is about a difficult medical history. Hansen's disease still carries the terrible antisocial stigma of leprosy. The progressive disease causes damage to the peripheral nerves, and patients suffer from the insensitivity that often leads to deformity. Nodules and lesions are often visible on the skin. Patients who were quarantined to Carville shared the experience of exile from family, community, and the rest of the world. The sample of patients' stories told in the museum, from the thousands of patients who once lived there, include accounts of personal losses. Patients often took false identities to protect their families. Other families disowned patients. The disease inflicted pain, suffering, blindness, deformities, and immobility on patients. Doctors and courts sentenced over five thousand patients suffering from the dreaded disease to live out their lives as quarantined patients at the "leper colony." Most families of the afflicted patients were ashamed of their relatives' fate and never told younger generations about their families' secrets. Repercussions from the forced quarantine are still felt today by former patients, their families, and their descendants. The museum is a testament to the legacy of criminalizing the victims of a misunderstood disease.

The museum hosts an average of two thousand visitors a year, including school groups. The tour of the museum includes displays about the illness, a history of treatments and medical research, the social life that evolved in the isolated community of patients and staff, and a sample of stories about suffering, medicine, defiance, and community building that took place here. The curator explains that some visitors come to tour the museum not

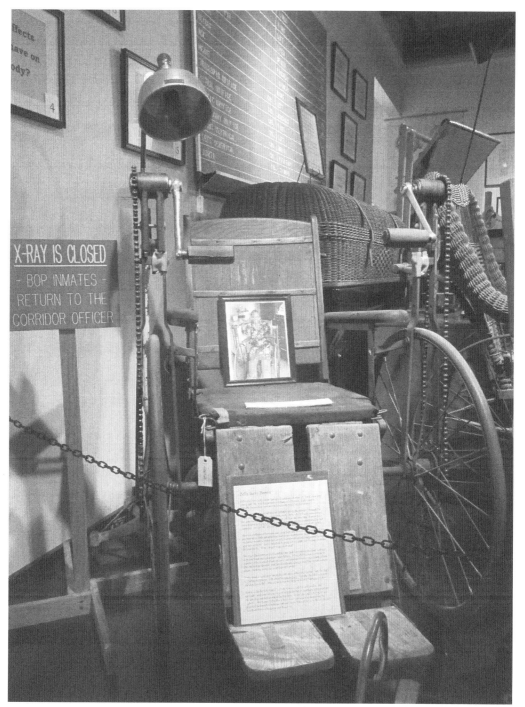

Patient's wheelchair next to an X-ray department sign that refers to "inmates." National Hansen's Disease Museum, Carville, Louisiana. Photograph by author.

knowing about the disease or of the concept of a leprosarium. Visitors can have emotional and extreme reactions to the history. Some visitors leave immediately, like the ten-year-old home-schooled boy who defiantly yelled to his classmates before exiting the museum building, "I just can't stay in here!" His class returned two years later for a second field trip, and the same student had the same reaction, saying he could not bear to learn about the disease or about the people who suffered.

These three anecdotes about museum experiences with three very different histories work to illustrate some of the key characteristics of interpretation that are distinctive to difficult histories. First, difficult histories serve as tools that are necessary for living and make us more self-aware by contributing to collective memory, identity making, commemoration, grieving, nation building, empathy, and trials for social justice and human rights. Second, difficult histories describe memories of pain, suffering, oppression, and grief that are emotive, thereby inciting anxiety, resistance, and stress for their audiences. Third, difficult histories can provide us with opportunities to learn about the formation of historical and current social structures. The current movement to interpret difficult histories, including the increased efforts of history organizations to uncover histories that had been traditionally marginalized or silenced, is a positive signal that the larger society recognizes that the histories of the oppressed, underprivileged, and minority populations matter. The movement to interpret difficult histories shows the good work history can do for society and for the improvement of lives globally.

Road Map to the Chapters

In this chapter, chapter 1, I look at the rising global demands on history organizations, including museums and historical sites, to interpret difficult histories. I discuss these increasing demands that have been embraced by many history workers seeking to use difficult history, for example, for commemorations, social justice education, and to advocate for civil and human rights. I also discuss how history organizations have been trending toward expanding their work from collecting and preserving to educating and supporting community issues. They are increasingly using their collections and historical sites to advocate for social change. In taking up the difficult histories that recall tragedy and suffering, I identify some of the challenges and obstacles to interpreting difficult history. History workers who are confronted with the difficult histories are finding that the stories are tough to tell and are recollections that can incite learners' resistances and can spur controversies in their communities. And yet, history workers are finding the difficult histories have important stories to tell.

In chapter 2, I describe the distinguishing characteristics of difficult histories as a unique genre of history and discuss some of the risks and benefits difficult history present to history workers and to visitors. Then, I discuss some of the compelling reasons why history workers take on the challenges and face the risks of interpreting difficult histories. I explore how difficult history interpretations can serve as tools for grieving, advocating, commemorating, and improving society. By considering the defining characteristics, risks, and benefits that are connected to difficult histories, readers will find in the subsequent chapters how necessary it is to use sensitive and ethical methods to represent and interpret the difficult histories. Readers will more readily understand the roles grief and empathy play in interpreting histories.

In chapter 3, I introduce Commemorative Museum Pedagogy (CMP), an approach to interpreting difficult histories that takes into account the learners' responses to the difficult histories and that allows for history workers to sensitively develop historical representations of the oppressed, victimized, and subjugated individuals and groups. This chapter describes the theoretical framework for CMP, which I call the 5Rs, for engaging learners in learning about difficult histories. I briefly present the underlying psychoanalytic concepts to explain how learners work through their resistances to difficult history and proceed nonlinearly through the five learning phases of difficult knowledge,[1] the 5Rs: reception, resistance, repetition, reflection, and reconsideration. I explain each of these five learning phases, and then provide examples and indicators for history workers to use in recognizing learners' progress in grappling with the difficult histories.

In chapter 4, I introduce, as part of the CMP approach to developing ethical representations of difficult histories, three building blocks. The three building blocks are conceptual components called the Face, the Real, and the Narrative, and when assembled, the ethical representations produce historical empathy in learners. I explain the basis for each of the three building blocks and offer examples and techniques on how to develop and use each component. Representations of difficult histories built with the three building blocks have the capacity to help learners (visitors and history workers) to shape their moral sensibilities and envision ways that they can take action to justly respond to the historical suffering in the present.

In chapter 5, I use an actual case study of history workers who grappled with the difficult history of plantation slavery.[2] Their challenge was to expand the historical interpretation of the historical site, Magnolia Mound Plantation in Baton Rouge, Louisiana, to increase and elevate the representations of slave life on their tours. The case study includes a ten-year followup review to critically consider the longer-term challenges to interpreting difficult histories. I provide descriptions of the specific types of learners' resistances that emerged from my study and that are common to history workers who were focused on learning and interpreting slavery history. Their experience led to the development and formalization of CMP and provides history workers with a valuable example of how expanding slavery history, and other difficult histories, can radically change the iconic meanings of well-established historical sites.

In chapter 6, I explain how CMP has five elements that are needed to develop and deliver interpretations of difficult histories. The five elements are 1) recognizing a history as a difficult history, 2) allowing for the dynamics of the 5Rs to unfold, 3) using the three building blocks to develop ethical representations, 4) providing safe and respectful environments in which learners can engage in learning difficult histories, and 5) making the institutional and individual commitments to responsibly interpret difficult history. I offer a discussion about how using CMP effectively will help sustain a sensitive and reflective culture within the history organizations. I close with a discussion about how especially pertinent our collective pursuit is to interpret difficult histories. My closing discussion was written just when the national news headlines were reporting the heated debates about the role and public presence of Confederate flags and Confederate statues. I discuss how this event illustrates well the need for CMP to interpret difficult histories and the important role history workers have to interpret difficult histories today and for the future.

Interpreting Difficult History Raises Challenges

History matters. Most often, without consciously thinking about it, we live historically. Our personal and political identities are woven from our lived experiences and are intimately tied to the historical experiences of our ancestors. Our geopolitical and cultural affiliations are informed by the history we accept and believe to be authentic. Our decisions on how we live within societies as families, communities, and nations are organized and informed by the past. Freud and Nietzsche remind us that remembering and forgetting both play important roles in the lives of individuals, communities, and cultures. Reading history, learning history, writing history, and even reflecting on history, difficult or otherwise, can trigger powerful reactions because we know that history matters, that it can be urgent, and that it is necessary for living as persons.

However, difficult histories in museums and historic sites can raise intense emotions and incite visitors' resistances to engaging in learning about a painful history. Many visitors resist or refuse to look at the displays, read the labels, or listen to a tour guide. They look away, leave, or talk about the discomfort that the exhibit causes them. History workers, the group of workers that includes a wide variety of paid and volunteer museum personnel and public historians, can also often be tentative or resistant to interpreting difficult histories. Reticent history workers often explain that they feel that the work brings risks of offending or hurting visitors' sensibilities. It is to the phenomenon of emotional and intellectual resistance to learning difficult history that I frame CMP.

Interpretations of difficult histories inevitably include the cultural and psychological components of identity at the personal, communal, national, and global levels. For history workers, the tasks of assembling representations and crafting interpretations for difficult histories are both personal and political. Learning from the historical interpretations is also personal and political for visitors and other audiences, be they students, visitors, scholars, history workers, or members of other audience groups. CMP asks history workers to recognize that all audiences of difficult history interpretations are positioned as learners who must grapple with the shocking and distressing content. As learners, history workers and visitors become more than recipients of information; they are learners who need to be allowed to express their individual forms of resistance. Their resistances are, in fact, natural responses and can be part of a productive learning experience. Learners' expressions of angst and discomfort begs history workers to responsibly help these learners work through their feelings of resistance in the process of engaging in the newly introduced history and in making the difficult history meaningful. Through this recognition, history workers can more effectively and sensitively address the extraordinary challenges of interpreting difficult history.

Public history venues, including museums and historical sites, take on the tremendous responsibilities of selecting and justly remembering people, places, and events that were set in motion by historical ideologies and decisions that most learners can only imagine, and never really know. History museums and historical sites that develop learning experiences about difficult histories use the surviving fragments of history and pieces of collective memories to shape narratives to show how the history is relevant today. The process of interpreting difficult histories culminates in commemorative presentations that are instructive and meaningful, while filled with unresolved tensions that represent the proud, the conflicted, and the complex realities that call history workers to "do" history.

Public memorials, historical sites, and history museums are steeped in educational commitments for now and for perpetuity, and yet they face immense challenges to sustain visitors and history workers in learning about the difficult histories. For every history of bravery, accomplishment, and pride, one can find related stories of oppression, violence, trauma, pain, and shame. Much of human history is not easy to recall. Both pride and pain are woven into recollections and remembrances that incite anxiety and resistances to facing the representations of the oppressive, violent, and painful episodes in history. Historic sites and history museums that are dedicated to commemorating difficult histories, or include representations of difficult historical experiences, face pronounced challenges to interpreting the histories. History workers at those sites must address how visitors (and fellow workers) likely find the difficult histories uncomfortable, shocking, and hard to learn. For some individuals, groups, and communities, it is easier to forget and "move on" than it is to remember and do the work of finding lessons and relevant meanings from the historic atrocities. Avoiding difficult histories, however, means missing learning opportunities that are otherwise ethically responsible, inclusive, and enlightening.

Histories of genocide, enslavement, and war, for example, are difficult histories because these events of gross human injustices go against our moral understanding of what it means to be part of civilized society. Historian James Oliver Horton calls our national memory of American slavery, for example, "the tough stuff" of history, and he calls for public historians to take the risk of engaging in "an uncomfortable national dialogue."[3] Philosopher Susan Sontag explains that fear can overwhelm viewers who are tasked with looking at images of violence.[4] So many emotions can arise from listening to and looking at representations of difficult histories, including fear, guilt, sympathy, empathy, disgust, and even melancholia. History workers' and visitors' resistances and angst in confronting and learning about difficult histories make the job of developing interpretations for exhibits, tours, and public programs especially challenging, intimidating, and at times untenable. But when historical interpretations engage learners in ways that illuminate how the difficult history is significant, learners are encouraged to rearrange their understandings and responses to oppression and injustices, attesting that the suffering is indeed meaningful in the present.

Current Trends Call for Elevated Interpretations of Difficult Histories

Social Justice Education Is a Good Thing

Museums and historical sites, since the last quarter of the past century, have increasingly recognized their social responsibilities as educational institutions and, more recently, are placing stronger emphasis on museums' relevance to social issues. These museums serve as advocates for social justice and responsible citizenship. "Fueled by both financial and ethical necessity, museum workers internationally are boldly proclaiming a critical role for museums in facilitating social inclusion, and their power as agents of change."[5] History workers' decisions to use their historical institutions to stimulate change for the betterment of mankind focus on the difficult histories embedded in their collections, landscapes, and buildings.

Social justice is based on the ideas of equality and equal opportunities in society. According to Matthew Robinson, social justice exists when "all people share a common humanity and therefore have a right to equitable treatment, support for their human rights, and a fair allocation of community resources."[6] Social justice ensures against discrimination and people's welfare being constrained on the basis of their gender, sexuality, religion, race, or other aspects of their background or group affiliations. John Rawls posits a theory of social justice commonly referred to as "justice as fairness." In this theory, social justice is about ensuring the protection of equal access to liberties, rights, and opportunities, as well as taking care of the least advantaged members of society.[7]

Museums and historical sites are emerging as social agents that can take on social responsibilities that go beyond collecting and preserving materials. They have the ability to positively influence and affect society.[8] Such a claim to social agency propels museums and historical sites into a wider and more urgent educational role of advocating for social justice. Sandell argues, "Museums can contribute to the combating of the causes and the amelioration of the symptoms of social inequality and disadvantage at three levels: with individuals, specific communities and wider society."[9]

Interpreting difficult histories is more than preserving and representing histories of human suffering. Interpretations of difficult histories can also be considered actions for social justice that are grounded in educational values to better understand social ills. Difficult histories recollected for public consumption, while painful and laden with risks of upsetting or offending audiences, are increasingly appearing in museums and historical sites around the globe. Educational philosophers Jennifer Bonnell and Roger I. Simon observe that over the last thirty years museums around the world have shown an increased willingness to take on what is often characterized as difficult subject matter.[10] Paul H. Williams observes that more memorial museums have opened since the turn of the twenty-first century than in the past one hundred years.[11]

The increasing emphasis on social justice education has prompted public historians to reflect on the dramatic shift to focus on difficult history within their field. Editor Randolph Bergstrom for the journal *The Public Historian* assembled an issue focused on the field's movement to interpret difficult histories.[12] A popular journal for museum workers, *Curator*, has dedicated several issues in recent years to difficult history exhibits and interpretations, including the 2012 issues titled "Remembering and Disremembering in Africa, also Australia, Turkey, Mexico, New York, Prague" and "Special Issue on Museums and International Human Rights."[13] The journal for the National Association for Museum Exhibition, *Exhibitionist*, has also dedicated issues to exhibiting and interpreting difficult history, including issues titled "The Unexhibitable" and "Museums, Memorials, and Sites of Conscience."[14] Candace Matelic, the 2013 keynote speaker at the Association of Nova Scotia Museums conference on Museums and Community Engagement, explained that museums with strong community engagement are institutions that robustly interpret difficult knowledge.[15] Richard Sandell, a leader in the social justice museum movement in the United Kingdom, contends that museums "are undeniably implicated in the dynamics of (in)equality and the power relations between different groups through their role in constructing and disseminating dominant social narratives."[16]

Well-known examples of contested interpretations about difficult histories include the *Enola Gay* exhibition at the Smithsonian Institution from 1995 to 1998[17] and aspects of the first-person slave life interpretations at Colonial Williamsburg Foundation in the 1980s and 1990s.[18] The *Enola Gay* exhibition was timed to mark the fiftieth anniversary of the dropping of the first atomic bombs, which concluded the World War II American conflict with Japan in 1945. The history workers at the Smithsonian Institution initially chose to frame the interpretation through an interpretive lens of the bombing victims to tell an otherwise familiar American heroic historical narrative about the role of the first dropping of atom bombs. The historical interpretation for the exhibit also addressed the amoral effects of nuclear war, which raised heated public and political debates among Congress, the Smithsonian Institution Board of Regents, veterans groups, and the public. The first-person slave life interpretations at Colonial Williamsburg Foundation in Virginia in the 1980s and the 1990s attempted to represent the oppressions of slavery. The interpretation included a slave auction, which was radically different than what many visitors had previously experienced at historical sites representing colonial life and slavery. The reenacted representations of the atrocity of human trafficking and enslavement disrupted the otherwise harmonious perception of the eighteenth-century colony and raised tensions among the site staff, visitors, and the general public.

A museum in Buenos Aires, Argentina, opened in 2007 to remember the victims of Argentina's "Dirty War." The museum reminds Argentinians and global visitors that the historical narrative about the Dirty War is still being written and that the books on the war cannot yet be closed. The museum exhibit is called *Space for the Memory, Promotion, and Defense of Human Rights* and is dedicated to commemorate those who were kidnapped and disappeared under the late twentieth-century dictatorship. The museum is located at the site of the former Navy Mechanical School, which was one of several death camps where people were tortured and killed. A few years before the museum opened, Paul H. Williams wrote that some people in Argentina preferred not to settle the memory of the Dirty War, while many others wanted to let the healing come to an end in order to forget the horrors and the losses. The country continues to wrestle with the losses and suffering caused by the Dirty War that took place under the military junta that held power in Argentina from 1976 to 1983.[19] The museums that are encumbered in controversy, like the examples from Argentina, Virginia, and Washington, D.C., can force history workers, stakeholders, and leaders to take a stance on which voices are chosen to be heard from history and to decide on the degree of detail and candor that their communities can bear in facing the past.

Museums today more profoundly recognize their responsibilities to use their collections, intellectual authority, and educational missions to address present-day social injustices and painful histories. Consider the influential exhibition *From Field to Factory: Afro-American Migration 1915–1940* developed by Spencer Crew at the National Museum of American History at the Smithsonian Institution in 1987. This landmark exhibition interpreted the Great Migration of African Americans from the sharecropping plantation South to the workers' struggles in the unionizing factories in the North. Crew's interpretation inspired many history workers to use their collections to recall social history through the stories of strife and struggle. The increase in historical representations of conflicts, pain, and oppression in museums has been growing in tandem with the museum field's growing willingness to address the difficult histories that can be confrontational and disruptive to present-day visitors and communities.

Workers in the public history field are more reflectively asking how and why the field is increasingly delving into difficult histories. Despite the increase of exhibitions and programs about mass violence and oppressive events, visitors' struggles and resistances to learning about these difficult histories continue to be challenging. The rationales that history workers provide for presenting difficult histories can be contradictory and controversial. Bergstrom observes, "As the assertive reclamation of troubling pasts has charged historians with presenting these pasts to the public, their horror and continuing consequence have made these histories as difficult to exhibit as they are important."[20] Given their cultural authority, history workers are charged with the responsibility to select the stories from the contested terrain of difficult histories.

Globalization Emboldens Difficult Histories

Histories of mass violence, trauma, and oppression matter even more as shifts in global demographics and economic powers are being rearranged through globalization, which is redefining minority populations and their political influence. The seismic shifts are increasing public demands and interest in remembering oppressed populations and subjugated histories. Museums and public history venues are more critically looking at their educational role to address difficult histories, in part, as a way to keep their institutions truly relevant to the communities they serve and to the larger society. As a result, an important role is growing for the thousands of history workers in large and small history organizations to respond to this increasing trend to uncover and represent the difficult histories.

In the American Alliance of Museums' magazine, *Museum*, James Cuno explains that the American Academy of Arts and Sciences stresses the essential roles the humanities and the social sciences play in American society and urges continued support of these endeavors at all levels of government.[21] The report argues, "We live in an increasingly global world. Being educated about one's own country or culture is not enough today. One must be curious and knowledgeable about the world. . . . In the globalized, polyglot, multiethnic world in which we daily confront our many differences, understanding and tolerance of difference is of the greatest importance. Museums, as humanist institutions, can contribute mightily to this."[22]

Exhibits on different continents are connecting world citizens through relevant issues and revelations about histories of war, violence, and oppression. For example, the exhibition *No Name Fever: AIDS in the Age of Globalization* was held from 2004 to 2006 at the Museum of World Culture in Gothenburg, Sweden. The museum emphasized the interdependencies and connections that ran across geographic boundaries in order to address controversial global topics. According to Bonnell and Simon, the exhibit included a photo essay by Gideon Mendel documenting individuals' experiences with the rising number of funerals in South Africa. Bonnell offers her personal response to one of the photographs included in the photo essay that deeply moved her. The photograph was an award-winning image titled "Coffin with Red Ribbons." It showed the coffin of a fifteen-year-old victim, Khanyisa Eugenia, being lowered into her grave. Bonnell says,

I felt overwhelmed by anger and sadness, by a sense of grief that was for a moment my grief. At the same time, I felt the distance of viewing this moment in time that was past now, the glass panel over the image reminding me of the giant chasm that separated her experience from mine, standing in the comfort of a museum exhibition in Sweden. I wrestled then, as I do now, with how to come to grips with the enormity of loss in this community, and with Khanyisa's courage in covering herself, even in death, with symbols of the fight against AIDS in a country where the disease is so stigmatized. . . . In thinking about her today I feel like I am nurturing the memory of my encounter with her, or traces of her, and by doing so I am trying to come to grips with my role and my responsibilities, as a witness.[23]

Indeed, the increasing rise of globalization has helped to spur international concern for present-day populations that are suffering. Museums and historical sites are emerging as significant advocates for learning about human suffering, social issues and ideologies, and the historical backgrounds that have enabled the injustices to persist.

The political outcomes and human losses of World War I and World War II, combined with the rise of electronic mass communications, have helped to drive the trend to recall and commemorate difficult histories worldwide. The global evolution of social justice education through interpreting difficult histories has emerged definitively over the past thirty years. Culture critic Andreas Huyssen explains,

If the 1980s were the decade of a happy postmodern pluralism, the 1990s seemed to be haunted by trauma as the dark underside of neoliberal triumphalism. The concern with trauma radiated out from a multinational, ever more ubiquitous Holocaust discourse. It was energized, in the United States as in Latin America or South Africa after apartheid, by the intense interest in witness and survivor testimonies, and it merged with the discourses, about AIDS, slavery, family violence, child abuse, recovered memory syndrome, and so on. The privileging of trauma formed a thick discursive network with those other master-signifiers of the 1990s, the abject and the uncanny, all of which have to do with repression, specters, and a present repetitively haunted by the past.[24]

The demand for historical representations of difficult histories and commemorative sites from around the world continues to mount. People want to know. Huyssen observes, "The desire for narratives of the past, for re-creations, re-readings, reproductions seems boundless at every level of our culture . . . but the seduction of the archive and its trove of stories of human achievement and suffering has never been greater."[25]

Consider the sites of historical traumas in New York where the World Trade Center towers once stood and the location where the Berlin Wall once stood in Germany. Both examples of commemorative sites illustrate how tangibly the memories of difficult histories have emerged today as major cultural effects of globalization. The mounting movement to memorialize and make knowable the difficult histories that connect the United States to the larger global community is, in large part, an educational outcome of globalization that elevates and exposes the consequences of human suffering.

Recovered from the demolished Berlin Wall, Germany, this original watchtower is open for visitors at the Newseum in Washington, D.C., to enter and view. Photograph by author.

A Humanist Museum Movement

David Fleming, chairman of the Federation of International Human Rights Museums and the director of the International Slavery Museum in Liverpool in the United Kingdom, observed that history museums have discovered that since their push to be more focused on education in the 1970s and 1980s, ultimately, the public positively responds to exhibits and programs that tackle human rights issues.[26] As the consummate museologist Stephen E. Weil explained in 2000, we have witnessed a metamorphosis of museums during the second half of the twentieth century. Museums have transformed from institutions that were primarily turned inward and concerned chiefly with the preservation and study of their collections into institutions that are turned predominantly outward and whose stated intent is to provide a service to the public.[27] The compelling humanist movement in the museum field that evolved as early as the 1970s continues to strengthen and includes projects to interpret difficult histories.

An overriding thematic thread among many exhibitions about difficult histories worldwide is the plethora of stories of common people who are identified historically and who are represented within the spatial and social parameters of horrific events. Museums have become more humanist as they become more tied to social justice education. In Brazil in 2013, for example, an exhibition opened at the University of Sao Paulo titled *Emancipation, Inclusion and Exclusion*, which was a photographic examination of the human condition of slaves and slavery in Brazil in the 1880s. The representations of the enslaved workers' faces transformed the once wet tears of the slaves into present-day pathos helping visitors and history workers make connections that can be so painful to recall that the oppressive experiences of slavery are nearly indescribable, yet are deeply felt. Fleming makes a call to museum workers worldwide to find ways for museums to break the silence on the past and to make human rights violations visible, and "to be as powerful as we can be as agents for change."[28]

The momentum for humanist interpretations from within the academic history field has also helped to propel the rise of exhibitions and programs about difficult histories in museums and historical sites. Over the past three decades, a vast array of difficult histories have been more often pulled from the margins of the historical canon to be featured in scholarly publications, museums, and at historical sites. The rise of social history, which started in earnest in the 1950s, has been slowly migrating into the American social consciousness and finding accepted, and yet provocative, places in history organizations. Rising interest in the history of civil rights, for example, has elevated the recognition of many common people, local activists, and grassroots organizations that participated in the American civil rights movement. In turn, such recognition and commemorative projects encourage deeper reflection about the localized sociohistorical context of the era and the institutionally supported oppressions that sustained the social injustices entrenched in American society.

The general realization that museum sustainability is largely dependent on the relevance of their exhibitions to museums' diverse audiences has contributed to the increase in exhibitions about subjugated histories. While the museums' internal drivers have expanded from collecting to collecting and educating, museum audiences have also transitioned. The broader makeup of museum audiences has encouraged museums to interpret more histories of minority communities and histories long pushed to the margins. Museums are more often serving audiences interested in the diversity of human survival. Susan Sontag observed, "A stepped-up recognition of the monstrousness of the slave system that once existed, unquestioned by most in the United States, is a national project of recent decades that many Euro-Americans feel some tug of obligation to join. This ongoing project is a great achievement, a benchmark of civic virtue."[29] The postmodern ethos of self-reflection and the ubiquitous social consciousness–raising of the latter half of the twentieth century have greatly contributed to museum audiences' interest in learning about difficult histories. This has led to the growth of archives and collections reflecting oppressed, subjugated, minority, and everyday people. As a result, museums, historical sites, and history organizations are responding to their visitors' growing interest in difficult histories.

Increasing Memorialization

Paul Williams and Kenneth E. Foote observe how our modern desire to commemorate historical traumas has the power to generate monuments and museums.[30] That desire focuses our search for meaning and reasons for the losses and suffering, and generates passionate endeavors to commemorate, remember, and honor the dead and the oppressed. The resulting monuments and museums help draw attention to the tragic events and turn the remembrances into lessons that can validate those memories as part of history. Spontaneous memorials are erected hours and days after tragedy strikes, as seen at the elementary school in 2012 in Newtown, Connecticut, where a shooter entered Sandy Hook Elementary and killed twenty-six people. Similar spontaneous memorials were observed at the perimeters of tragedies, such as the fence memorials surrounding the bombing site at the Murrah Federal Building in Oklahoma City in 1995 and the area called Ground Zero in lower Manhattan where the World Trade Center was destroyed by terrorist attacks in 2001. Williams uses the word *memorial* to describe the remembrance of a person or event, *memorial museum* to describe a museum dedicated to a historic event commemorating mass suffering of some kind, and *memorial site* as a physical location that serves a commemorative function.[31] Williams explains that the rise of memorial museums since the end of World War II has produced an expectation that ordinary and often conflicted attitudes toward struggles can be materially represented.

Geographer Kenneth E. Foote observes that it was only during the mid- to late nineteenth century that Americans began to look back on their history with a view toward formal commemoration.[32] The swell to memorialize landscapes and buildings where tragedies and injustices happened has unlocked self-protective social and psychological barriers to discussing and representing violence, not just contemporary violence, but episodes from the past as well. Of all the sites in America that Foote has studied, he believes those relating to Native American and African American history may be the most important to monitor over the next several decades.[33] These changes are impressive given the invisibility of such commemorative sites as recently as the 1980s. Foote predicts that the growing number of difficult history sites, sites he terms *shadowed ground*, can provide common ground for efforts toward reconciliation of political factions and serve as rallying points for change.[34] Foote also predicts the next wave of scarred landscapes that will be interpreted for social good will be the unmarked battlefields and war zones.[35] Battlefields and war zones are filled with competing meanings between histories of valor and achievements and histories of loss and aggression.

Foote explains that people tend to rally around common goals and shared losses as a way to organize for social action and civic betterment. It is possible that the work to remember the tragedies can help cement community bonds and inspire allegiances around shared traditions and common visions of history. Marking sites of tragedies seems like a natural response for a grieving community. The creation of memorials honors the victims and helps the community to mourn. However, most sites go unmarked, and only those events that touched a relatively homogeneous, self-identified community that views the tragedy as a common public loss will come together and invest in commemorative acts. Members of such communities often share a sense of identity based on civic pride, or ethnic or religious affiliations or occupations.

Such places for war remembrances contain parallel messages about accomplishments and idealistic desires, while simultaneously commemorating virtuous behavior and acknowledging human losses. History workers must consider how sites of war and mass violence reflect widely ranging attitudes toward violence and tragedy and society's work toward peace. History workers and visitors are tempted to look for single messages and unequivocal answers that the sites can somehow represent. The interpretations of the difficult histories, however, can mix together the stories and lessons about tolerance and intolerance, of violence and oppression, acceptance and rejection, and pride and shame. Some learners feel pride for particular events and shame in others, and at other times, some learners prefer not to confront the issues.

Consider sites of violence, massacres, and wars on American soil that are now popular historical parks and memorials, including Harper's Ferry in Virginia, where John Brown and his followers made their attack on slavery and where the largest surrender of federal troops during the Civil War took place. The histories at such sites are closely bound to underlying social tensions and political competition over meaning.[36] Stories of bravery and treason are mixed together, as are the human dramas of death and survival. Many of these historical sites are among the most powerful national symbols for Americans and engender a sense of community and shared sacrifices made by many groups in contemporary society.[37] The "enshrinement" of these sites asks history workers and visitors to contend with the meanings of the past in ways that they might wish to avoid. Many sites of tragedies are conflicted or provide contradictory historical interpretations of how events were traditionally told. Sites of tragedies can evoke such extreme feelings of shame or emotional pain for some learners that they continue to be too difficult to address.

Communities and cultures have many ways to sustain their collective memories and beliefs, including ritual and oral traditions, landscapes, literature, art, and monuments. Retrospection is a tool for memory as much as it is a tool for writing history. The movement to commemorate tragedies also creates traditions and writes histories that are consistent with the scripting communities' beliefs and expectations. These conceived traditions and stories develop as the historical details are sifted through and the stories are repeated. Over time, only certain key memories are singled out and remembered generations later.

Memorialization as a form of cultural expression in the latter part of the twentieth century has proliferated in ways that more emphatically focus on the individuals who suffered from unjust and violent events, such as the victims at the Oklahoma City bombing in 1995. Edward Linenthal explains, "[T]he bombing occurred at a time when memorialization had become a significant form of cultural expression. Much more than a gesture of remembrance, memorialization was a way to stake one's claim to visible presence in the culture."[38] In addition, events of human suffering are gaining a new kind of public attention through mass media and social media. The new attention has allowed millions of people to bear witness, and in some cases in real time, to the plights, violence, and oppression.

The focus on individual suffering in the context of mass violence and oppression is seeding a cultural shift on how society remembers tragedies. Edward Linenthal observes, "We have moved from a desire to see loved ones memorialized in stone to a larger vision of what a memorial is and what it does. We moved from unfocused emotion to reflection on what it means to us, and from 'what do I do' to 'what do we want to give as a gift to the world.'"[39] The shift is breaking down memories of group identifications to a culture that values the ethical representations of persons who have suffered and allows for multiple interpretations of what the tragedy means historically, socially, and pedagogically.

On April 19, 1995, the Murrah Federal Building in Oklahoma City was bombed, killing 168 men, women, and children and injuring at least 680 more. It was the most destructive act of terrorism committed in the United States until the September 11 attacks of 2001. The tragedy is remembered as the Oklahoma City bombing, and today the 3.3-acre site is home to the Oklahoma City National Memorial & Museum, a place that honors the memory of the victims, survivors, and rescue workers, and promotes peace education. The mission of the memorial and museum reflects the growing trend to interpret difficult history through the stories of the people who died, suffered, and witnessed the events. The mission reads, "We come here to remember those who were killed, those who survived and those changed forever. May all who leave here know the impact of violence. May this memorial offer comfort, strength, peace, hope and serenity." The mission statement was developed soon after the tragedy by a 350-member commission who used the statement to guide the interpretation and the design of the memorial and museum. The statement is a remarkable document that represents the Oklahoma City community's consensus, which was brought together under extremely stressful circumstances.

In Edward Linenthal's 2001 study of the creation of the Oklahoma City National Memorial & Museum, he found "contending memorial visions" quickly surfaced in the process of deciding on "how to remember and commemorate the victims and survivors and the events surrounding the horrific losses."[40] Oklahoma City's experience helps to demonstrate the shift in how we remember. Remembering mass traumas has broadened to allow multiple memories of the past, conflicted or uncomplicated, to exist side by side. The realization that the perpetrators of the malicious bombing were Americans "resurrected alternative histories and paid attention to violent values and events that were understood to be as defining of the American experience as were the virtues revealed in the rescue and recovery efforts in Oklahoma City."[41]

In fact, Linenthal demands that we should not let any one narrative be "the story" because the differing perspectives offer valuable and significant memories of what happened, who was impacted, and what the tragedy means to many different people. The realization that the multiple perspectives on the tragedy were all valid interpretations of the tragic events led the National Memorial Foundation to broaden their mission by writing it to

Former site of the Murrah Federal Building is the location of the Oklahoma City National Memorial & Museum, Oklahoma City, Oklahoma. Photograph courtesy of the Library of Congress.

be more inclusive when they planned the museum and memorial park. The impact of the violence, damages, deaths, and injuries meant different things to the many planners as they were as diverse as the citizens grieving around the nation.[42]

Difficult Histories Can Rattle Longstanding Collective Memories

The increasing trend of interpreting difficult histories disrupts long-held collective memories. The disruption to collective memories can be in turn difficult for learners to understand or accept, particularly when learners are asked to consider new historical perspectives from often long-silenced historical voices.

Collective memory, according to Maurice Halbwachs, is a socially constructed notion that draws strength from a coherent body of people.[43] There are as many collective memories as there are groups in a society. Social classes, families, associations, and armies all have distinctive memories that their members have constructed, typically over long periods of time. Individuals do the remembering, and those located in a specific group draw on that group context to remember and re-create representations of the past. Collective memory needs to be repeated. In repetition, memories are conflated, as they are continually being revised. Over time, individual memories coalesce into conformed images that sustain collective memories.[44] Collective memory is bound up to the extent that our respective relationships, commitments, and promises of a shared past are, to some degree, mutually constitutive.[45] The tears and pain of even momentarily losing one's ties to the past-one-knows are strong enough to generate feelings of loss, a traumatic event that could evoke refusals and resistances from individuals tasked with learning new historical information.

When museums present an alternative viewpoint or a revised interpretation of a patently accepted story of how "it" happened, learners can be challenged to accept the new knowledge. Alternative viewpoints and revised interpretations can disrupt learners' long-accepted understandings of a history that was taught in school, for example, and can change how individuals understand their connections to a history, thereby disrupting the learners' identities. Changing how histories are told and revealing long-forgotten or silenced stories can rattle the collective memories learners have relied on, making learners anxious and even fearful.

The rising trend and demands to interpret difficult histories has serious consequences on the reshaping of collective memories. Huyssen explains that while formerly the historical past was used to give coherence and legitimacy to family, community, and nation, as described by Eric Hobsbawm as the "invention of tradition,"[46] those formerly stable links have weakened today. National traditions and historical pasts are increasingly deprived of their geographic and political groundings, which are being reorganized through the processes of cultural globalization.[47] Collective memories can both challenge or enforce our understandings of difficult histories. It depends on who is doing the telling and who is listening.

Barbie Zelizer explains that collective memories implicitly value forgetting and remembering.[48] Collective memories value the kind of remembering that reflects the choices we have made in deciding what no longer matters. Collective memories are unpredictable, and they are not necessarily stable, linear, rational, or logical.[49] The important point is not how accurately a recollection represents some past reality, but why historical actors and their descendants constructed their memories in a particular way at a particular time. The embodiment of memory can rouse controversy, both politically and personally.

Andreas Huyssen doubts the current relevance of Halbwach's mid-twentieth-century approach to collective memory that depended on the relatively stable formations of social group memories. The older sociological notion of collective memory might no longer be adequate to grasp the current dynamics of the media, the immediacy of communication, and globalization. "The clashing and ever more fragmented memory politics of specific social and ethnic groups raises the question whether forms of collective consensual memory are even still possible today, and if not, whether and in what form social and cultural cohesion can be guaranteed with them."[50] From this perspective about memory, remembering is a cultural artifact that has emerged as a force for living, a force that works against forgetting. Sigmund Freud, the father of psychoanalysis, has taught us that memory and forgetting are inextricably linked. The current fervor to remember is made that much more difficult when many of the histories of tragedies and suffering are buried, subjugated, marginalized, or repressed. Difficult histories are made challenging by the learners' resistances to facing the pain of others, and the task to represent difficult histories is made more complicated by the political and emotional pushes to avoid them.

Pierre Nora investigates the history of memory through an extensive study of French history and collective memory. Nora explains that collective memory informs history, while history seeks to describe "true memory."[51] It is fair to reason then that interpreting history in museums and historical sites remains an essential component of the power of memory discourse. Huyssen explains, "After all, the act of remembering is always in and of the present, while its referent is of the past and thus absent. Inevitably, every act of memory carries with it a dimension of betrayal, forgetting, and absence."[52]

Collective memory can work toward or against a just society. Collective memories are learned, inherited, and functional. While racism, for instance, is an inherited evil from previous generations, patriotism can also be inherited but is an attribute that is valued by nations. Collective memories inform history workers' decisions to select particular representations in order to interpret difficult histories. History workers' experiences within their families, communities, and nations, in turn, shape their inclinations and decisions about how to interpret histories for exhibitions and programs. Consequently, how history workers interpret particular histories can influence how visitors will understand societal functions and morality.

Interpreting Difficult Histories Is a Pedagogical Challenge

What role do museums and historical sites play in shaping our personal and political relationships relative to society? Social institutions including schools, churches, temples, and governments strive in varying ways to promote and teach civil rights, moral behavior, citizenship, and social justice values. Museums and historical sites attempt to move visitors to live more consciously by raising visitors' awareness of their relationships and responsibilities to others from the past and in the present. Sandell explains that museums' social responsibilities lie within the interplay of social inequality and cultural authority.[53] Museum interpretations of difficult histories are valuable pedagogical strategies to address social justice education, to advocate for human rights, and to serve as memorials and commemorations. By exposing and elevating the stories of the oppressed and the victimized, difficult histories in museums and historical sites become tools for advocacy, civility, and education.

Interpreting difficult histories in museums and at historical sites is a compelling job. It is an important job laden with responsibilities that reach beyond the walls and fences of those history organizations. Commemoration of difficult histories is an act of collective instruction to render the remains of tragedies and the memories of survivors into meaningful and productive teachings. Because remembering is an ethical act, history workers are accountable to those remembered. Remembering can be overwhelming. Understandably, history workers can feel discouraged or even stymied by the awesome and painful challenge to resurrect the stories of suffering. And yet the high interest and relevance of difficult histories to today's audiences are encouraging more and more history workers to consider ways to interpret difficult and marginalized histories.

Eresh Naidu, program director for Africa, Asia, the Middle East, and North Africa of the International Committee of Sites of Conscience, considers the good that comes from interpreting difficult histories. "Are mass graves, burial grounds, and memorial sites merely the markers of all that is wrong in our world? Or can these sites of death, mourning and ending actually give life, fostering new beginnings and rebirth?"[54] Naidu's provocative question implores history workers to explore the possibilities for goodwill work and for expanding the meanings and lessons of difficult histories. The promise of commemorations, of new beginnings, can emerge from the effects of remembering and teaching. In this way, difficult histories are rich in opportunities to inspire and influence a large and diverse audience to live more consciously and to be more aware and prepared to contribute to unlimited opportunities for social improvement.

A "just remembrance"[55] does more than honor the memory of the oppressed. Interpretations of difficult histories help visitors to understand the significance of the historical suffering and how that can be translated into good citizenship and productive empathy today. Interpretations about difficult histories serve as remembrances and are instructive. Interpretations can be positioned as warnings against future violence, and they can offer support to those who are mourning losses. Interpretations of difficult histories are pragmatic encounters with history, making the history practical and political in the moment and for the future. Naidu concludes that Rwandans want a memorial to tell their story to the international community through the voices of survivors because there are more stories to be told and many more oppressive events to be exposed to the world.[56]

Museums are self-regulating institutions that can use interpretations of difficult histories to promote critical thinking and to provide forums for social improvement, community engagement, and education. The authority invested in historical sites and museums, and their ownership of the materials that authenticate that authority, are some of the ingredients available to history workers for civic good. Lois Silverman explains, "Despite successful programs in which museums are playing key roles in their communities, institution-wide commitment to museums as agents for social change is not yet the norm. . . . What is clearly needed now is a critical grasp of the knowledge and competencies required to 'walk the talk' of the changing vision."[57] A persistent challenge in the public history field is to convince resistant history workers to take on the challenges and to commit to interpreting difficult histories, histories that can be hard to tackle.

Over the centuries and around the globe, communities and institutions have marginalized and silenced select histories. Sometimes the histories of the defeated factions in war and at other times populations that were oppressed and subjugated were not formally recorded. Such deferments put the task of researching and facing the painful knowledge of the historical suffering onto later generations to represent. Much scholarly research is still needed to interpret many of these difficult histories. Due to the long tradition of silencing, dismissing, and avoiding painful and oppressive histories, the respective artifacts and archives are sparse and memories are faded or fading. The revelations and findings that have yet to be done still hold great potential for commemorating, mourning, teaching, and for advocating for change.

The resistance and discomfort that can be experienced by history workers and visitors confronted with learning difficult histories needs to be addressed in order to "walk the talk," and to bring more difficult histories in from the margins in order to use those histories for civic good. Nightingale and Sandell stated, "There can be no equality of opportunity if difference is not understood, taken account of, valued and harnessed."[58] There is more to the assumption that if public history venues present exhibits and programs about difficult histories in ways that are emotionally engaging and elicit empathy, then those histories will enrich the visitors' consideration of civic life.[59] The call is out for more in-depth discussions from the public history field about the demands difficult history interpretations ask of learners. What can history organizations expect from learners' engagement, and to what capacity are learners able to engage in learning about difficult histories? How, when, and why are such demands pedagogically productive?

Commemorative Museum Pedagogy

This book presents CMP, a sensitive and responsible interpretation strategy for visitors and history workers to engage in learning about difficult histories. The pedagogical challenge is to develop history learning experiences that support learners in their moments of resistance. CMP provides a method for history workers and visitors to grapple with their resistances. This learning method specifically recognizes that difficult history likely startles, upsets, or even implicates visitors and history workers who are being asked to acknowledge and come to terms with painful content. History workers need to respectfully challenge the hegemonic recollections that are supported by the standing collective memories and the long-held traditions of interpretations that can buffer visitors from the difficulties in learning histories of violence, tragedy, and oppression. History workers need to thoughtfully assist their visitors toward making productive and meaningful connections to the difficult histories. History workers can use CMP to assist visitors to overcome their ambivalence and emotional distress, and to support their colleagues who are impacted by the discomfort of the difficult histories they are charged with interpreting. A key challenge to interpreting difficult histories is to sustain visitors' and history workers' engagement in learning by addressing their resistances.

Two pedagogical paths shape the work of interpreting difficult histories and the experience of engaging in difficult histories—cognitive learning and emotional learning. CMP was developed to enable history workers, from board members and directors to curators and frontline tour guides, to interpret difficult histories given the extraordinary challenges of engaging learners with content that can be shocking and uncomfortable, and yet compelling, meaningful, and useful.

One key to interpreting difficult histories, according to CMP, is my readers' willingness to recognize and accept that visitors and history workers are both learners. By recognizing that difficult histories can be hard for just about anyone to grasp who encounters sites, images, stories, and artifacts about suffering, we can begin to consider the cognitive and emotional learning enveloped around recollections of pain and suffering.

CMP addresses both history workers' tentative responses to interpreting difficult histories and visitors' resistances to engaging in learning about difficult histories. Consider how history workers are learners who must first grapple with their personal resistances to the difficult histories and then must imagine how their visitors might respond to the difficult histories. At first glance, history workers' resistive responses might be viewed as biased or even insensitive reactions, but consider how history workers must make the decision to take on the risks and challenges of developing interpretations for difficult histories. Sandell and Nightingale observe, "Museum work to interpret difficult history is emotionally demanding work with opportunities for insensitivity, embarrassment and failings of insight."[60] Hence, the movement to address difficult histories in public history venues is, in part, also cautionary and measured due to history workers' resistances to working with the difficult histories. History workers are also positioned as pedagogues who not only consider their own fears, angst, and feelings of risk but must also consider the risks of inflicting discomfort on their visitors. Finding the confidence and courage to interpret difficult histories is an opportunity for history workers to practice diversity, social justice education, and human rights advocacy in the spirit of goodwill and as expressions of solidarity with the human condition. Ironically, the history workers' and visitors' fears and anxieties are simultaneously restrained by the emerging trend for increased representations of difficult histories in museums and historical sites. It is this paradox of individual resistance to the otherwise much-desired difficult history interpretations that is addressed by CMP.

Notes

1. Julia Rose, "Rethinking Representations of Slave Life at Historical Plantation Museums: Towards a Commemorative Museum Pedagogy" (PhD diss., Louisiana State University, 2006).
2. Ibid.
3. James Oliver Horton and Lois E. Horton, ed., *Slavery and Public History: The Tough Stuff of American Memory* (New York: The New Press, 2006).
4. Susan Sontag, *Regarding the Pain of Others* (New York: Farrar, Straus and Giroux, 2003).
5. Lois Silverman, "The Therapeutic Potential of Museums as Pathways of Inclusion," in *Museums, Society, Inequality*, ed. Richard Sandell (London: Routledge, 2002), 69.
6. Matthew Robinson, "What Is Social Justice?" *Appalachian State University*, March 3, 2014, http://gjs.appstate.edu/social-justice-and-human-rights/what-social-justice.

7. John Rawls, *Justice as Fairness: A Restatement*, ed. Erin Kelly (Cambridge, MA: Harvard College, 2003).

8. Richard Sandell, ed., *Museums, Society, Inequality* (London: Routledge, 2002), 3.

9. Ibid., 4.

10. Jennifer Bonnell and Roger I. Simon, "'Difficult Exhibitions' and Intimate Encounters," *Museums and Society* 5, no. 2 (2007): 65.

11. Paul H. Williams, *Memorial Museums: The Global Rush to Commemorate Atrocities* (New York: Berg, 2007).

12. Randolph Bergstrom, "Tough Telling," *The Public Historian* 35, no. 3 (2013): 5–7.

13. Zahava Doering, ed., "Remembering and Disremembering in Africa, also Australia, Turkey, Mexico, New York, Prague," *Curator* 55, no. 2 (2012) and "Special Issue on Museums and International Human Rights," *Curator* 55, no. 3 (2012).

14. Gretchen Jennings, ed., "The Unexhibitable," *Exhibitionist* 27, no. 2 (2008); and Gretchen Jennings, ed., "Museums, Memorials, and Sites of Conscience," *Exhibitionist* 30, no. 2 (2011).

15. Candace Tangorra Matelic, "Museums and Community Engagement," keynote address at the Annual Meeting for the Association of Nova Scotia Museums, Canada, September 19, 2013.

16. Sandell, *Museums, Society, Inequality*, 8.

17. Kyo Maclear, *Beclouded Visions: Hiroshima-Nagasaki and the Art of Witness* (Albany: State University of New York Press, Albany, 1999).

18. Christy Coleman Matthews, "Twenty Years Interpreting African American History: A Colonial Williamsburg Revolution," *History News* 54, no. 2 (1999): 6–11.

19. Williams, *Memorial Museums*, 109.

20. Bergstrom, "Tough Telling," 5.

21. James Cuno, "What Matters Most: Museums Play a Crucial Role as Humanist Institutions," *Museum* 92, no. 6 (2013): 27–29.

22. Ibid., 28.

23. Bonnell and Simon, "'Difficult Exhibitions' and Intimate Encounters," 80.

24. Andreas Huyssen, *Present Pasts: Urban Palimpsests and the Politics of Memory* (Redwood City, CA: Stanford University Press, 2003), 8.

25. Ibid., 5.

26. David Fleming, "Human Rights Museums: An Overview," *Curator* 55, no. 3 (2002): 251–56.

27. See Joanne Hirsch and Lois Silverman, ed., *Transforming Practice* (Walnut Creek, CA: Left Coast Press, 2006).

28. Fleming, "Human Rights Museums," 251.

29. Sontag, *Regarding the Pain of Others*, 93.

30. See Williams in Kenneth E. Foote, *Shadowed Ground: America's Landscapes of Violence and Tragedy* (Austin: University of Texas Press, 2003).

31. Williams, *Memorial Museums*, 8.

32. Foote, *Shadowed Ground*, 50.

33. Ibid., 332.

34. Ibid., 353.

35. Ibid., 354.

36. Ibid., 284.

37. Ibid., 292.

38. Edward Linenthal, *The Unfinished Bombing: Oklahoma City in American Memory* (New York: Oxford University Press, 2001), 4.

39. Ibid., 229.
40. Linenthal, *The Unfinished Bombing*.
41. Ibid., 21.
42. Ibid., 185.
43. Maurice Halbwachs, *Maurice Halbwachs on Collective Memory*, ed. & trans. Lewis A. Coser (Chicago: University of Chicago Press, 1992).
44. Patrick H. Hutton, *History as an Art of Memory* (Hanover, NH: University Press of New England, 1993), 7.
45. Richard Terdiman, *Present Past: Modernity and the Memory of Crisis* (Ithaca, NY: Cornell University Press, 1993).
46. Eric Hobsbawm and Terence Ranger, ed., *The Invention of Tradition* (UK: Cambridge University Press, 1992).
47. Huyssen, *Present Pasts*, 4.
48. Barbie Zelizer, *Remembering to Forget: Holocaust Memory through the Camera's Eye* (Chicago: University of Chicago Press, 1998).
49. See James Wertsch, "Epistemological Issues about Objects," in *Perspectives on Object-Centered Learning in Museums*, ed. Scott G. Paris (Mahwah, NJ: Lawrence Erlbaum, 2002), 113–18.
50. Huyssen, *Present Pasts*, 17.
51. Pierre Nora, "Between Memory and History: *Les Lieux de Mémoire*," in *History and Memory in African-American Culture*, ed. Geneviéve Fabre and Robert O'Meally (New York: Oxford University Press, 1996), 4.
52. Huyssen, *Present Pasts*, 3.
53. Sandell, *Museums, Society, Inequality*.
54. Eresh Naidu, "Endings, and Beginnings," *International Coalition of Sites of Conscience*, July 25, 2013, http://www.sitesofconscience.org/category/featured-african-network/.
55. Claudia Eppert, "Entertaining History: (Un)Heroic Identifications, Apt Pupils, and an Ethical Imagination," *New German Critique* 86 (Spring/Summer 2002): 71–101.
56. Naidu, "Endings, and Beginnings."
57. Silverman, "The Therapeutic Potential of Museums as Pathways of Inclusion," 70.
58. Eithne Nightingale and Richard Sandell, introduction to *Museums, Equality and Social Justice*, ed. Richard Sandell and Eithne Nightingale (London: Routledge, 2012), 3.
59. See Bonnell and Simon, "'Difficult Exhibitions' and Intimate Encounters."
60. Nightingale and Sandell, introduction to *Museums, Equality and Social Justice*, xxi.

Defining Difficult History

Risks, Reasons, and Tools

Introduction

MANY MUSEUM workers and public historians are asking how we can overcome the observable resistances and challenges to interpreting histories of oppression, violence, and trauma, a genre of history known as difficult history. This is a central concern to thousands of workers at museums and historical sites who are presently wrestling with developing equitable practices to serve increasingly broad and diverse audiences. The histories can be stories of tragedies, suffering, and injustices. They are woven through with layers of emotion and tangled with eternally unresolved questions about what actually occurred, about right and wrong, about choices and fate. Difficult histories are both challenged by and shaped by the instability of memories and the ebb and flow of testimonials, which rest on the reality that traumatic histories can never be fully known.

The histories of the victors often overshadow the histories of the oppressed, the marginalized, and the underclasses by burying the subjugated stories further away into memory. The artifacts and the archives are not saved or appreciated, and they become more scarce over time as historical actors and their descendants discard objects and memories of tragedies, allowing younger generations to forget the stories these items hold. The work of uncovering, expanding, and elevating the long-silenced, forgotten, and painful histories requires history workers to readdress mainstream histories. The newly introduced difficult histories often conflict with or blur present generations' understandings of particular pasts or present generations' moral understandings of daily life.

The disruption to visitors' understandings of moral behavior and the changes to the longstanding collective memories of how the histories happened are often, and with some predictability, met with skepticism, challenges, denials, and emotional resistance from many visitors and history workers. The shocking and unpleasant images and stories that describe difficult histories can easily elevate political and personal tensions and raise anxiety for individual visitors and history workers. Interpretations of difficult histories require the representations and the delivery of the interpretations to be sensitive, ethical, and responsible.

Certainly, history workers want to avoid upsetting visitors and still present difficult histories honestly, accurately, and fully. Key challenges to interpreting difficult histories are devising the best methods to sustain visitors' interest and attention throughout difficult history programs and exhibits, and addressing visitors' emotional responses to the histories. The possibility of some visitors' resisting the difficult histories must be taken into consideration. While visitors are expected to flinch at the shocking content on display, pedagogical strategies are needed to sensitively support visitors in listening, reading, viewing, and contemplating the difficult history presented. How, then, do history workers respond and support visitors who are upset and resistant to engaging in learning about a difficult history?

This book is written for history workers (including museum workers and public historians) who are charged with interpreting difficult histories. The task to interpret difficult history cannot be taken lightly, especially when committed professionals recognize the risks of unintentionally disrespecting the memory of individuals or groups, or of offending or upsetting visitors.

Interpreting difficult history in a museum exhibition, a restored historical house, or on a battlefield, a few of many examples, are acts of remembrance. Acts of remembrance in museums and at historical sites can pose potential conflicts when history workers decide whose perspective to use to see the past. Whose stories do museums tell, and whose voices do the telling? These are ethical questions that are both political and personal for history workers, their institutions, and their supporting communities. The recalled voices of the historical actors who have suffered might be unfamiliar or upsetting to learners, which can disrupt learners' understandings of a moral world, making history that much more difficult for visitors to learn.

In their effort to develop historical interpretations, history workers are charged with finding and selecting persuasive evidence to demonstrate why particular histories matter today. By design, museums and historical sites are self-regulated. They accept and use their privilege to interpret history, a privilege that grants history workers power to determine how history is recalled and to explain how that history is significant. However, in order to implement best practices, history workers must also acknowledge and recognize their responsibility to ethically, productively, and purposefully interpret difficult history. Determining the "how and why" a difficult history is selected to be represented in a museum or historical site, for example, are foundational steps to bringing a difficult history to the public's attention. While difficult histories are useful, they are also filled with inherent risks. While difficult histories can serve as tools for advocacy, new paths forward, remembrances, grieving, apologies, education, and commemoration, on one hand, the interpretations of difficult histories can also be disruptive, upsetting, shocking, and even painful, on the other hand.

Two often emphatically used phrases in history museums and historical sites to justify exhibits about violence, trauma, and oppression are good starting points to look closely at the "how and why" we interpret difficult histories. The two phrases are "Never forget!" and

"Never let that happen again!" These expressive phrases are cries for memory to be pedagogical. They are calls for lessons to be learned from tragedies. They are calls for commemorations and calls for articulating moral responses to human suffering. Humanist Susan Sontag describes U.S. Civil War photographer Alexander Gardner's response to his images of the dead and dying soldiers on the bloody battlefields. He said, "Here are the dreadful details! Let them aid in preventing such another calamity from falling upon the nation."[1] Gardner's imperative, like the command from survivors and witnesses of so many tragedies to "never forget!" the human suffering of the many historical events, is framed by ethics, education, and hope. They are words asking future generations to remember in order to improve society. They are words of hope embedded with the emotions of sadness, indignation, fear, and grief, and filled with the loss that we feel in the present while viewing traces of death and oppression in historical photographs and artifacts. Like Gardner, many history workers and visitors today are thinking earnestly about how future generations can learn through representations of difficult histories.

History workers are hopeful that the suffering being remembered through commemorative exhibits and memorials offer teachable moments fostering new understandings of what humankind is capable of doing and how present generations can be uplifted through an ethical response for a more just society. History workers use courage when they interpret difficult histories by taking the risks of feeling sadness and emotional loss. History workers use courage to face their fear of upsetting the public or offending the memory of historical populations.

In order to engage learners in sustained involvement in exhibits and programs about a difficult history, history workers need to anticipate, respect, and respond to visitors' possible resistances to the difficult history. Difficult histories are indeed rendered difficult by the challenges faced by history workers to engage visitors in stories that are upsetting and even painful to learn. For example, shame and the self-conscious realities of the underclasses and downtrodden are memories and stories some descendants wish away. A white senior citizen tourist from New Jersey visiting historical plantations in Baton Rouge in 2006 discussed with her tour guide whether she wanted to see the "ugly past" of slavery or only view the well-appointed planter's mansion. An African American parent chaperoning her child's field trip that included a stop inside a slave cabin exhibit in Port Allen, Louisiana, in 2010 told the children in her charge that they did not want to view that exhibit and should enjoy the playground nearby instead. Holocaust child survivor Felicia Liban explained that living in poverty as a refugee after immigrating to the United States in 1948 felt shameful. It was not until she visited the U.S. National Holocaust Memorial Museum in Washington, D.C., in 2001 that Mrs. Liban felt validated that indeed her life story was important and that she was connected to world history in an important way.

Chapter 2 Road Map

In the following section, I offer a definition and description of difficult histories in order to highlight some of the more poignant characteristics of this important genre of history. In the third section, I highlight some of the risks that can discourage history workers from tackling difficult histories. Considering some of the defining characteristics and risks that are germane to difficult histories will later help readers to address sensitive and ethical methods to represent difficult histories and more deeply understand the role grief plays in interpreting histories. Understanding the fundamental features of difficult histories will shed light on the real challenges and perceived limitations of interpreting these tough histories.

In the fourth section of this chapter, I explore the benefits of why history workers take on the risks of interpreting difficult histories and how difficult history interpretations can serve as tools for healing, advocating, commemorating, and improving society. Difficult histories have been tools for remembrances that have been valued by societies for centuries. Recollections of violent pasts and oppression have often been tools for nations to shape ideologies, governments, allegiances, and patriotism. Interpretations of difficult histories touch people in the psychological process of grieving and can serve as tools to help people find explanations for the sacrifices and the losses of the events.

Defining Difficult History

What are difficult histories? For the purpose of history workers in museums, history organizations, and other public history venues, I broadly define difficult histories as histories of oppression, violence, and trauma. Difficult histories are a category of recollections that are filled with pathos, and are surrounded with intellectual and political risks that make the telling of difficult histories, well, difficult! Histories about slavery, genocide, mass murder, war, disease, racism, and sexism are a few examples of the types of histories that recall oppression and tragedies that are not only hard to tell because of the pain and suffering experienced by the victims but also because the histories, however long ago, continue to impact our lives today. History workers, including museum workers and public historians, have referred to difficult histories as tough stories to tell.[2] Some history workers and visitors find the histories of pain and suffering uncomfortable, stressful, and shocking to encounter. Other history workers and visitors explain that the difficult histories are validating, useful, and necessary to represent. Difficult histories recall a broad range of injustices and atrocities that demonstrate the capacity for human wickedness and cruelty. Simultaneously, recalled difficult histories can also include stories of survival, ingenuity, bravery, and goodwill, and enable us to envision pathways to social justice.

Difficult histories touch the present, making history workers and visitors sorely more aware of the suffering around us today. History workers and visitors often resist looking at painful history, or express skepticism or disbelief, because the very idea that the difficult history was real is hard to conceive. More implicating, and perhaps more uncomfortable, is the presence of immorality in our everyday lives that evolved from the difficult history on display. In the context of visitors learning about slavery in the Caribbean, historian Michel-Rolph Trouillot explains,

> And [while] we should not ask these tourists to be true to that past, they were not responsible for slavery. . . . What needs to be denounced here to restore authenticity is much less slavery than the racist present within which representations of slavery are produced. The moral incongruence stems from this uneasy overlap of the two sides of historicity.[3]

The authenticity of the historical suffering and tragic losses is necessary, "lest the representation becomes a fake, a morally repugnant spectacle."[4] Difficult history must be recalled purposely and accurately especially because of the aching relationship the knowledge has to the present and future.

Difficult histories can be hard to interpret and can be hard to learn because they require history workers and visitors to bear witness to human traumas and immorality, and subsequently they require some learners (including visitors and history workers) to consider how the new information may contradict their understanding of the past and present. The responsibility to address and acknowledge the historical person's pain or suffering can shake our beliefs in a moral society and shake our internal understandings of right and wrong.

Learners internalize the disruption as a psychic loss in how the immorality or cruelty jeopardizes what the learner has understood to be true history or to be moral behavior. This kind of disruption is described by the educational concept of "loss in learning," which is key to understanding history workers' and visitors' resistances and abilities to engage in learning about traumatic histories.[5] History workers are a set of learners who have to learn the difficult histories in order to develop and deliver the interpretations to visitors. Visitors are another set of learners who most often self-select the histories they want to learn. And yet, despite the observable desire to learn the difficult histories, individuals within both sets of learners will demonstrate resistance to the histories.

Difficult histories can be so disruptive to learners that the new knowledge is actually upsetting or shocking. The new knowledge about a difficult history can be internally felt as a disruption to what the learner believes to be true or possible. And the learner might exclaim, "I can't believe that!" The disruption is felt as a kind of psychic loss by the learner who then has to grapple with the new knowledge in order to make sense of it and has to consider how the new knowledge changes the learner's understandings of the world. The educational psychology concept of loss in learning will be further described in chapter 3.

Traumatic History: Stories That Are Painful to Remember

The Greek word *trauma*, meaning "wound," as in a bodily injury, is used by Sigmund Freud to describe a wound inflicted upon the mind. According to Laplanche and Pontalis, the term *trauma* adopted in psychoanalysis describes three ideas: "the idea of a violent shock, the idea of a wound and the idea of consequences affecting the whole organisation [*sic*]."[6] The Freudian concept of traumatic memories are those memories that are buried deep into the subject's memory and are too painful to bring into his or her conscious realm.

Difficult histories can include accounts of human trauma, which are especially complex to interpret. In order to begin thinking about how to interpret traumatic histories, we need to explore briefly how traumatic events are remembered and, frankly, not remembered. Traumatic histories are framed by the partiality of how they can be remembered. Most often, victims and witnesses of violence and oppression explain that they do not remember the events or are unable to tell the whole story. Cathy Caruth examines the complex ways "knowing and not knowing" are entangled in the language of trauma and in narratives associated with trauma.[7] When survivors are asked to recall a traumatic event, they might only remember parts of the story or setting. Survivors often explain they are at a loss for words to describe what happened, saying, "I cannot talk about it" or "I only remember the moments before the event," for example. At times, surviving victims and traumatized witnesses might rely on other witnesses to explain what happened.

Dori Laub, professor and an expert on interviews and survivor testimonies, reported a particular recollection from a Holocaust survivor from the Auschwitz concentration camp.[8] The recollection is a good example of how traumatic memories are fragile and incomplete even though they are extremely useful oral histories. A woman in her late sixties was telling interviewers about her experience in the camp for the Video Archive for Holocaust Testimonies at Yale University. She was describing the Auschwitz uprising when prisoners attacked the camp guards and destroyed many portions of the camp. Dori Laub explains that months after the interview at a conference, historians, psychoanalysts, and artists engaged in a lively debate about whether the woman's testimony was accurate.

> The testimony was not accurate, historians claimed. The number of chimneys was misrepresented. Historically, only one chimney was blown up, not all four. Since the memory of the testifying woman turned out to be, in this way, fallible, one could not accept—nor give credence—to her whole account of the events. It was utterly important to remain accurate, least the revisionists in history discredit everything.
>
> A psychoanalyst, who had been one of the interviewers of this woman, profoundly disagreed. "The woman was testifying," he insisted, "not to the number of the chimneys blown up, but to something else, more radical, more crucial; the reality of an unimaginable occurrence."[9]

Laub explains that traumatic memories are useful and meaningful testimony not simply to present empirical historical facts, but to explain the very secret of survival and of victims' resistances. The woman who survived Auschwitz had come to testify, not to the empirical number of chimneys, Laub explains further, but to the prisoners' resistance and to the affirmation of survival.[10]

Subjugated History: Difficult History in the Learner's External World

Subjugation is a characteristic of many difficult histories.[11] Subjugated histories are the silenced, ignored, and marginalized histories. Victors often subjugate history told from the perspective of the underdogs, the victimized, the oppressed, and the defeated, while the dominant voices are the authors of the hegemonic recollections. Histories that have been ignored or marginalized by historians, museums, educators, governments, and communities are examples of subjugated histories. Such histories are positioned to seem less important than mainstream history, or are in opposition to familiar historical accounts and collective memory. Once elevated, the subjugated histories can be resisted by history workers and visitors because they might run counter to what people learned in school or at home, because the histories come from a new historical perspective in a voice that had not been heard before. For example, American slave life histories, which include accounts of oppression, have been marginalized and overshadowed by the histories of the wealthy free planter class.[12]

Consider how different perspectives and alternate voices from history can shape and reshape historical facts by highlighting some histories and suppressing other histories. In regard to subjugating the history of slavery, Trouillot argues that in the process of writing history, historians can prioritize traumas and select historical significance, thus generating legacies of the past. "At first glance, it would seem obvious that the historical relevance of slavery in the United States proceeds from the horrors of the past."[13] The slavery era is often evoked as the starting point of an ongoing traumatism and is a necessary explanation to current inequalities suffered by blacks. However, he argues, outside of the United States millions more Africans were sent to the Americas as slaves and "in no way can we say that the magnitude of U.S. slavery out did that of Brazil or the Caribbean."[14] Trouillot contends that today the histories of slavery in Brazil and in the Caribbean are subjugated histories, and he compares that subjugation to the more elevated history of slavery represented in the United States.

Social Forgetting

Iwona Irwin-Zarecka's notion of social forgetting, in the context of popular culture and in museums, is another component of difficult histories that accounts for some of the omissions and absences of particular people and events in public memory.[15] Randolph Bergstrom observes that the paucity of the material record of those who lived the oppressions works to keep the painful memories from public knowledge, thereby limiting the possibilities for history workers to write and exhibit representations from the subjugated perspectives.[16] The histories retrieved from the margins or from the depths of long-overlooked archives can disrupt history workers' and visitors' understandings of the histories that they thought were factual, making the newly introduced historical information all the more difficult to accept and learn. One danger of social forgetting is when history workers and even visitors foreclose on learning about a difficult history.[17] Social forgetting is a collective loss that allows the social groups (e.g., governments) to value some artifacts and allow other artifacts to be vanquished to attics or to underfunded repositories, or worse left to deteriorate or be thrown away.

An example of a deliberate act of fighting social forgetting is illustrated through the successful establishment of the June 4th Museum in Hong Kong, which is dedicated to preserving the memory of the deadly prodemocracy protests in Tiananmen Square. This small museum hosts two hundred visitors each weekday and one thousand visitors each weekend. While the history of the 1989 protests in Tiananmen Square remains a controversial topic, even taboo, in Mainland China, people from around the world want to discuss, remember, mourn, and connect to this difficult history. The reported global public interest in the history of the 1989 protests shows that even though Chinese authorities have deleted the events from China's official record, public demand for dialog about this massacre has persevered in Hong Kong.[18]

Another exhibition that worked to address social forgetting was the temporary exhibition that was held at the Contemporary Art Center (CAC) in New Orleans in 2008 titled *Remember the Upstairs Lounge*. The exhibition attempted to elevate a difficult history that has been passively disremembered. It was an art installation that recalled the history of the deadliest fire in New Orleans. An arsonist set a fire in the stairway to the Upstairs Lounge on June 24, 1973, a popular gay men's club in the French Quarter. Artist Skylar Fein created the exhibit that was displayed on the fourth floor of the CAC thirty-five years later. Journalist Doug MacCash described the exhibition as a "haunting memorial" of an event that claimed thirty-two lives and injured many who were trapped in the burning bar.[19]

The museum installation was an art piece with hallways and small rooms that alluded to the club interior and recalled the tragedy through period memorabilia, popular-culture posters, historical newspaper clippings, news reports, and an audio track that took museum visitors back in time into a space that recalled the madness and tragedy of that night in 1973. The news accounts described the fire attack as arson committed by an angry gay patron, and not as a hate crime. The artwork combined real and imagined artifacts of the lounge where museum visitors learned about the social setting of New Orleans and the city's mid-twentieth-century intolerance.

The fire at the Upstairs Lounge was among the deadliest attacks on LGBTQ people in U.S. history. The official investigation did not yield any convictions. Filmmaker Robert L. Camina said in 2003, "I was shocked at the disproportionate reaction by the city government. The city declared days of mourning for victims of other mass tragedies in the city. It shocked me that despite the magnitude of the fire it was largely ignored."[20] Some witnesses remember the fire as a tragic event that emotionally bonded the city's gay community. Others remember the fire as a senseless loss of life and little more.

How is the history of the deadly fire in the Upstairs Lounge significant to the current LGBTQ civil rights movement? Do the citizens of New Orleans remember that tragedy, or is the memory fading? Ignored largely by the government of New Orleans as merely an incident among many fires in the Crescent City, the history of the mass murder of gay men quickly became a closed case left unresolved.

Social forgetting adds to the struggle over the meanings of sites where violence of many kinds took place, including fires, battles, crimes, slave auctions, and assassinations. Events of human suffering are remembered and forgotten historically by the choices made by collectivities influenced by power and grief. Consider, for example, the historic site called The Forks of the Road in Natchez, Mississippi, which was one of the largest inland slave markets in the mid-nineteenth century. While slave sales in Natchez were held in a number of places, The Forks of the Road eclipsed the others. In 1830, thirty-two slave dealers were listed in Natchez along five city blocks. The slave market was last used for slave trading in 1863. The following year, when Union soldiers occupied Natchez, the site served as a refugee camp for newly freed slaves. After the war, the market buildings were torn down. By the middle of the twentieth century, the five-block area no longer resembled a major commercial center. Only a gas station and groves of overgrown trees cloaked the site of earlier horrific human oppression.

The slave trade center nearly faded from memory. In 1998, a group of concerned Natchez citizens approached the National Park Service and the Mississippi Department of Archives and History in an effort to have the site designated as a historic landmark. In 2003, the Natchez Juneteenth Committee successfully installed a state historic marker to resuscitate the memory of The Forks of the Road slave market from near oblivion. The action took courage in order to face the community opposition, the local government's resistance, and years of debate and struggle to justify, clarify, and agree on the meanings of the scarred landscape.

Difficult Knowledge: Difficult History in the Learner's Internal World

For many learners, difficult histories are considered difficult knowledge. A key to understanding how learners engage in difficult histories is Deborah P. Britzman's concept of "difficult knowledge."[21] Difficult knowledge includes difficult histories and other knowledge that is upsetting, stressful, or too hard to bear. Difficult history can be considered difficult knowledge when the learner resists the presented history. Britzman explains that the learning from difficult knowledge recognizes the discontinuities between the new information and the learner's status quo. Learning from difficult knowledge asks something intimate of the learner, and it requires the learner to recognize how he or she might be implicated in the new knowledge and to recognize his or her attachments that organize his or her self-identity. Resisting difficult knowledge is, in large part, a learner's reaction to psychic self-preservation. Difficult knowledge disrupts the status quo of the learner's internal world and disrupts how the learner understands the external world. In the context of history workers and visitors engaging in interpretations of difficult histories, newly introduced tragic histories can be perceived as difficult knowledge.

A difficult history may be too intense for the learner to consciously assimilate into memory. Britzman describes her students' painful reception of difficult knowledge in reading about the history of the Holocaust, which required "an exploration of the vicissitudes of loss and attachment and the woeful insufficiency of the belated response."[22] In her research, which is focused on classroom learning, Britzman draws from psychoanalysis in the context of teaching historical accounts of trauma, specifically the Holocaust and the HIV/AIDS epidemic. Britzman concluded that the painful, difficult histories are repressed into the learner's unconscious memory and remain uncomprehended; the emotional energy of the loss or pain is contained in the learner's memory, which can cause the learner anxiety and stress.

Repressed memories are held in the unconscious to protect the learner's ego from painful disruptions of the individual's ego ideal.[23] Briefly, the ego ideal is a Freudian notion that describes the part of the mind that includes the rules and standards for moral behavior. Newly introduced difficult knowledge can disrupt the learner's moral compass, which forms at a young age. The learner's concept of ideal behavior, and specifically his or her concern for others, evolves as early as eighteen to twenty-four months of age, and continues to evolve through adulthood.[24] A child's growing sense of self underlies his or her concern for others. The unconscious part of the mind that Freud calls the superego imposes on itself concepts of moral behavior developed from parental and social standards. These rules and moral concepts help the learner distinguish his or her moral understandings of good behavior within society.

The fabric of each individual's social life, his or her relationships and concern for others, is exceedingly fragile, and the threads can be damaged in the humblest of ways through, for example, disagreements, fear, shame, or guilt. When difficult knowledge asks learners to consider immoral and shocking events, the learner is pressed to make sense of the new information. When the knowledge is too difficult, emotional disruption can be extreme and can shake the learner. The effects of self-preservation (the desire to protect the learner's ego ideal) can render the historical trauma unknowable to the learner because it is held repressed in his or her unconscious memory.[25]

Britzman argues that learning difficult knowledge is painful in the way it jeopardizes the learner's psychic balance and thereby creates truly felt scenarios of loss. This feeling of loss requires the learner to work through the difficult knowledge in order to make sense of the history.[26] The feelings of loss, anxiety, and other troubling emotions are the types of emotional pain difficult knowledge can elicit within learners. The discomfort felt by the learner upon encountering difficult knowledge is often expressed as resistance to further engagement with the knowledge, which the learner perceives as too difficult to understand or to accept as knowable.

Risks of Interpreting Difficult Histories

We call histories of oppression, trauma, and mass violence "difficult" in part because the work of interpreting these histories has associated risks. The risks of interpreting difficult histories vary greatly; the risks are personal and political. Understanding the risks that cause learners' resistances is especially pertinent to history workers who are tasked with developing historical interpretations that must simultaneously be sensitive, accurate, purposeful, and productive.

Public history venues take on political risks in exhibits and programs about difficult histories that can offend or contest a collective memory of a valued history. An interpretation of a difficult history can potentially challenge political viewpoints or subvert an accepted ideology. Funding and support can be put at risk when museums and historical sites present a controversial exhibit or program. Difficult history interpretations can upset the political status quo in a community or for society at large, and sway public opinion on current issues.

Refusing to engage in learning about a difficult history is a way for learners to avoid feeling discomfort, or to keep others from knowing about a tragedy. In both instances, such resistance puts that history at risk of social forgetting, or worse, of putting the history at risk of annihilation.[27] The risks of learners not learning about a difficult history include the endangerment of the larger collective memory of the events; the lack of future understanding for the historical conditions upon which the present-day social structures rest; and the loss of the memories of the people who were the victims, the oppressors, and the witnesses. Widespread social forgetting and subjugation of a difficult history by history workers, educators, civic leaders, religious leaders, and communities puts subsequent historical, sociological, and political information and the respective empirical material culture at risk of being lost or trivialized. The silencing of select difficult histories risks a great loss of the foundational historical background of later histories that were the result of the earlier tragic past.

Controversial historical content can be difficult knowledge for individuals, groups, communities, and governments. Yet controversies are an integral part of the collective production of knowledge.[28] Disagreements and intellectual tensions can productively motivate further investigations and dialogs to further the search for the meanings of historical events and related evidence. Controversial histories can also spawn heated and passionate differences. Interpretations of a difficult history can raise political risks for the presenting history organization and for the organization's supporting communities. Interpretations of difficult histories can upset and ignite community outrage and, for better or worse, impact public policy. Collective resistance can emerge from politically volatile exhibitions and programs.

Resistance is a natural response from individual learners who are faced with a subject that is unpleasant or even shocking. Learners who engage in difficult histories take the risk of stirring deep emotional responses or of finding controversial political effects between the past and present that learners find compelling, even offensive or outrageous.

Much is at stake in learning difficult histories for individuals personally. Learners might come to an exhibition about a difficult history with certain expectations about what the exhibit will mean to them. Such visitors might be grieving, searching for meanings, or looking to further define their cultural identities. But when they find that the historical interpretation does not meet their expectations or fit their understandings of how that history happened or what the history represents, learners are uncomfortable, distraught, even shaken, offended, or angered. Even more specific to difficult histories is the risk of visitors finding that their expectations are shattered, so much so that the visitors are at risk of shutting down and refusing further engagement with the museum experience. Learners of difficult histories are at an increased risk of a variety of resistant feelings, such as feeling remorseful, astonished, confused, frustrated, guilty, grieved, angered, shocked, and shamed.

History workers are compelled to ask whether their interpretation respects their visitors' well-being and respects the historical individuals or groups they intend to represent. Is there a risk that visitors might be harmed by the history learning experience? At the same time, another important risk for history workers to consider is whether parts of a difficult history will be silenced, avoided, or forgotten. History workers are faced with finding a balance of interpreting a difficult history accurately and ethically while not offending or overwhelming their visitors.

The work to interpret a difficult history is emotionally demanding, filled with chances for insensitivity, embarrassment, and failings of insight. History workers take the risk of raising strong emotions in learners in their efforts to interpret difficult histories. The emotional risks are as equally alarming for visitors as they are for history workers.

Risk: Persistent Resistance

Psychoanalyst Shoshana Felman explains that ignorance is a form of resistance to a difficult knowledge.[29] When museum visitors choose not to pursue reading the label copy of a traumatic history because it is too hard to bear, the visitors are choosing not to know the information at that moment. Trouillot contends that when history is simply ignored "this ignorance produces a silence of trivialization."[30] If the learner chooses not to learn a difficult history, then he or she can believe the history did not happen or that the history does not matter to him or her. The learner can avoid feeling upset or uncomfortable, believing that he or she is relieved of taking responsibility for knowing about that trauma or immorality.

When learners do engage in representations of difficult histories, philosopher Susan Sontag concedes, there can be shame as well as shock in looking at images and the material evidence of tragedies. Sontag explains that when looking at images of real horror there are essentially two groups of viewers.[31] There are viewers who look at images of suffering who can do something to alleviate the suffering, like doctors, social workers, policy makers, and activists who have the skills to respond responsibly. Then there are the viewers who gaze at the images like voyeurs, whether or not they mean to be. Let us add a subset of viewers to Sontag's two groups of viewers; namely, empathetic learners. Empathetic learners include children who are interested in expanding their understanding of the world.

The grisly and frightening representations of difficult histories can invite viewers to be spectators and cowards, or to be more engaged as activists and learners. The possibility of these responses includes both history workers and visitors. The actively engaged viewer is a responsible learner who moves past his or her initial shock, repulsion, or intrigue about the historical representations to develop empathy for the victims. The engaged learner actively seeks how the recalled history is relevant and how it fits into the realities of our world today.

Difficult histories can be deeply felt by learners who are imagining the historical settings and thinking about how they feel about the tragedies described. However, the learner is at risk of projecting his or her own life onto the suffering of the historical persons being recalled. Learners might think about their personal understandings of pain and oppression in the sense-making process. However, unlike other genres of history, difficult histories engender feelings of loss that can be so profound that the learner can submerge himself or herself exclusively into how the tragedy makes him or her feel. A learner might search his or her memory for other histories that the learner can compare it to and attempt to reconcile which hell is worse. When does solipsism surpass empathy? Sontag explains, "It is intolerable to have one's own sufferings twinned with anybody else's."[32] The learner who focuses on the extent of his or her own pain is not yet ethically or responsibly responding to the history.

One of the challenges of interpreting difficult histories is helping learners overcome their narcissistic tendencies to project their own pain and suffering onto the histories on display. Because human suffering is unique, the learner is tasked to separate the learner's psychological distress from his or her perceived losses that were aroused by the representations of the tragedies experienced by the historical individuals and communities. History workers are therefore not only tasked with researching multiple voices and searching for authentic historical evidence to interpret a difficult history; history workers are also responsible for developing interpretations that enable learners to make connections that are both ethical and empathetic responses to the historical persons' suffering.

Risk: Traumatizing Effects of Difficult Histories

Difficult histories include accounts of human suffering that could be traumatic for present-day learners to bear witness to. The pedagogical strategies used in museums and historic sites to interpret difficult histories can be shaped by the history workers' sensitivity to understanding the potential for visitors' traumatic responses to difficult histories and to adjust for the serious possibility that visitors can be greatly impacted, and possibly even traumatized, by the history learning experiences.

Learning about a tragic event from eyewitnesses, for example, can overwhelm recipients of those accounts. Consider the scenario described by Edward Linenthal about the mental health workers who were positioned at the recovery stations located in Oklahoma City immediately after the bombing that killed and injured hundreds of people and destroyed the Murrah Federal Building. Many of the mental health workers were traumatized by the stories they heard, and like many survivors were even diagnosed with post-traumatic stress disorder. (PTSD)[33]

Witnesses and victims of traumatic events, including terrorist attacks, are vulnerable to PTSD, which can trigger nightmares, flashbacks, and panic attacks. According to psychiatrist Sarah Roff, one of the cardinal symptoms of PTSD is avoidance of people, places, or activities, which can become extremely impairing symptoms. However, Roff explains, "The current *Diagnostic and Statistical Manual of Mental Disorders* specifically excludes exposure to media depicting traumatic events as a cause of PTSD."[34] In addition, Roff contends that learning about traumatic events in college classes, for example, will not incite PTSD for students. The difficult history could, however, impact students who arrive on college campuses suffering from the aftereffects of childhood trauma, as well as for returning veterans trying to go back to school who are burdened with symptoms of PTSD. Therefore, it seems good practice for history workers to be sensitive to the visitors who suffer from PTSD and are vulnerable to exhibits and programs about difficult histories.

While visitors and history workers unlikely will become sufferers of PTSD as a result of learning about difficult histories in museums and historic sites, these learners are still vulnerable to emotional stress and feeling traumatized by the stories, recollections, images, artifacts, films, and historical settings. Witnesses' accounts, images of suffering, artifacts from the events, and places where events took place are still only partial and secondary to the actual suffering experienced by the victims.

In museum settings or on historical landscapes, listening to visitors' verbal remarks and watching visitors' physical responses to a difficult history helps history workers assess the impact the history has on visitors. Is the visitor upset or shocked? Is the exhibit or presentation too much for the visitor to bear? Are visitors refusing or resisting further engagement in learning about the history? For example, I observed visitors in a World War II museum exhibit that displayed images of prisoners in a concentration camp exclaim, "This is unbelievable!" Andrea Liss watched museum visitors avoid a boxcar on display, which once was used to transport Polish men, women, and children to death camps in Nazi-occupied Poland.[35] At the LSU Rural Life Museum, I listened to visitors' expressions of disbelief while touring a historical plantation slave quarter cabin. An older woman said to her husband, "Two families lived in this one cabin? No way!" Traumatic histories can be difficult for learners to accept as true and have the potential to greatly upset visitors.

The learner, who could be a visitor or a history worker, troubled with receiving the historical testimony of suffering might go into an emotional state, even so far as being traumatized by the reading of testimonies. Reading exhibit labels or viewing images of difficult histories asks learners to partially know the horror that was faced by the historical witnesses and victims. Felman explains this concept in the context of the 1974 book *Kafka's Other Trial* by Elias Canetti. Canetti writes that he was so emotionally affected by the testimonials in Kafka's writing that Canetti concluded, "I can only say that these letters have penetrated me like an actual life."[36]

In using Felman's framework for educators,[37] history workers need to consider how the act of writing historical interpretations is tied to the act of bearing witness. In some interpretations, history workers are asking visitors to receive the historical testimonies of victims and survivors. If the historical interpretations of difficult histories are the alignment among three sets of witnesses (the historical actors, the history workers, and the visitors), then what do these alignments mean? And what extent of history workers' agency is actually allotted to them to bear witness?

The classic symptoms of trauma range from feelings of restlessness and agitation to the more extreme feelings of numbness and melancholia. A documentary film with scenes from a difficult history or a lethal weapon on display in an exhibit can impact learners who might, for example, subsequently have recurring nightmares or be upset by the images that frightened or disturbed them well after the museum experience. An exhibit about a difficult history has the potential to make the learner feel despondent, melancholic, or overwhelmed.

Some learners are inadvertently put to a task that they did not elect to take on—the difficult and ethical task of witnessing when asked to engage in an exhibit about a difficult history. The personal crisis of receiving testimony when encountering difficult knowledge can be traumatizing, causing a learner to experience a range of disturbing emotions. Some difficult history interpretations can put learners at risk of being traumatized, raising the risk of suffering long-term effects that can influence learners' daily living.

Risk: Shock

Difficult histories can be shocking and raise the risks of emotionally harming visitors or even offending audiences. How much is too much? Difficult histories can be overwhelming for some learners. Shocking stories that recall tragedies that impacted massive populations can make the learner feel powerless or helpless.[38] Visitors-as-learners stunned by a history can be numbed by the encounter, which becomes a way of not thinking further about the historic oppression.[39] History workers run the risk of visitors being shocked by the content, which can prevent some visitors from engaging in the difficult history. However, shocking images and content can raise tensions, which in turn can be productive in moving learners to care about the history and the effects of the history.

The emotional impact that difficult histories set in motion is likely stressful for learners. Paul H. Williams explains that there is a close connection between the theory of trauma and the visual aesthetic of shock:

> When the human psyche tries to process a traumatic event, it will endlessly replay it, struggling to find meaning, or resolution through the replay. Hence, traumatic memory, like the camera, has been described as consisting of an arrested moment that is disconnected from the forward motion of linear time, and lacks the ability to take part in some story that can offer resolution or sense to terrible events. When we gain *information* [italics sic] by establishing the context of any image, we do not necessarily understand the subject's traumatic experience, since not only is it not the sum of what an outsider can adduce from the contextual signs in an image, but moreover, it denotes something that may not even have been fully experienced, in a contextual-historical sense, by the traumatized subject.[40]

Shocking images or graphic representations can startle and even terrify viewers. Viewing an exhibit or listening to a guided tour narrative can be intensely personal, and the feelings that shocking content can generate can be deeply private. When the content on view represents a difficult history that is violent, graphic, or extremely sad or frightening, the learner is at risk of being shocked.

Risk: Guilt and Shame

History workers who interpret difficult histories are possibly faced with shameful histories that are packed with meanings that have great potential to disturb learners, both co-workers and visitors, emotionally. The difficult histories can matter deeply to learners, sometimes productively, and more perilously, the difficult histories can matter negatively to learners. The histories carry the risk of potentially implicating, humiliating, disgracing, or humbling learners. Consider the shame that the former mayor of Dallas, R. L. Thornton, expressed when President Kennedy was assassinated in Dallas. Mayor Thornton admitted, "For my part, I don't want anything to remind me that a President was killed on the streets of Dallas, I want to forget."[41]

Educational psychoanalyst Sharon Todd explains that learners often verbally express their feelings of guilt through declaring their degree of responsibility to a history. Todd explains that "guilt connects the self to the external world, to the real of the social."[42] Expressions of guilt describe how the learner perceives his or her answerability or remorse for another's suffering. Learners are envisioning another's risk of well-being, and the learner is compelled to declare that he or she is not responsible. Learners who feel guilt are concerned with how they perceive their ties to an event or to other people in terms of the quality of their relationships.

Todd describes three kinds of guilt that are expressed by classroom students.[43] These types of guilt are applicable to learners in museums and historical sites. The first type of guilt feels like "my fault." For example, the learner's response might be, "I am a bad person for not helping." The learner believes he or she did not do enough. The second type of guilt overwhelms the learner who believes he or she deserves to suffer too. This is akin to survivor's guilt as expressed by some descendants of Holocaust survivors, or post-traumatic slavery syndrome, which is a type of guilt expressed by present generations of African Americans who describe the residual impacts of generations of slavery.[44] The learner refocuses the knowledge about the particular suffering on his or her own lack of suffering. The learner might say, "I do not deserve a full plate of food." The third type of guilt emerges as anger. The learner is angry because he or she was made to feel guilty. The learner recognizes something unjust had occurred, feels angry, and then declares how incensed the injustice makes him or her feel.

While guilt is generally tied to the external world, shame is more closely tied to the individual's internal world. Learners who feel shamed by a difficult history are focused on how the learner perceives himself or herself. The difficult history puts some learners at risk of feeling ashamed, implicated, humiliated, or embarrassed. Those learners are at a higher risk of foreclosing on learning anything more about that history. The learners feeling shame are concerned with their personal relationship to an event. The learner might ask, "How does this history make me look?" Todd explains that while shame remains confined within the self's parameters of self-idealization, feelings of shame are more likely indicative of how the learner holds herself or himself in severe disregard; shame often involves a revelation or belief that one cannot bring oneself to admit to another person.

The shamed learner might be resisting responsible engagement or empathy for a history. A learner's expressed shame might be an indication that he or she believes that he or she is distant from the injustice. For example, upon viewing a southern plantation slave cabin a visitor declared, "My family did not immigrate to the United States until 1900. That was after slavery." Learners who feel shamed by a difficult history are more likely to be aware of their relationship to the difficult history. A shamed learner might actually recognize the roots of his or her feelings of humiliation, regret, embarrassment, or unease.

Difficult history can trigger shame that can engender forgetting, thus raising the risk that the history might be lost to time. The desire to forget a shameful past can be negotiated by the oppressors, survivors, and witnesses and later generations. Shame can encourage resistance to preserving difficult history. Historian James Oliver Horton points to the shame of slavery that has jeopardized America's healing. "The history of American slavery is a shameful tale of inhumanity and human exploitation and of the attempt to hide national hypocrisy behind tortured theories of racial inequalities."[45]

Shame also invades more recent history. For example, Americans' collective shame slowed down the eventual opening of the Manzanar National Park Interpretation Center. It was a nearly sixty-year endeavor to convince the U.S. government to openly commemorate and represent the World War II–era internment of 110,000 Japanese Americans at the historic site that eventually became a commemorative landscape within the National Park Service. Many former detainees and their descendants from Manzanar and nine other internment camps eventually gained historic site recognition. In the 1990s, the advocate groups shepherded an act of Congress to establish the Manzanar National Historic Site that provides protection and interpretation of the historical, cultural, and natural resources associated with the relocation of Japanese Americans during World War II.

At the time of the establishment of the Manzanar National Historic Site, historian Robin Winks argued,

> With the recent addition of Manzanar National Historic Site to the National Park System, the public has been introduced more dramatically than ever before to a fundamental debate. Should the national parks commemorate and protect only places and events in which we take pride, or should the parks strive to mark events and places that many agree represent shameful episodes in our national experience? . . . The question is, should we commemorate or should we strive to forget, indeed should we bury from the national consciousness, these fearful times in our history? . . . Education is best done with examples. These examples must include that which we regret, that which is to be avoided, as well as that for which we strive. No effective system of education can be based on unqualified praise, for all education instructs people of the difference between moral and wanton acts and how to distinguish between the desirable and the undesirable. If this premise is correct, we cannot omit the negative lessons of history.[46]

From a pedagogical standpoint, learners' responses of guilt and shame to difficult histories reveal to history workers extremely significant moments, moments that Shoshana

Felman and Deborah Britzman and other educational philosophers qualify as learning crises.[47] The learning crisis is also a pivotal moment when the learner could resist and quit going any further with the learning encounter. However, history workers should not avoid or disregard the learning potential tied to the risks of learning crises. Benefits could outweigh the risks. Guilt and shame are two important responses to the learning process for emerging empathy, for making reparations, and for the formation of responsibility, which eventuate ethical responses derived from learning about difficult histories.

Todd contends that guilt and shame are pedagogical forces to be reckoned with, "where learning about another's pain becomes refracted through one's declared sense of responsibility (or lack thereof)."[48] These emotional responses suggest to observing history workers that the learner feels implicated in the context of the described wrong committed against another.

The overriding emphasis on good behavior and bad behavior in difficult history interpretations stems from narratives that clarify what is meant by "doing the right thing." In the Western moral tradition we can understand the idea of the "moral ought," which Kitwood explains is the idea of what one knows one *should* do.[49] When the concern for others is thought of in these moralistic terms, and attached to the category of ought, Kitwood says, "Psychologically, a whole range of feelings of personal inadequacy and unworthiness are often aroused, depriving a person of confidence and spontaneity."[50] The moral ought arouses a range of feelings of guilt, inadequacy, and unworthiness and can shake the learner who faces a difficult history.

The stress of feeling shame or guilt in learning difficult histories can evolve from the tensions learners can feel in wanting to both remember and to forget. Consider the Nazi pogrom terror in Germany, Austria, and the occupied region of Czechoslovakia on November 9, 1938, often remembered as *Kristallnacht*. In an AP story about the seventy-fifth anniversary, Deidre Berger, director of the American Jewish Committee in Berlin, explains how she works to ensure that Germans do not forget that night and the descent into inhumanity it represented.[51] "It's important to understand why the veneer of civilization was easily cracked," she said. Berger notes that there were many who stood against the massive violence inflicted against their longtime friends and neighbors. But there were more people who joined in or stood by passively. Berger explains, "It really shows the fragility of political systems. In one night, so many who had grown up together turned and attacked the dignity and the safety of their neighbors, laughed as they were arrested." So many witnesses saw the horror and looked the other way, explained Berlin's mayor Klaus Wowereit. He went on to question the inaction of the bystanders: "Many neighbors remained indifferent, and I'm asking myself why over the years, so few came out and admitted: 'I saw it, and looked the other way. Today I am ashamed.'"[52]

Difficult histories can make visitors feel implicated or self-conscious. Remembering and forgetting the shame of neighbors and bystanders who did nothing can cause anxiety and tension for present-day learners. Learners can be asked to consider the immediacy of oppression, war, and genocide in our present day when learning about *Kristallnacht*, and can be led to ask, "Am I a silent bystander, too?" The recollections of the Nazi resistance and the martyrs and heroes who did take action to help victims are hopeful and positive accounts of the difficult history that serve as models for moral behavior. However, can visitors be asked to imagine bystanders' compliance or complacency? Was the instinct for personal survival at play, or was institutional racism empowering the bystanders to let the oppressors wage war on Jews? Interpreting this difficult history raises the risk for learners to feel guilt or shame as learners become more aware of their personal complacencies, indifferences, and inaction to social injustices. The guilt and shame of our present-day insensitivities, inactions, or ignorance about current-day oppressions can make the tragic histories more difficult to learn.

Risk: Apathy, Irrelevance, and Passive Empathy

When the learner decides that a history is not relevant to him or her, or the learner's response is indifference, the learner becomes apathetic and unable to see how the history matters and the risk of depreciating that history increases. Apathy is a form of resistance. In one scenario in which an interpretation shakes the learner's beliefs about a history, the learner might imagine that the history is not relevant to him or her. Alternative scenarios can arise as well, for instance, when the images on display are too foreign to the learner's visual vocabulary and the learner passes by the content, saying, "This is not relevant to me" or "I can't tell what this is."

Time and space can disconnect learners from the significance of a difficult history. Past events can seem unrelated to a learner's life. Events that happened continents away can feel like a safe distance from a learner's present living routines. Passive learners have a kind of contentment in knowing that they are not presently in harm's way. Sontag asks, "What to do with such knowledge as photographs bring of faraway suffering?"[53] Sontag suggests that, possibly, a viewer has a kind of satisfaction in knowing that this horror is not happening to me. I am not ill; I am not dying. I am not trapped in a war. Sontag concludes, "[I]t seems normal for people to fend off thinking about the ordeals of others, even others with whom it would be easy to identify."[54]

Indifferent learners' passive empathy can prompt a disingenuous satisfaction in knowing, which merely empowers learners to say that they have heard of the difficult history without being moved by that history. Another nullifying scenario tied to the learner's temporal distance from a historical event and the learner's geographic distance from a history is the mistaken usefulness of passive empathy, the empty pity or sympathy the visitor shows for a history. Expressions of "how sad" or "wasn't that a shame" provide little more than a false sense of achievement because the learner has acknowledged something graphic or sensational occurred but without changing how the learner views the world.

Risk: Controversy

Controversies in museums and historical sites can cast a shadow over histories that are defined as difficult history. Exhibits that attempt to interpret difficult histories engender disagreements about what the history means and how the history is best represented. Debates can be heated, putting the host institution at increased risk of offending audiences, jeopardizing financial and community support, and putting the history workers under public scrutiny in ways that can challenge the institution's authority. Controversies can be prolonged, public, and passionate. Critics of difficult history interpretations, including community groups, museum patrons, civic groups, religious groups, governments, and social activist organizations will fervently voice their opinions and viewpoints, and argue their disagreements often through the media and even through legal channels.

Ivan Karp and Steven Lavine contend that the very nature of exhibiting overlays the contested terrain of interpretations.[55] The inherent contestability of museum interpretations comes with risks that have high stakes for social change and political power. Controversial exhibits can be met and altered by community demands and governmental actions. Interpretations of controversial history can jeopardize a museum's or a historical site's highly valued public trust. It has been seen multiple times in recent history.[56] A museum's risk of encountering controversy needs to be weighed against how useful the difficult history interpretation will be for social good, including advocating for justice, education, commemoration, and mourning.

Not all controversy is bad. Public controversy also has great positive potential to generate public engagement and initiate dialogs that can eventually prove to be powerful tools to change cultural understandings, political positions, and energize social movements.

A well-known example of a controversial difficult history interpretation is the *Enola Gay* affair at the Smithsonian Institution's National Air and Space Museum.[57] At risk were the museum's funding, reputation, authority, and the quality of the American national narrative for the first atomic bomb used in war. Between 1993 and 1995, the National Air and Space Museum in Washington, D.C., prepared the commemorative exhibition that was to mark the fiftieth anniversary of the end of World War II through the aeronautic history of the B-29 bomber that carried the first atomic bomb, which was dropped on Hiroshima, Japan, in 1945. The original exhibit script and title, *The Crossroads: The End of World War II, the Atomic Bomb and the Cold War*, were drafted by the museum's curatorial staff. The exhibit was arranged around the restored fuselage of the *Enola Gay* and discussed the powerful destruction and massive loss of human life as a result of the atomic explosion. According to Vera Zolberg, the original exhibit script questioned the significance, necessity, and morality of the decision to drop atomic bombs on cities of large civilian populations.[58]

Instead of a commemorative exhibition that paid tribute to the bravery of the American veterans who served to end the war, the then Smithsonian secretary, Robert McCormick Adams, found the original interpretation unbalanced and, if installed, would put the Smithsonian Institution at an unacceptable risk of public controversy. The less-than-patriotic theme was deemed unacceptable. Expressing his difficulties with the planned exhibit, which focused on the horrors of the bombing and omitted the horrors experienced by the Americans in the Pacific campaign, the secretary urged his curators to revise the exhibit to commemorate the successful American conclusion of the war.

However, before the 1995 anniversary year, the internal controversy was leaked to the public. The internal debate as to whose memory could account for the atomic ending of World War II spread out into the public domain, pulling in the museum's community advisory board, the local and national press, academics, veterans, and members of Congress. The Smithsonian Institution, which received over 75 percent of its budget from Congress, came under congressional scrutiny. The Smithsonian Institution reports to a board of regents that is chaired by the chief justice of the Supreme Court, who decided to scale back the exhibit to its bare bones, according to social critic Zolberg.

Part of the fuselage of the Enola Gay, accompanied by a plaque and video interviews with its flight crew, are all that remain. Gone will be any evidence of the 600-page script (even revised); no museum catalogue; no discussions of the issues influencing President Truman's decision; no arguments over the morality of using atomic weapons; no testimony from survivors; no photos of the victims, and nothing about the beginnings of the Cold War.[59]

The decision about how to interpret the *Enola Gay* became the center of the public controversy because the stakeholders deeply cared about the history and the artifacts and how the memory of that historical event would be shaped. The results of the heated public controversy was how the *Enola Gay* was ultimately used to patriotically remember the atomic end of World War II, and the revelations on how the revised interpretation restrained alternative meanings of the B-29 bomber.

Linda Ferguson reported the results of an international study that identified topics that visitors considered controversial for museum exhibitions in the United States, Canada, United Kingdom, New Zealand, and Australia. Ferguson reported, for example, that American visitors identified six topics as being potentially controversial: scientific topics that confront people's ethics or beliefs, issues of national identity, issues that are perceived to be about mortality, differing perspectives about history, and terrorism and the war against terrorism.[60] Ferguson and her colleagues found that many museum staff members were deeply concerned about how certain topics could be displayed in museums, and they feared the possible outcomes of hosting controversial exhibitions.

One of the foremost fears expressed by staff in the study was loss of funding support.[61] Other fears of hosting controversial exhibitions that permeated the international museum community were the risk that museums would engage in self-censorship to avoid controversy, and that the exhibition content would be unduly influenced by corporate or political sponsors. Also, museum workers feared that overinfluence would shape exhibit content and heighten political correctness in exhibition messages. Ferguson found that museum staff members were fearful about how controversial exhibitions would potentially impact visitors, and that controversial exhibitions would potentially bring hate into their museums.[62]

However, avoiding controversy is not necessarily an optimal practice. Controversial topics in museums and at historical sites can be valuable tools to generate public engagement and to initiate discussions about critical issues. Tensions raised through difficult history interpretations promote problem solving and critical thinking. Indeed, the call from within the museum profession since the last half of the twentieth century to expand museum practice to include civic dialogs resonates with the increasing number of exhibits and programs about difficult histories in museums and historic sites worldwide.

Museologist Richard Sandell rightly contends that "if a museum is unreflective, unmoved or not humbled by this type of contact with people's lives then these are sure signs this is work with which it should not be engaged."[63] Humility and courage are necessary for history workers and visitors in order to interpret and learn from controversial, difficult histories.

Controversial museum exhibitions about difficult histories raise significant risks for museums and communities. Education philosopher Megan Boler contends, "The educator who endeavors to rattle complacent cages, who attempts to 'wrest us anew' from the threat of conformism, undoubtedly faces the treacherous ghosts of the other's fear and terrors, which in turn evokes one's own demons."[64] Interpretations of difficult histories can upset and ignite individual and community outrage, and negatively impact public policy and critical institutional funding. However, as Crew and Sims maintain, confrontation is alienation that allows space for reflection, argument, and understanding of a problem.[65]

Risk: Public Safety

Safety is a primary consideration for institutions that serve the public. Both the emotional and physical safety of visitors need to be considered in planning difficult history interpretations. Sadly, too many violent incidents have occurred at memorial museums. Take, for example, the shooting death of Museum Special Police Officer Stephen Tyrone Johns at the U.S. National Memorial Holocaust Museum in Washington, D.C., in 2009 and the shooting deaths of visitors at the Jewish Museum in Brussels, Belgium, in 2014. Many difficult history exhibits and programs are political and reach hate groups and can become focal points for those seeking attention for their causes. While public safety precautions and planning are extremely important aspects of planning for difficult history interpretations, they are not covered in this book, which is focused on educational and ethical approaches to interpreting difficult histories. History workers need to plan for appropriate security measures as well.[66]

Risk: Not Knowing Your Visitors

History workers accept the risk of preparing exhibitions and programs about difficult histories for learners they personally know little about. Unlike classroom education, public history interpretations attempt to address a much more broad and diverse audience who come to the learning experience of a difficult history with life experiences and knowledge unknown to the history workers. While surveys of visitors' responses to museums and public history programs are commonplace today, the information about visitors' emotions is less common.[67]

In addition, failure to meet visitors' expectations raises the risk of further discouraging visitors' interest in a difficult history. Paul H. Williams offers the example of a group of African American visitors who identified their ancestral heritage with the Elmina Slave Castle historic site in Ghana, located in West Africa. The group reported that they were disappointed with their visit. Even though the African American visitors saw the trip as a pilgrimage to their ancestral homeland, the overriding interpretation lumped all of the American visitors—including them—as foreigners. The tour experience did not acknowledge the African Americans' identification with their ancestral homeland. The African American visitors who had anticipated finding validation for their affinity-based heritage in West Africa left sorely disappointed.[68]

While evaluation tools from visitor studies can assist history workers in learning about their visitors, and assist in planning and anticipating audiences' responses to difficult histories, evaluation tools are hard-pressed to address the unpredictable personalities of visitors and the anomalies of public access. Thorough research efforts can help history workers see that the majority of visitors' interests and concerns are addressed in exhibit designs and historical interpretation strategies. But history workers can never fully know the infinitely diverse emotive nature of the individuals who will encounter the difficult history representations.

Ultimately, each history worker and every visitor will respond uniquely to difficult histories. Gaynor Kavanagh explains that museums have difficulty predicting, with a high degree of accuracy, how people really will respond to painful resurfacing memories. It puts the institutions' relationships with their history workers, visitors, donors, and the people with whom they work at some amount of risk.[69] Difficult history interpretations can heighten the anxiety that can accompany learners' identification with the victims as well as potentially retraumatize those who have experienced past violence themselves.[70]

A risk is raised by visitors' narcissistic anxieties that can move the visitors to dismiss or dislike the presenting institution for the choices the history workers made. In 2005, I visited the Iberville Museum, which is located in a charming restored rural courthouse in Iberville Parish, Louisiana. On that visit, I was turned off by the history museum's displays because of the authentic and large Nazi flag that was then hanging in the center of the main gallery. Why, I wondered, would this farming community choose to tell its local history this way? The curator explained to me that the donor of the flag was a World War II veteran who was a resident of Iberville Parish. He was proud of the war booty and saw the artifact as a symbol of the American victory over Germany. However, I felt extremely uncomfortable with the battlefield souvenir, which overshadowed the showcases filled with Louisiana rural life ephemera. I felt distanced from that museum believing in the moment that the organization's supporting community felt differently about the Nazi flag than I felt.[71]

Similarly, a California visitor to the West Baton Rouge Museum in Port Allen, Louisiana, wrote a comment card about the temporary exhibition *Portraits in Gray: A Civil War Photography Exhibition*.[72] The exhibit featured seventy striking historical portraits organized into several themes, including Citizen Soldiers, Civil War Photography, Dressed for the Photographer, Brothers in Arms, Youth at War, and Bowie Knives and Muskets, illustrating the broad range of relationships among the soldiers to one another and to the events of the war. The visitor wrote that the museum was a racist institution for featuring the Confederate portraits. Did the California visitor judge the exhibit as racist because the Confederacy defended slavery and by association saw the museum as a defender of slavery? Can the museum really know whether the visitor actively read the exhibit content and came away with a message about racism, or by association implicated the museum as racist for displaying photographs of Confederate soldiers?

Expectations about difficult history interpretations stem from the learner's personal attachments and memories of that history, meanings that can sometimes be misunderstood, ignored, or denied. Visitors who are not inquisitive or not willing to invest energy in moving past their initial assumptions or familiarity with a difficult history are at risk of being offended by the names, symbols, or images associated with a difficult history. The Iberville Museum example and the West Baton Rouge Museum example illustrate the risk of unengaged visitors who dismiss the deeper historical content by not understanding or agreeing with the meanings the history workers intended for their historical interpretations of the difficult histories.

Visitors can feel deep emotions in the presence of a physical space where a difficult history happened. Visitors in the fall of 2014 to the then newly opened National September 11 Memorial and Museum in New York entered into the areas called Ground Zero. During his visit to the National September 11 Memorial and Museum that fall, visitor Ian Rose, who was originally from Louisiana, explained that he felt connected to the people who perished in the attacks on the World Trade Center over thirteen years earlier. Ian explained that being inside the same spaces where the victims called for help, left messages, ran, and ultimately died made him feel deeply sad, reverent, and grieved by standing in those same spaces. Geographer Kenneth E. Foote explains that a "sense of place" can refer to a learner's deep bonds that develop for environments the learner appreciates. A sense of place can provide some learners with empathy, and at times, even comfort. On the other hand, individuals can experience a sense of "placelessness," what Foote describes as "feelings of alienation, anomie, and even anxiety and fear in situations where these strong positive bonds are missing."[73] For example, sociologist Stephen Small visited a selection of slave cabin exhibits in the Southeast region of the United States and found the history of the people who lived as slaves was "annihilated" by the tour narratives, which trivialized the oppressive experience of their bondage.[74]

In another scenario, visitors can feel estranged or excluded at historic sites where a difficult history took place. Visitors can feel uncomfortable, unwelcome, or denied. Visitors' bonds of attachment can feel disrupted when they enter the spaces that make it difficult for the learner to find ways to connect to the history. Consider my sense of placelessness when I was on a tour in Vienna, Austria, and the strong tension I felt between feeling connected and ashamed in my response to the former Nazi amphitheater. Alternating bonds to historic places are indicative of the wavering tensions incited by difficult histories.

History workers take the responsibility for the interpretations that bequeath the testamentary traces of a difficult history to the public with the expectations that the visitors will care about the history well after their museum visit. Difficult history interpretations are a big "ask" of visitors. Without knowing their visitors personally, history workers are asking visitors to take responsibility for receiving the knowledge about those who suffered. "Each exhibition enacts the giving of a gift that carries with it the demand that visitors attend to and assess the significance of what they are being given."[75] Visitors' responses to difficult knowledge are more than a social interaction with history; the historical accounting demands that visitors assess the significance of the information. Visitors are being asked to learn and take care of the knowledge, respond to the history, work to assess its importance, and to take that knowledge into account as they go about living their lives.

Discussion of Risks

Interpreting difficult history is a form of memory work that is laden with risks and demands sensitivity. Working with memories includes the risk of handling people's emotions from the past, present, and in the future. This is not easy work. Ethical responsibilities cannot be avoided. Working with emotional content raises hard questions and exposes the dangers of good intentions that have not been thoroughly vetted. Kavanagh explains, "This is never more true when memories of trauma are stimulated; when this occurs nothing less than serious reassessment and realignment of museum work is required."[76]

Interpreting afflictions and achievements, cowardice and bravery, human suffering and evil agents raises history workers' concerns to tell difficult histories perceptively in order not to hurt visitors' sensibilities and not to turn off visitors from engaging in museum exhibits and public history programs. While visitors choose to visit exhibits and historical sites about difficult histories, their contentment is merged with sometimes painful memories. Dean MacCannell observes, "For a starting point, let me suggest that pleasurable and painful memory converge in every attraction and that every attraction stages an ethical meeting ground of the wonderful and the dreadful."[77] Visitors can be heard saying that they were glad they visited the Hiroshima National Memorial Museum, for example, even though they had to engage in seeing horrifying images and artifacts, and read frightening accounts of the violent history. Learning about a difficult history can offer learners hopefulness and reconciliation. Learning difficult history can be a burden, and it can be stimulating.

Benefits of Interpreting Difficult History

Reasons and Tools

Given the potential and variety of the risks involved in interpreting difficult histories, history workers can feel hard-pressed to consider why they should pursue interpreting such painful histories. Interpreting difficult histories is a retrospective enterprise that also has valuable social, emotional, and political consequences. The reasons to interpret difficult history are couched in education, politics, and hope. The reasons are not dependent on naive optimism but on a kind of advocacy that is based on a genuine desire to make the difficult history matter, to help individuals and to ultimately help society lead better, more productive lives. There is no basis to believe that interpreting difficult histories can be easy, or to assume that the history workers' efforts will guarantee that all learners will make meaningful connections or feel critical empathy for those who suffered in the past or in distant parts of the world. The interpretations, however, have the great potential to give learners a more accurate record for the capacity of humankind for goodness and evil in order to recognize learners' complicities and affiliations, and to imagine possibilities for alternative futures.

Lonnie Bunch, the founding director for the Smithsonian Institution's National Museum of African American History and Culture, explains the sweeping role museums serve by interpreting difficult histories. "Museums all over the country are working to create opportunities that allow visitors to see our institutions as places of healing, education, affirmation and reflection; cultural entities that are ripe with contemporary resonance; and sources for historical knowledge . . . for people wrestling with despair and uncertainty."[78]

Some of the more superficial explanations of history workers' and visitors' resistances to difficult histories are that the individuals are biased, prejudiced, or uninformed. I argue that the majority of today's twenty-first-century history workers and visitors, while tending to express fear or to show resistance to difficult histories, are more likely responding to the internal psychological learning crises that difficult knowledge incites within learners. As described in chapter 1, the growing trend to interpret war, mass violence, oppression, and tragedies is evidence that despite the risks, history workers and visitors are nevertheless seeking socially responsible historical interpretations and educational opportunities to better understand the world—information that can admittedly be extremely difficult to bear.

Another explanation for history workers avoiding difficult histories is that they are apprehensive, and at times fearful, of the public's possible reactions to exhibits and programs about difficult histories. Janet Marstine observes that museums are generally not risk takers.[79] Former museum director Ruth Abram counters by saying, "At its base is the mistaken idea that the public cannot bear the truth, but the results of Rosenzweig and Thelen's (1998) survey and our own experience at the Tenement Museum say otherwise. The public is clamoring for the truth."[80] David Simpson argues that difficult histories need to be represented, and even commemorated, because no universal consciousness or sympathy is likely to emerge from repressing those memories and that people want to walk where others actually died, in part to pay homage to the dead and partly in a commitment to an authenticity of memorialization.[81]

Interpretations of difficult histories in museums and at historic sites have the power to inform the public, offering authentic evidence and authoritative interpretations of oppression and suffering. Difficult history interpretations can be therapeutic, even cathartic, for learners who are connected to and grieving a difficult history. Difficult history interpretations can provide learners with validation or expand their understandings of the history. Interpretations of difficult histories can influence political views of events or present-day social circumstances. Interpretations of difficult histories can provide legal basis for reparations, and promote reparation and reconciliation processes by revealing consequences for future practices and social changes. Interpretations of difficult histories can expand and elevate subjugated knowledge that can impact the lives of present-day learners and their vision for the future.

Interpretations of difficult histories, Abram explains, are opportunities for history workers and their institutions to actively promote social change and inclusion by taking a leadership role in dealing with complex, controversial, and difficult issues, and therefore shaping a future that has equal and inclusive partnerships with a diverse range of communities.[82] Representations of subjugated histories have the potential to more accurately reflect the composition of public audiences than highly synthesized and overly simplified mainstream historical interpretations and can attract a more diverse set of visitors. A fuller, more diverse audience is then provided with opportunities to further define their individual and social identities and strengthen their affiliations within society. When public history venues are more willing to take on a role in polemics, the public history venues can more productively serve as mediators through which difficult histories can be explored.

Honoring the memory of those who suffered through commemorations and public history endeavors is a form of memory work. Collective memory scholars explain that perpetual remembering of a historical event signifies that the history is imperative to shaping ideologies, traditions, allegiances, and personal and communal identities.[83] The society's drive to sustain particular identities and ideologies is supported by creating and substantiating institutional collections of artifacts and images that encapsulate common ideas of significance and trigger memories and feelings that Sontag calls "perpetual recirculation."[84]

The purpose, Sontag argues, for preserving archival and museum collections related to these historical events is to ensure that the difficult stories they depict will continue to figure in people's consciousness.

Perpetual recirculation, however, is more than remembering. Perpetuating the renewal and recollection of memories assuages the pain of grieving communities in their efforts to make sense of their suffering and losses. The persistent call that this tragedy will never happen again is hopeful and adamant and woeful. The visions stirred by commemorative acts are a hope for peace and a call for collective instruction. Historical representations of suffering invoke the miracle of survival. The role of commemoration is the articulated lessons about how the suffering was not in vain, that the suffering matters to us today and for the future. How often we hear the insistent cry of the bereaved, "Never again!" The lessons from difficult histories can be simultaneously pragmatic, spiritual, and instructive. The ethics of commemoration are designed from fragments of what was left of the losses and from the imagination of the survivors who ask, "What have we learned?"

When learners come to understand the circumstances of mass violence and oppression, they are more likely to ask questions and demand to know more about the history and the people affected by the history, then and now. Empathy for the historical victims and their descendants can emerge from learners when they are moved to respond to the injustices described in an exhibition or historical venue. Visitors' subsequent actions are indicators that the visitors-as-learners have an empathetic vision for a more just world, sometimes by making personal or local changes. Such reactions are indicators of the kind of hopefulness that interpretations of difficult histories can ignite. Active empathy can stimulate present-day learners' actualization to influence policy and politics, inspiring changes in society. The responses can be wide ranging from simply changing one learner's opinion to moving a group of learners to become advocates for a cause. Learners can be influenced to change their personal behavior, perhaps sign a petition, donate funds to a social cause, or register to vote. Learners can have a change of mind and no longer associate with an entity or consume particular products.

There are sensitive, productive, and meaningful ways of interpreting difficult histories that can be instructive, useful, and even empowering and life changing. Sandell explains,

> [W]orking with both the memories and the people to whom they truly belong, museums can bear witness to the best and the worst, the extraordinary and mundane, the innovative and the traditional. They can enable others in their own explorations of life's experiences. They can create environments that may precipitate the sharing of talk and reflection on the past hitherto not expressed. Where this is handled with tact, knowledge, emotional honesty, and a genuine quality of understanding, the ability of museums to be socially relevant is increased beyond measure. Indeed, their ability to be socially inclusive cannot proceed without it.[85]

Ongoing List of Reasons to Interpret Difficult Histories

Advocacy

Citizenship

Commemorate

Create memories

Create, sustain, or modify identities

Demonstrate respect

Educate

Grieve

Honor

Hope

Inform

Inspire critical action, advocacy, and social improvement

Inspire empathy

Instruct

Moral concern for others

Motivate research

Offer of an apology

Offer of reparations

Peace education

Provide examples of inspirational resolve

Provide social affirmation

Raise tensions for learning

Remember

Render compassionate justice

Renew memories

Resolve

Social justice education

Therapeutic reminiscence work

Validate visitors' understandings or challenge understandings

Warn against future violence

Work through suffering

Difficult histories can serve as tools for a number of positive objectives, some political, some personal, some scholarly, and some emotional. The above list of potential reasons to pursue interpreting and learning difficult histories is merely a start. The reasons help to explain why we risk predictable discomforts in learning about the histories of suffering and injustice. Each reason is worthy of further discussion. The following sections look more closely at some of the more commonly cited reasons for interpreting difficult histories.

Engendering Hope

Hopefulness is embedded in historical interpretations of difficult histories. The decision to interpret difficult history is part of a hopeful enterprise that encourages a positive antic-ipation that the interpretations of the difficult history will improve our collective under-standing of humankind. History workers' actions in conducting research, designing exhibits and programs, writing publications, and producing films are focused on showing how the difficult histories are relevant and meaningful to visitors.

New interpretations of difficult histories are contributions to the language of possibili-ties. A theme of hope can come from the telling of new stories, or from updating interpreta-tions or from helping learners locate their place within a tradition, or can be found in rede-fined relationships to an ethical code. Newly introduced interpretations of difficult histories are not meant to collapse the past into the present but to highlight the mutually referential tensions. When history workers can present new comparisons, draw fresh parallels, identify previously little-known relationships, and reveal forgotten histories, new perspectives and questions emerge and hopeful visions of a better world without the painful and oppressive structures will make that difficult history matter even more.

Practical, ethical, personal, and political imaginations are rooted in our understanding of human dignity. And descriptions and images of compassionate justice encourage learn-ers to further their commitments to families, communities, and nations. While empathy is essential to learning about difficult histories, so are learners' abilities to imagine perspec-tives about the future. Reflecting on and conversing about a difficult history are avenues to imagining possibilities for what the history means today and for the future. Educator Roger I. Simon contends, "A language of possibility does not have to dissolve into a reified utopianism; instead it can be developed as a precondition for nourishing convictions that summon up the courage to imagine a different and more just world and to struggle for it."[86] Interpretations of difficult histories profoundly ask learners to envision what is and what will be possible.

Serving as Commemorations

Interpretations of difficult history can commemorate and remember. The promise of re-membrance and new beginnings is inherent in the work of commemoration, a core promise that energizes historical research and innovations in the work of history. David Simpson explains, "The routines of commemorative culture, whether private or public, exist to medi-ate and accommodate the unbearably dissonant agonies of the survivors into a larger picture that can be metaphysical or national-political and is often both at once."[87]

Acts of commemoration are contained in education. The promise of remembrance is the work of commemoration, the responsibility to mark, research, and teach the meanings of our ancestors' achievements and afflictions. Our ancestors' monuments and moments are the promise they left to us to build the next generation of new beginnings. The process of designing commemorative markers and programs demands reflection, discussion, and planning, all with the goal of teaching others about the select meanings sown from a history. Our emotional and intellectual desires to make meanings from pieces of history are part of memory work, and part of the work of creating identities from personal affiliations to global identifications. The lessons from commemorations hold infinite possibilities, which are as varied as the multiple viewpoints learners bring to a particular commemorative representation. Yet regardless of the chosen partialities for any commemoration, the act of collectively remembering is imbued with a promise to teach others and a promise to keep learning. Kenneth E. Foote explains that retrospective examinations of historic sites offer useful lessons that can rally citizens around the idea of a shared heroic past.[88] This can contribute greatly to building a sense of community and nationhood, and help to build upon commemorations that honor the dead to expand on the lessons of the event in which the lives were lost. Foote gives the example of the historic site at Bunker Hill, arguing that the site was commemorated less to honor the 140 soldiers who died there than to teach about the American Revolution and its consequences.[89]

Advocating for Social Justice

We can use the histories of injustices for social good. Interpretations of difficult histories that are shaped as lessons, as examples, as art, and as sources for dialogs about social justice serve as history tools. Like the drive to find lessons and reasons to honor loss through commemoration, history workers search for moral and practical connections to explain how difficult histories are relevant for the living. Museums and history venues, it is generally believed, are endowed with the public's trust and can exercise their authority to educate for social justice.

Often, memorialization interpreted in museums illustrates triumph over adversity through vindicating messages showing resolve and constructive outcomes. The Hiroshima Peace Museum, the Oklahoma City Memorial Museum, and the National September 11 Memorial and Museum all interpret difficult histories as memorials that offer examples of violence and triumph, and, as much, lessons about violence and peace. Historical interpretations about difficult histories can be used as lessons to show the continuation of threats of oppression. In this way, Paul H. Williams argues, "Visitors possessing a diversity of culturally informed and historically situated identities respond to this 'moral education'—the cluster of ideas concerning personal culpability, victimhood, and responsibility as it relates to past remembrance and future vigilance."[90]

The Manzanar Japanese Internment Camp historic site, while marking the tragic losses and oppressions inflicted on Americans, has expanded to teach contemporary lessons relevant to twenty-first-century social justice issues. The immediate meanings of the historic buildings, barbed wire fences, and historical photographs of the Japanese American internment camp have expanded from remembering the individuals who were hurt by the oppression and imprisonment to teachable lessons about American values of citizenship and freedom from violence and oppression and the extreme harm of racial prejudice and racial profiling.

Memorial museums, peace museums, and social justice museums, including the National Center for Civil and Human Rights in Atlanta, Georgia, use histories of oppression and injustices to illustrate lessons for peace education. Dina Bailey at the National Center for Civil and Human Rights explains that the center "uses difficult stories from the past (and present) to illustrate positive lessons for today. Supporting the development of global citizens who are committed to peaceful interactions is a thread that ties all museums of conscience together."[91] Nancy Gillette at the U.S. Memorial Holocaust Museum in Washington, D.C., said the museum is expanding its interpretation and work for social justice education to address genocide in other parts of the world.[92] Richard Cooper at the National Underground Railroad Freedom Center in Cincinnati, Ohio, said the center is expanding its interpretation beyond Africans and African Americans who were enslaved in the nineteenth century in North America to include slavery in the twenty-first century to advocate for the global modern abolition movement.[93]

The concept of difficult histories as a tool for social good is well articulated by Ruth Abram. Abram is a founding member of the International Coalition of Sites of Conscience and former director of the Tenement Museum in New York. Abram recognizes that while history in general is integral to the human experience, difficult history has practical instructional and advocacy value.[94] Abram gives the example of using an historic slave cabin to teach learners about the relevance of slavery from the past to slavery in our present. "If through the Slave House, we understand the circumstances and the thought process that can lead one human being to regard another human being as property, we can fight against the factors that encourage this insidious view."[95] Abram explains that embedded in the histories are lessons that are so powerful that, if taken to bear, could inform, guide, and improve our future. The concept of history as a tool for social good gives history workers further justification to face the risks of interpreting difficult histories and to explore, with great sensitivity, methods to represent oppression and mass trauma. Williams explains, "More than almost any other institution, memorial museums purport to be morally guided. They invariably cherish public education as it is geared towards the future avoidance of comparable tragedies."[96]

Mark O'Neill and Lois Silverman contend that the global awakening of a public who more broadly recognizes their power to claim and exercise their human rights has encouraged museums to tackle difficult histories.[97] The external social pressures being felt by museums and the global tourism industry has supported museums to more boldly serve as agents of cultural activism. With a bold agenda to interpret difficult histories, history workers are more willing to interpret difficult histories for the purpose of social justice education and advocacy. This path is leading history workers to more critically assess how they can attempt to teach compassion.

Museums and historic site interpretations, which are assembled with material culture, narratives, and landscapes, can cultivate compassion and offer lessons that explain how human suffering is a constant regrettable and painful reality that is relevant in the present. David Simpson compares the power of literature to the power of museum interpretation as a medium to cultivate compassionate identification with the demise of physical suffering.[98] Difficult history interpretations have the capacity to inspire compassion and can serve as an available tool for learning to live ethically.[99]

Grieving

Survivors and witnesses often search for meanings of the deaths that they are grieving. Mourning the loss of loved ones, friends, communities, and even ideologies (e.g., loss of freedoms, political power, or censorship) is a necessary psychological response for the survivors. How will the losses change the way we live? Can the bereaved make sense of the losses so that the bereaved can go on to live their lives? The plaques and statues that serve as memorial markers on historic landscapes and on preserved historic buildings sometimes signify that the tragedies that took place within those walls can be valuable to the bereaved. The artifacts in cases that are assembled to recall the memories of the dead are set in places that can be sites for mourning. Public art dedicated to the memory of the deceased are placed in locations that mourners can visit to reflect on their losses and sorrow. Exhibitions that recall human losses can provide spaces for conversations, validation, reflection, and working through grief. These interpreted spaces about difficult histories are conceived with the purpose of engaging visitors, some who are grieving and some who are concerned or curious about how the losses impact the world. And even though the historical interpretations are planned, the ways visitors will connect to the histories and grieve will be unique to each individual.

In discussing memorial museums, Williams explains that mourning sites are socially necessary, and they eventually evolve as ideological statements.[100] Ritualized mourning customs, like unveiling a historic marker or opening a memorial museum, can help to liberate the bereaved from what can be paralyzing grief and enable them to go forward with their lives. Memorial museums, for example, can be an extension of the mourning process for entire communities who choose to examine and reflect on the losses. Memorial museums also provide learning experiences for a broader range of visitors who are usually interested in learning about the impact of the losses historically and about finding how the losses are relevant today. Survivors and later generations look for the causes of the losses and for reasons they might be able to attribute to their losses in their mournful search for explanations for the tragedies. In the case of the memorial and museum in Oklahoma City, Edward Linenthal explains,

> The elevation of those killed in Oklahoma City to the hierarchical status of culturally meaningful public deaths reminded some that there were victims of everyday violence who remained largely forgotten, their deaths counting only as by-products of everyday American violence. Their lives and deaths were consigned to oblivion by the vagaries of what registered as culturally meaningful death. Intense public mourning for the children murdered in Oklahoma City, for example, provided an opportunity for some to call for a "remembrance" for these forgotten child victims through increased efforts to end domestic abuse in the United States and child slavery in various countries.[101]

As part of the grieving process, mourners and empathetic learners can work through their pain productively through historical interpretations, raising public awareness of the tragedies and informing others about the victims' travails and connecting those stories to populations who are presently being afflicted by offenses.

The unplanned exhibits of grief, tribute fences, roadside markers, and fence memorials acknowledge specific difficult histories and appear as spontaneous places for the public to grieve, pray, give testimonials, and offer condolences. Such public grieving has grown more demonstrably in the past decades. The fence memorial around the front of Kensington Palace in London spontaneously grew emotional when mourners left flowers, candles, and condolences in 1997 when Princess Diana died. Twenty years later, a tribute fence was decorated with flowers, condolences, and sentimental offerings on the campus at Virginia Tech in Blacksburg, Virginia, in 2007 immediately following the mass shootings. After a period of mourning, the university's administration encouraged the collection of the material offerings and the preservation of the grief objects.

Memorial museums and public sites for grieving provide visitors with a place to physically connect to and mourn the losses of a difficult history. As part of a Jewish custom, mourners visiting a gravesite will leave a stone on the headstone each time they visit. The message of concern and grief grows with the mounting number of stones on the edges and corners of the gravesite. Mourners of many cultures leave flowers, food, tobacco, and other gifts on gravesites. These symbolic gestures are physical demonstrations of grief that can be seen by others. The act of placing something as a "gift" on a fence or memorial allows the mourner to connect to the deceased and to the event, as if to say, "I remember you and I am showing the world that I care about you." The act of giving something to the memorial space is also a part of the bereaved person's mourning, a prescribed way of emotionally connecting to the deceased.

The Vietnam Veterans Memorial in Washington, D.C., is a long-accepted site for public grieving where visitors have continuously left over two million items and written sentiments for over thirty years. The public mourning phenomenon materialized at the perimeter of the elementary school in Newtown, Connecticut, in 2012 after the mass shooting, and along the fences of the Murrah Federal Building in 1995 after the bombing. Public mourning occurs spontaneously, person by person, as mourners make their offerings of condolences and memories with thoughtful materials and written sentiments placed on the fences or on the perimeters of the sites of violence. The interactive experience provides mourners with a ritual space that allows individuals to express their sorrow and articulate their connections to the event and to the victims by allowing mourners to creatively and physically contribute to the memorial.

Fence memorials can also emerge as sites for advocacy, as one grieving survivor wrote in a letter left on the fence at the remains of the Murrah Federal Building, "Deborah Ferrell-Lynn, whose cousin Susan was murdered, informed visitors that Susan would want her death to 'stand for something.' She then offered a challenge: 'How will you change because of this place and the people who died in years to come?' Or will you ask, 'How can I stop the pain, the suffering, the tears?'"[102]

Public sites of grief carry messages from the bereaved that the losses were not in vain, that the losses have meaning in the present. The phenomenon of public grieving appears within the interaction between grief-stricken visitors and historical interpretations about difficult histories, especially within the spaces of memorials and commemorations.[103] At memorials, exhibits, and historic sites, visitors' responses can help history workers see how the visitors are mournfully invested in engaging in the memorials, exhibits, or sites. Visitors might be working through their grief, in part, through the public history experience. In these settings, the visitors are often looking for evidence and explanations, and through the history learning experience can be encouraged to find connections to what was lost. The dedicated spaces to interpreting difficult histories are tools that can provide mourners with opportunities to grieve, talk, learn, and reflect.

Offering Pedagogical Reparations

Museums and memorials about difficult histories can serve as pedagogical reparations that are indeed subjective remedies to render compensation and discourse for forgiveness. Historic sites, museums, documentaries, and public art focused on difficult histories can be examples of reparations to begin the healing processes for victims, perpetrators, witnesses, and descendants. Calls of "Never again!" and "Never forget!" sound loudly with each dose of restitution offered through public history venues, however uncertain the offering might redress the oppressed.

Extensive history exhibitions like those at the National Museum of African American History and Culture and the National Museum of the American Indian, both components of the Smithsonian Institution in Washington, D.C., contain within them a deeply felt sub-text of regret and expressions of apologies and loss. While the interpretations include celebrations of two distinct cultural heritages, historical journeys, and achievements, the very placement of these particular massive museums among the other highly valued museums are also expressions of the elevated value these histories now hold for Americans. The two newer museums, in part, serve as national reparative statements for the history of oppression endured by millions of men, women, and children over centuries in America.

The public history offerings of exhibits, preserved historic sites, and memorial museums about difficult histories can serve as attempts at reparations, even at the risk of appearing perfunctory. Mary Kurihara spoke about the World War II–era Japanese internment camps to the presidential commission whose findings led to the passage of the Civil Liberties Act of 1988. She relayed her husband's testimony to the commission about the years he was forced to live in the camps Santa Anita and Post. Quoting her husband, she read, "I remember having to stay at the dirty horse stables at Santa Anita." . . . "I remember thinking, 'Am I a human being? Why are we being treated like this?'" . . . "I was treated like an enemy by other Americans."[104] Kurihara concluded by saying, "This government can never repay all the people who suffered. But, this should not be an excuse for token apologies. I hope this country will never forget what happened . . . and do what it can to make sure that future generations will never forget."[105] The reparative value of interpretations of difficult histories is that they have the potential to elevate the nation's awareness of the history, recognize the significance of the history, and inspire learning and advocacy for the prevention of future oppressions. The historical interpretations offer survivors and the descendants of the victims the promise that the history is not forgotten.

Reparations for the injustices suffered in difficult histories are a responsibility for the living to negotiate. Ta-Nehisi Coates argues, "One cannot escape the question by hand-waving at the past, disavowing the acts of one's ancestors, nor by citing a recent date of ancestral immigration. The last slaveholder has been dead for a very long time. The last soldier to endure Valley Forge has been dead much longer. To proudly claim the veteran and disown the slaveholder is patriotism à la carte."[106]

Museum encounters with historical suffering can be pedagogical reparations in the form of supporting learners' concern and responsibility toward others. In this way, guilt can be viewed as a necessary emotion for the moral work of making reparations. History workers can consider how visitors' feelings of guilt are entwined in responsible historical interpretations.

Sharon Todd looks to the writings of philosopher Emmanuel Levinas, who emphasizes that the living need to be less concerned with how guilt is tied to our past experiences and more concerned with our openness to ethical gestures made toward others for the future. Todd explains, "Lévinas draws attention to the metaphysical aspects of guilt and susceptibility and how these give rise to an inevitable responsibility."[107] Through a learning experience about a difficult history, the visitor might be moved from feeling guilt toward feeling empathy and is then better positioned to productively respond to present-day injustices.

Todd contends, "Unlike empathy, for example, guilt is a response that is seen to represent a pedagogical failure of sorts, for guilt is not generally held to be morally or politically productive, and certainly is not viewed as having much education value."[108] However, history workers can consider guilt as it is tied to the act of offering reparations. History workers can consider the ethical significance of how guilt engages learners with the suffering of others. While feelings of guilt are one form of resistance to difficult knowledge, guilt is also a step in learning how to morally respond to others, to understand how the history is relevant to the learners' present, and possibly a prelude to how the learner can make a positive difference in the future.

Interpretations of difficult histories can serve as a way for the culpable agents to offer a reparative response for the historical injustices. Civil rights activist and former internment camp detainee Sue Kunitomi Embrey recognized the fragility of memory of the internment of Japanese Americans in her remarks at the opening ceremony in 2004 of the Interpretive Center at the Manzanar National Historic Site. She said, "My answer is that stories like this need to be told, and too many of us have passed away without telling our stories. The Interpretive Center is important because it needs to show to the world that America is strong as it makes amends for the wrongs it has committed, and that we will always remember Manzanar because of that."[109]

Memory Work: Tools for Historians and Therapists

A benefit of memory work is to improve historiography. For historians, memory work is a critical view of how we recall the past. It allows us to question the past that we recognize. Memory work questions familiar histories and lets us imagine what voices are not being heard or reimagine and critically research the historian's long-held tradition about how or why a history happened. Historian Michael Kammen writes about memory work in the context of how nations remember, in particular, the United States. As Kammen reminds us, there has never truly been one American history, and the what, the how, and the why events happened are open to debate.[110] Critic Peter Ling says Kammen explains how memory work addresses the "changing configurations of recognized and contending pasts, and Kammen assumes that his treatment of the afterlife of past events will be elaborately reticulated."[111] Midcentury philosophers, including Walter Benjamin and Jacques Derrida, wrote extensively on memory work, encouraging scholars in multiple fields, including historians, to be willing to read histories through the prisms of different eras. In the context of museum work, Ruth Abram emphasizes that everyone is invited to regard history with skepticism because it is an ongoing process of discovery and correction.[112]

Lev Grossman wrote a touching obituary for author and poet Maya Angelou, calling her a legendary voice. Angelou was a deeply reflective storyteller. So many of her works are based on personal and historical accounts and are her responses to the oppression of black Americans.[113] Grossman tells us that Angelou could transform her stories of suffering into "a hymn of glorious human endurance that profoundly influenced generations of memoirists."[114] Writing is a form of memory work, and Angelou explained that memories of human suffering are tools for building trust and crumbling antagonism. "What I would really like said about me [when I die] is that I dared to love. . . . By love I mean that condition in the human spirit so profound, it encourages us to develop courage and build bridges, and then to trust those bridges and cross the bridges in attempt to reach other human beings."[115] It might seem fitting to add memory worker to Angelou's list of accomplishments. While history is partial and memory is fallible, memory work is healing, creative, and educational.

Andreas Huyssen reminds us that the past is not simply held in our memories but must be articulated in order to become memory. The chasm between living through an event and remembering it in representation is that space that is open to tremendous cultural and artistic creativity.[116] What comes to my mind immediately when I reflect on memory work are novels based on difficult histories that inspire readers to feel empathy for the fictional victims, and then move readers to see how the real history matters; for example, *Obasan* by Joy Kogawa[117] and Toni Morrison's *Beloved*.[118]

Another benefit of memory work about difficult histories is it can be therapeutic. Museums, historical sites, and their collections are of value to individuals wrestling with their memories of difficult histories, and are of great use to those who want to help those who are struggling to live with those memories.[119] Reminiscence work is a form of memory work that is therapeutic by design.[120] Museum theorist Gaynor Kavanagh writes about therapeutic reminiscence work with veterans who are grappling with their traumatic war experiences. Kavanagh explains, "Memories are like scar tissue: they stay with us through life."[121] Memories are used to communicate and define who we are. However, traumatic memories are buried deep into subconscious memory. Consider veterans who do not often talk about their wartime experiences. Kavanagh describes a couple that visited a museum that encouraged the husband, a war veteran, to talk about a wartime experience. Kavanagh said, "The visit, coupled with the opportunity to talk with other veterans, appeared to have lifted a burden from him. He seemed to be quite relaxed when recalling his experiences, whereas hitherto he had been ill at ease when the war in the Far East had been raised in routine conversation. For the veteran's wife, the visit to the museum had been a catalyst, acting on her husband and other veterans in a way that no other environment or setting could have done."[122]

Museums and other public history venues foster interactions between people and artifacts that can open learners' imaginations and deepen their understandings of reality. Imagining and critically reflecting on how a history happened through the aid of an exhibit, a program, or a film can greatly expand the capacity of difficult history interpretations to serve as agents of change, healing, and social inclusion.[123] Developing interpretations for difficult histories is a form of memory work that demands creativity, multiple viewpoints, and dialog that can help those who are struggling to heal.

Accessing Truth, Individual Morality, and Authenticity

Interpretations of difficult histories are tools for learners who are seeking truth and for shaping one's moral self. The power of a museum's authority to interpret history is found within the relationships among an institution's history workers who make the interpretive decisions. A persuasive unified voice in an exhibit interpretation can constitute an authoritative tone, which impresses upon visitors that this information is true. According to Hooper-Greenhill,

> We [museum workers] approach experience and/or material matter with certain prejudices [prejudice here means selective rather than biased], or foreknowledge, given by our own position in history, and with a certain openness. This receptiveness to our "object," allowing it to speak for itself, creates a balance or dialectic between prejudice and openness. . . . The dialectic permits revision of our prejudices towards a greater "truth," but this truth is still relative, historical and social.[124]

History workers eventually decide what may be viewed, how it should be seen, and when the interpretation will be available. Museum interpretations mediate authority and truth through representations of ideas, events, and people through visual and discursive systems. While the viewpoints presented in any given history are open for discussion, the interpretations of difficult histories can provide learners with valuable opportunities for authentic experiences and fact finding.

Public history rests on the authenticity of the evidence history workers bring to bear through their interpretations of the history. Jim Loewen reminds us that to do otherwise is immoral: "[T]he concealment of historical truth is a crime against the people."[125] Learners who feel they have been lied to or deceived in museums or in public history venues can be offended. Abram explains, "Those who learn they have been lied to in an important matter are . . . resentful, disappointed and suspicious. They see that they were manipulated, that the deceit made them unable to make choices for themselves according to the most adequate information available, unable to act as they would have wanted to act had they known all along."[126] Visitors to museums and other public history venues are learners who expect truthful historical representations and are also positioned to question the given histories.

A morning newspaper comic, "Mallard Fillmore," shows an image of a middle-aged man sitting in front of a television. The text bubble coming from the television says, "WARNING: The following story may contain some facts that don't jibe with our preconceived narrative; viewer discretion is advised."[127] While the daily comic is poking fun at the idea that history is negotiable and viewers will be resistant to new information, it also tells us that postmodern sensibilities have filtered out to mainstream daily life. History workers who recognize the holding power of collective memory and the likely scenario of visitors resisting new historical interpretations will be better prepared to address visitor resistance. Indeed, history workers can encourage learners to challenge facts and to critically listen to stories. Newly introduced difficult history interpretations can help prepare learners to change their understandings of the world by emphasizing that what we know about the social world is ever changing.

Learning about a difficult history is a kind of personal memory work when visitors and history workers are in search for truth and moral identification. The individual learner will look through the prisms of historicity and determine what he or she assesses as true. The learner will determine how he or she is connected to the evidence and consider if the learner can identify with the evidence. "Do I believe this?" "Is this relevant to me?" "Does this make sense to me?" The interaction between learner and historical interpretation is an opportunity for the learner to validate or change what the learner believes. Learners, especially young learners, who engage with newly introduced information about a difficult history are collecting examples of good and evil and right and wrong as the historical interpretations unfold. Accumulated examples of difficult histories provide an ever more complex matrix for moral living for individuals who are learning how to live in a civil society.

Interpretations of difficult histories are tools for informing the public as a response to the call to "Never forget!" that the tragedies happened. The interpretations ask learners to take responsibility for learning about the history and to make that knowledge matter. Abram explains, "By insisting on the 'truth,' we help illuminate some important concepts, which, if taken to heart, could inform and improve lives."[128] Interpretations of difficult histories are tools to help learners make informed decisions on how to vote or how to teach family members about right and wrong, and about warning students about the existing evil realities that impact our lives. Difficult histories can be revealing to learners who are just finding out about who has suffered in the past, who is suffering now, and who is at risk of suffering in the future. Learning about the Holocaust, for example, provides learners with a historical context to understand the need for aid and refuge for populations threatened with genocidal war in Africa at the opening of the twenty-first century.

For young learners, difficult histories serve as illustrations of immortality and mass violence that enable them to understand the meaning of the calls of "Never again!" Children who learn about wickedness in the world through sensitive and appropriate historical interpretations are learning what behaviors are immoral and what reactions to injustice are helpful to society.

Interpretations of difficult histories can play a role in identity negotiations. We live historically and depend on our personal and collective memories to move through life, always reflecting, "Who am I?" Recovery of the past is a part of a lifelong process of constructing our identities. Difficult histories are some of the stories that shape cultural responses to identity formation, such as posttraumatic slavery syndrome and survivor's guilt, discussed earlier in this chapter. Historical interpretations can strengthen an individual's and a community's sense of belonging, as much as they can clarify social differences. Interpreted difficult histories can amplify diversity and power struggles through examples of social systems that identify consensual and conflicting ideologies. Relevant historical interpretations can show shared and biased positions in society that can help us define who the "other" was and help learners assess what populations are being targeted as outsiders today.

Subjugated histories and venerated histories are sifted, mixed, and calibrated in historical interpretations. Museums and public history venues are places where people can actively make and refine their identities by finding content and characteristics among difficult historical events and histories of oppressed populations that they find meaningful and useful.

In Closing: Reasons and Tools for Interpreting Difficult Histories

History workers sensitive to the powerful tools of history interpretation can use difficult histories to elevate and remember the forgotten communities, shape social justice ideologies and educational aims, advocate for human rights, reveal silenced histories, aid those who are grieving, keep history current and relevant, strengthen individual and community identities, teach concern for others, and help society distinguish between immoral and moral living. Difficult history interpretations are hopeful enterprises that help to commemorate, honor, and remember those who suffered, and bring to the forefront of our present-day attentions those who are suffering now. Difficult history interpretations are relevant history projects that serve as tools for improving lives and society. Through historical interpretations of difficult histories, history workers can answer the call of victims and survivors to "Never forget!" and to teach present generations why victims, survivors, witnesses, and their descendants cry out "Never again!"

Addressing the Learning Process for Difficult Histories

Understanding the risks of interpreting difficult histories in museums and other public history venues and recognizing the reasons, benefits, and tools difficult histories afford learners and their communities demand that history workers develop methods for best practice to address the resistance this genre of history provokes among history workers and visitors.

The next chapter explains Commemorative Museum Pedagogy, which addresses visitors' resistances. CMP is a method that enables history workers to recognize the risks and address learners' emotional distress. The approach allows for the unpredictable, nonlinear, and recursive nature of learning and accounts for the need for the ethical engagement of learners in remembering victims from the past.

Historian Michel-Rolph Trouillot rightly asks, "If some events cannot be accepted even as they occur, how can they be accessed later? In other words, can historical narratives convey plots that are unthinkable in the world within which these narratives take place? How does one write a history of the impossible?"[129]

Psychoanalysis has attained a significant role among educational theorists as an analytic methodology dedicated to understanding how new information such as traumatic histories of violence or group aggression is known. Difficult history is always a combination of that which is knowable and that which is unknowable. It is wrapped in the dynamics of grieving implicated through the rhetorical expressions and actions of history workers and visitors. Psychoanalytic curriculum theories search within pedagogies and interpretation traditions to better understand socially repressed motives, fears, and desires that shape interpretation practices and learning environments.

CMP uses this group of scholarship and focuses on trauma studies to address questions about how learners engage in learning about histories of mass violence and oppression. What happens when stories are too much for the learner to bear? Deborah Britzman, Claudia Eppert, Roger I. Simon et al.,[130] and others offer insights into this kind of difficult learning—theoretical insights that are central to CMP and my analysis for exploring history workers' and visitors' responses to interpretations of difficult histories.

Notes

1. Susan Sontag, *Regarding the Pain of Others* (New York: Farrar, Straus and Giroux, 2003), 53.
2. See, for example, James O. Horton and Lois E. Horton, ed., *Slavery and Public History: The Tough Stuff of American Memory* (New York: The New Press, 2006).
3. Michel-Rolph Trouillot, *Silencing the Past: Power and the Production of History* (Boston, MA: Beacon Press, 1995), 148.
4. Ibid., 149.
5. See Deborah P. Britzman and Alice J. Pitt, "Pedagogy in Transferential Time: Casting the Past of Learning in the Presence of Teaching," in *Action Research as Living Practice*, ed. Terrance Carson and Dennis Sumara (New York: Peter Lang, 1997), 65–76; Deborah P. Britzman, *After-Education: Anna Freud, Melanie Klein, and Psychoanalytic Histories of Learning* (Albany: State University of New York Press, 2003); Claudia Eppert, "Relearning Questions: Responding to the Ethical Address of Past and Present Others," in *Between Hope and Despair: Pedagogy and the Remembrance of Historical Trauma*, ed. Roger I. Simon, Sharon Rosenberg, and Claudia Eppert (Lanham, MD: Rowman & Littlefield, 2000), 213–46. These references offer examples of loss in learning in classroom settings. See Juliet Mitchell, ed., *The Selected Melanie Klein* (New York: The Free Press, 1986) for a theoretical description of loss in learning in young children.
6. J. Laplanche and J. B. Pontalis, *The Language of Psycho-Analysis*, trans. Donald Nicholson-Smith (New York: W. W. Norton, 1973), 466.
7. Cathy Caruth, "Trauma and Experience: Introduction," in *Trauma: Explorations of Memory* (Baltimore, MD: Johns Hopkins University Press, 1995), 3–4.
8. Dori Laub, "Bearing Witness, or the Vicissitudes of Listening," in *Testimony: Crises of Witnessing in Literature, Psychoanalysis and History*, ed. Shoshana Felman and Dori Laub (New York: Routledge, 1992), 57–74.
9. Ibid., 59–60.
10. Ibid., 62.
11. See Trouillot, *Silencing the Past*, and Antoinette T. Jackson, *Speaking for the Enslaved* (Walnut Creek, CA: Left Coast Press, 2012).
12. See Drew Faust, *The Creation of Confederate Nationalism: Ideology and Identity in the Civil War South* (Baton Rouge: Louisiana State University Press, 1988); Eric Gable, Richard Handler, and Anna Lawson, "On the Uses of Relativism: Fact, Conjecture and Black and White Histories at Colonial Williamsburg," *American Ethnologist* 19, no. 4 (1992): 791–805; Trouillot, *Silencing the Past*; Katherine Bankole, "Plantations without Slaves: The Legacy of Louisiana Culture," in *Plantation Society and Race Relations: The Origins of Inequality*, ed. Thomas J.

Durant Jr. and J. David Knottnerus (Westport, CT: Praeger, 1999); Jennifer L. Eichstedt and Stephen Small, *Representations of Slavery: Race and Ideology in Southern Plantation Museums* (Washington, DC: Smithsonian Institution, 2002); Julia Rose, "Preserving Southern Feminism: The Veiled Nexus of Race, Class and Gender at Louisiana Historical Plantation Home Sites," *Taboo: Journal of Culture and Education* 8, no. 1 (2004): 57–75.

13. Trouillot, *Silencing the Past*, 16.
14. Ibid.
15. Iwona Irwin-Zarecka, *Frames of Remembrance: The Dynamics of Collective Memory* (New Brunswick, NJ: Transaction, 1994).
16. Randolph Bergstrom, "Tough Telling," *The Public Historian* 35, no. 3 (2013): 5.
17. Irwin-Zarecka, *Frames of Remembrance*.
18. Kelvin Chan, "Tiananmen Memory Flickers in Tiny Museum," *The Advocate* (Baton Rouge, LA), June 8, 2014, 9D.
19. Douglas MacCash, "Skylar Fein: Installation Reignites Memory of a Deadly Fire," *Times-Picayune*, December 1, 2013, http://blog.nola.com/dougmaccash/2008/11/fein_pages.html.
20. Diane Anderson-Minshall, "Remembering the Worst Mass Killing of LGBT People in U.S. History," *The Advocate* (Baton Rouge, LA), June 24, 2013, http://www.advocate.com/crime/2013/11/15/remembering-worst-mass-killing-lgbt-people-us-history.
21. Deborah P. Britzman, *Lost Subjects, Contested Objects: Toward a Psychoanalytic Inquiry of Learning* (Albany: State University of New York Press, 1998).
22. Ibid., 117 and 134.
23. See James Strachey, *The Standard Edition of the Complete Psychological Works of Sigmund Freud*, Vol. 14 (London: Hogarth Press, 1972); Melanie Klein, "The Early Stages of the Oedipus Conflict," in *The Selected Melanie Klein*, ed. Juliet Mitchell (New York: The Free Press, 1986), 69–83; Donald W. Winnicott, "D. W. Winnicott: The Fate of the Transitional Object," in *D. W. Winnicott: Psycho-Analytic Explorations*, ed. Clare Winnicott, Ray Shepherd, and Madeleine Davis (Cambridge, MA: Harvard University Press, 1989), 53–58; Pamela Thurschwell, *Sigmund Freud: Routledge Critical Thinkers' Essential Guides for Literary Studies* (London: Routledge, 2000).
24. Tom M. Kitwood, *Concern for Others: A New Psychology of Conscience and Morality* (London: Routledge, 1990).
25. See Sigmund Freud, *Beyond the Pleasure Principle*, trans. C. J. M. Hubback (London: The International Psychoanalytical Press, 1922); Caruth, "Trauma and Experience: Introduction"; Britzman, *Lost Subjects*.
26. Britzman, *Lost Subjects*, 117.
27. See Eichstedt and Small, *Representations of Slavery*.
28. Everett Mendelsohn, "The Political Anatomy of Controversy in the Sciences," in *Scientific Controversies: Case Studies in the Resolution and Closure of Disputes in Science and Technology*, ed. H. Tristram Engelhardt Jr. and Arthur L. Caplan (UK: Cambridge University Press, 1989), 93.
29. Shoshana Felman, *Jacques Lacan and the Adventure of Insight: Psychoanalysis in Contemporary Culture* (Cambridge, MA: Harvard University Press, 1987), 78.
30. Trouillot, *Silencing the Past*, 104.
31. Sontag, *Regarding the Pain of Others*, 41.
32. Ibid., 113.
33. Edward Linenthal, *The Unfinished Bombing: Oklahoma City in American Memory* (New York: Oxford University Press, 2001), 90.
34. Sarah Roff, "Treatment, Not Trigger Warnings," *Chronicle of Higher Education* LX, no. 38 (2014): B2.

35. Andrea Liss, *Trespassing through Shadows: Memory, Photography and the Holocaust* (Minneapolis: University of Minnesota Press, 1998).

36. Shoshana Felman, "Education and Crisis, or the Vicissitudes of Teaching," in *Testimony: Crises of Witnessing in Literature, Psychoanalysis, and History*, ed. Shoshana Felman and Dori Laub (New York: Routledge, 1995), 2.

37. Ibid., 1–56.

38. Sontag, *Regarding the Pain of Others*, 99.

39. David Simpson, *9/11: The Culture of Commemoration* (Chicago: University of Chicago Press, 2006), 116.

40. Paul H. Williams, *Memorial Museums: The Global Rush to Commemorate Atrocities* (New York: Berg, 2007), 75.

41. Kenneth E. Foote, *Shadowed Ground: America's Landscapes of Violence and Tragedy* (Austin: University of Texas Press, 2003), 59.

42. Sharon Todd, "Guilt, Suffering and Responsibility," *Journal of Philosophy of Education* 35, no. 4 (2001): 600.

43. Ibid., 599–600.

44. See, for the latter example, Joy Angela DeGruy, "Post Traumatic Slave Syndrome," in *Post Traumatic Slave Syndrome: America's Legacy of Enduring Injury and Healing* (Baltimore, MD: Uptone Press, 2005).

45. James Oliver Horton, introduction to *Slavery and Public History: The Tough Stuff of American Memory*, ed. James Oliver Horton and Lois Horton (New York: The New Press, 2006), x.

46. Robin Winks, "Sites of Shame: Disgraceful Episodes from Our Past Should Be Included in the Park System to Present a Complete Picture of Our History," *National Parks* LXVIII, no. 68 (1994): 22.

47. Felman, "Education and Crisis," and Britzman, *Lost Subjects*.

48. Todd, "Guilt, Suffering and Responsibility," 600.

49. Kitwood, *Concern for Others*.

50. Ibid., 14.

51. Matthew Schofield and McClatchy Foreign Staff, "Germany Marks Kristallnacht's 75th Anniversary Asking: What Tips a Society into Madness?" *The Advocate* (Baton Rouge, LA), November 9, 2013.

52. Ibid., 9A.

53. Sontag, *Regarding the Pain of Others*, 99.

54. Ibid.

55. Ivan Karp and Steven D. Lavine, ed., *Exhibiting Cultures: The Poetics and Politics of Museum Display* (Washington, DC: Smithsonian Institution, 1991), 1.

56. See, for example, Kyo Maclear, *Beclouded Visions: Hiroshima-Nagasaki and the Art of Witness* (Albany: State University of New York Press, 1999); Léontine Meijer van Mensch, "New Challenges, New Priorities: Analyzing Ethical Dilemmas from a Stakeholder's Perspective in the Netherlands," *Museum Management and Curatorship* 26, no. 2 (2011): 113–28; Lawrence Rothfeld, ed., *Unsettling "Sensation": Arts-Policy Lessons from the Brooklyn Museum of Art Controversy* (New Brunswick, NJ: Rutgers University Press, 2001).

57. See MacClear, *Beclouded Visions*; and Vera Zolberg, "Museums as Contested Sites of Remembrance: The Enola Gay Affair," in *Theorizing Museums*, ed. Sharon MacDonald and Gordon Fyfe (Oxford, UK: Blackwell, 1996), 69–82.

58. Zolberg, "Museums as Contested Sites of Remembrance," 72.

59. Ibid., 76.

60. Linda Ferguson, "Pushing Buttons: Controversial Topics in Museums," *Open Museum Journal* 8, http://pandora.nla.gov.au/tep/10293.

61. Ibid., 5.

62. Ibid., 6.

63. Richard Sandell, ed., *Museums, Society, Inequality* (New York: Routledge, 2002), 120.

64. Megan Boler, *Feeling Power: Emotions and Education* (New York: Routledge, 1999), 175.

65. Spencer R. Crew and James E. Sims, "Locating Authenticity: Fragments of a Dialogue," in *Exhibiting Cultures: The Poetics and Politics of Museum Display*, ed. Ivan Karp and Steven D. Lavine (Washington, DC: Smithsonian Institution, 1991), 159–75.

66. See, for example, Lawrence Fennelly, *Effective Physical Security*, 4th ed. (Oxford, UK: Butterworth-Heinemann, 2013); and Steven P. Layne, "An Ounce of Preservation—Worth More Than a Pound," *History News* 66, no. 1 (2011): Technical Leaflet #253.

67. Williams, *Memorial Museums*, 146.

68. Ibid., 140.

69. Gaynor Kavanagh, "Remembering Ourselves in the Work of Museums: Trauma and the Place of the Personal in the Public," in *Museums, Society, Inequality*, ed. Richard Sandell (London: Routledge, 2002), 110.

70. Jennifer Bonnell and Roger I. Simon, "'Difficult' Exhibitions and Intimate Encounters," *Museum and Society* 5, no. 2 (2007): 67.

71. The World War II Nazi flag was not prominently displayed at this museum in 2014.

72. This exhibition was organized by the Southern Museum of Civil War and Locomotive History of Kennesaw in Georgia.

73. Foote, *Shadowed Ground*, 208.

74. Eichstedt and Small, *Representations of Slavery*.

75. Bonnell and Simon, "'Difficult' Exhibitions and Intimate Encounters," 68.

76. Kavanagh, "Remembering Ourselves in the Work of Museums," 111.

77. Dean MacCannell, *The Ethics of Sightseeing* (Berkeley: University of California Press, 2011), 168.

78. Lonnie Bunch quoted in Marjorie Schwarzer, *Riches, Rivals and Radicals: 100 Years of Museums in America* (Washington, DC: American Association of Museums, 2006), 26.

79. Janet Marstine, "Museologically Speaking: An Interview with Fred Wilson," in *Museums, Equality and Social Justice*, ed. Richard Sandell and Eithne Nightingale (London: Routledge, 2012), 38.

80. Ruth Abram, "Harnessing the Power of History," in *Museums, Society, Inequality*, ed. Richard Sandell (New York: Routledge, 2002), 133.

81. Simpson, *9/11: The Culture of Commemoration*, 53 and 91.

82. Abram, "Harnessing the Power of History," 170.

83. See, for example, Maurice Halbwachs, *Maurice Halbwachs on Collective Memory*, ed. & trans. Lewis A. Coser (Chicago: University of Chicago Press, 1992); Pierre Nora, "Between Memory and History: *Les Lieux de Mémoire*," in *History and Memory in African-American Culture*, ed. Geneviéve Fabre and Robert O'Meally (New York: Oxford University Press, 1996), 284–300; Patrick H. Hutton, *History as an Art of Memory* (Hanover, NH: University Press of New England, 1993).

84. Sontag, *Regarding the Pain of Others*, 86–87.

85. Sandell, *Museums, Society, Inequality*, 120.

86. Roger I. Simon, *Teaching against the Grain: Texts for a Pedagogy of Possibility* (New York: Bergin & Garvey, 1992), 13.

87. Simpson, *9/11: The Culture of Commemoration*, 2.

88. Foote, *Shadowed Ground*, 120.

89. Ibid., 122.

90. Williams, *Memorial Museums*, 131.

91. Personal communication, 2015.

92. Personal communication, 2014.

93. Personal communication, 2014.

94. Abram, "Harnessing the Power of History," 129.

95. Ibid., 127.

96. Williams, *Memorial Museums*, 131.

97. Mark O'Neill and Lois Silverman, "Foreword," in *Museums, Equality and Social Justice*, ed. Richard Sandell and Eithne Nightingale (London: Routledge, 2012), xx.

98. Simpson, *9/11: The Culture of Commemoration*, 125.

99. Ibid., 126.

100. Williams, *Memorial Museums*, 128.

101. Linenthal, *The Unfinished Bombing*, 196.

102. Ibid., 171.

103. See James Young, *The Texture of Memory: Holocaust Memorials and Meaning* (New Haven, CT: Yale University Press, 1993).

104. Linda Gordon and Gary Y. Okihiro, ed., *Impounded: Dorothea Lange and the Censored Images of Japanese American Internment* (New York: W. W. Norton and Company, 2006), 80.

105. Ibid.

106. Ta-Nehisi Coates, "In Case for Reparations," *The Atlantic* 313, no. 5 (2014): 62.

107. Todd, "Guilt, Suffering and Responsibility," 598.

108. Ibid., 597.

109. Nao Gunji and Gwen Muranaka, "Sue Embrey, 83, Led Movement to Preserve Manzanar," *Rafu Shimpo L.A. Japanese Daily News*, December 14, 2013, http://archive.is/UNIzR.

110. Michael Kammen, *Mystic Chords of Memory: The Transformation of Tradition in American Culture* (New York: Alfred A. Knoff, 1991).

111. Peter Ling, review of *Mystic Chords of Memory: The Transformation of Tradition in American Culture*, by Michael Kammen, *Journal of American Studies* 27, no. 2 (1993): 249.

112. Abram, "Harnessing the Power of History," 135.

113. For example, Maya Angelou, *I Know Why the Caged Bird Sings* (New York: Random House, 1969).

114. Lev Grossman, "Maya Angelou: A Hymn to Human Endurance," *Time* 185, no. 1 (May 28, 2014): 16.

115. Ibid.," 16.

116. Andreas Huyssen, *Twilight Memories: Marking Time in a Culture of Amnesia* (New York: Routledge, 1995), 3.

117. Joy Kogawa, *Obasan* (New York: Anchor, 1993).

118. Toni Morrison, *Beloved* (New York: Alfred A. Knopf, 1987).

119. Kavanagh, "Remembering Ourselves in the Work of Museums," 116.

120. See also Lois H. Silverman, *The Social Work of Museums* (New York: Routledge, 2009).

121. Kavanagh, "Remembering Ourselves in the Work of Museums," 114.

122. Ibid., 113.

123. Lois H. Silverman, "The Therapeutic Potential of Museums as Pathways for Inclusion," in *Museums, Society, Inequality*, ed. Richard Sandell (New York: Routledge, 2002), 81.

124. Eilean Hooper-Greenhill, ed., *The Educational Role of the Museum*, 2nd ed. (London: Routledge, 2002), 12.

125. Loewen, cited in Abram, "Harnessing the Power of History," 130.

126. Sissela, cited in Abram, "Harnessing the Power of History," 135.

127. Bruce Tinsely, "Mallard Fillmore," *The Advocate* (Baton Rouge, LA), September 1, 2014.

128. Abram, "Harnessing the Power of History," 136.

129. Trouillot, *Silencing the Past*, 73.

130. Britzman, *Lost Subjects*; Eppert, "Relearning Questions"; Roger I. Simon, Sharon Rosenberg, and Claudia Eppert, *Between Hope and Despair*.

CHAPTER 3

Loss in Learning

Psychoanalytic Framework for Commemorative Museum Pedagogy

Introduction

A PHOTOGRAPH of Anne Frank and a playbill from the 1955 stage production of *The Diary of Anne Frank* illustrate a large text panel in a gallery in the Anne Frank House museum in Amsterdam, The Netherlands. The large, multisection gallery is adjacent to the building that is the historic hiding place where the Jewish Frank family hid through most of World War II. After visitors complete the self-guided tour of the historic house that included the secret Frank family apartment above a store and warehouse, visitors enter a gallery where visitors are engaged in an exhibit about Otto Frank's work to publish his daughter's diary and about the worldwide impact the published diary has had for subsequent generations.

In the closing gallery, in front of the large seven-foot-by-three-foot text panel, a young girl, perhaps five or six years old, in English asked, "Daddy, is that Anne Frank?" Her father, holding the girl's hand, answered, "Yes." His daughter then asked, "What is she doing?" He answered, "Working." The inquisitive girl pointed to the text panel, asking, "Can you read that to me?" Her father read the text panel title: "This play is part of my life . . . Otto Frank, October 1955." Then the young girl's father bent down on one knee and quietly read aloud the full panel to his daughter:

> Otto Frank himself sees neither the play nor the film. It's too painful for him. But he does want as many people as possible to get to know his daughter's diary. This is his

most important goal in his life. So he is closely involved in the realization of the script and helps the actors prepare for their roles.

The father then read the text bubble above the photograph of Anne Frank to his daughter: "I hope the play will reach as many people as possible and awaken their sense of responsibility to humanity." The father asked his attentive daughter, "Do you know what that means?" She shook her head no. He patiently looked at her and explained, "It means that he hopes many people see the play. People will learn to be nice to each other, as many as possible."

Nurturing children's moral development through the stories of difficult histories is one critical and relevant role for difficult history. And realistically, people of all ages are constantly shaping and cultivating their moral compasses as they are exposed to and learn about how people have historically helped and hurt one another, how groups have been oppressed and rescued from harm. Interpretations of difficult histories illustrate ways people have diminished and improved society. Learning from and about difficult histories also helps individuals learn about themselves and how they might identify with the recalled history.

A small audience gathered at the West Baton Rouge Museum in Port Allen, Louisiana, to listen to history professor Aaron Sheehan-Dean present a lecture called "Was the Civil War a Just War?" The lecture was part of a public series to mark the sesquicentennial of the American Civil War. The lecture focused on the evolution of the conventions and international rules of war leading up to the time of the American Civil War. The history professor explained his thesis that emphasized the major pressure for armies to behave responsibly in wartime in the mid-nineteenth century that came from the philosophical and religious beliefs behind the theory of "just wars." He unpacked historical writings from the *Law of Nations* written in 1758 by Emerich de Vattel that explained when nations could legitimately resort to armed conflict and how they could behave once engaged.

A gray-haired gentleman stood up several times during the lecture to stretch and twice left the room. The professor was animated, and the audience was deeply engaged in the illustrated and dynamic lecture. When the lecture was over, I met the gray-haired gentleman in another gallery in the museum. Again, he was stretching his back. I asked him if he was all right and if I could be of help. The gentleman sighed and explained that his back was hurting him and it was difficult to sit still during the lecture. He went on to explain that he suffers from war wounds and he has shrapnel in his back that continues to bother him. Then the gentleman spoke to me almost apologetically for not being able to sit in the room throughout the lecture, intimating that his aching back was not the only reason he could not sit still in the lecture. He raised his eyebrows when he expressed his disbelief in the concept of fighting a "just war." He said, "I am sorry. I could not just sit there and accept the concept of a 'just war.' How can I believe in a 'just war'? What wars are good wars, what wars are just? There are no such things as just wars! I cannot accept that concept."

At an American Association for State and Local History (AASLH) meeting an enthusiastic speaker presented a talk about her experiences giving tours about slave life at a historical house in Virginia. She was a professional museum interpreter trained to interpret slave life history on house tours. The speaker, an African American woman, described her frustration over the seemingly misinformed nature of her house-tour visitors. She said to the AASLH group, "You would not believe the questions I was getting!" The speaker went on to recount a particular confrontational interaction she had with a visitor who doubted the information she offered about food rations given to enslaved families. The visitor had responded, "You are not telling the truth! That is not all they had to eat." The speaker explained that she was taken aback at the visitor's challenge to her interpretation. She told the visitor that the description of the slaves' meager food rations was accurate information based on archival research that came from the site's historical records. This tension-filled museum experience illustrates a visitor's initial resistance to the difficult knowledge about the malnourished slave population and a history worker's resistive reaction to the visitor's skepticism. The museum interpreter found the visitor's questions both astounding and, as she described, "humorous." While the visitor was resistant to the difficult knowledge of the impoverished diets forced on the slaves, the museum interpreter was resistant to fully recognizing that her visitors will, likely, not be knowledgeable about slave life when they first come on her tours.

The house museum interpreter said a technique she uses when working with visitors who ask questions that seemed to be outrageous or misguided was to keep a sense of humor. Laughingly, she recalled when visitors asked her if she was ever enslaved or if her ancestors had been enslaved. Rather than be distraught by visitors' ignorance or naiveté, she recommends that history workers find humor in their work. I have heard other African American museum interpreters report that the same phenomenon happened to them when they were telling the public about slave life history. However, can history workers' laughter and joking be more than a method to get through the uncomfortable interactions with visitors?

Why are visitors of all ages and varying backgrounds often asking what seems to be silly, inexperienced, challenging, or outrageous questions at sites of difficult histories? History worker Azie Mira Dungey[1] recalls visitors reacting to her first-person interactions in the Greenhouse Program at Mount Vernon in Virginia where she was stationed to talk to visitors about slavery on their walk through a historical building. Dungey describes the challenges of interpreting difficult history. "I saw a lot of emotion about it and a lot of defensiveness and a lot of resistance and a lot of shame."[2]

The anxious veteran attending the "Just War" lecture wanted to learn but was conflicted by the lecture's logic and the historical house visitor who was contradicting the tour content about slave life were both thinking hard, and with emotion, about histories that were difficult to comprehend because the tough stories went against their moral understandings of right and wrong. At those moments of disbelief or confusion, each visitor risked losing what he and she thought was true about a history. In these examples, the little girl visiting the Anne Frank House museum, the veteran attending the lecture, and the house museum interpreter were engaged in learning about human nature and how people can be in the same world and yet not see the world the same way. These episodes in learning difficult histories are tense and filled with anxiety for the visitors and for the history workers. The new information can be disruptive and shake our understandings of what is true and right. These tense moments, these often innocent yet powerful questions from visitors, and the defensive and even indignant history workers' responses, are cues that something big, really big, is happening within the internal psychological and cognitive world of each of those visitors and history workers. As learners, the visitors and the history workers were trying to figure out how the new difficult knowledge, however dissonant the history was felt to be or however radical the learners' reactions were to the tension-filled moments, could be fit into each individual's view of the world.

Road Map to Commemorative Museum Pedagogy

Commemorative Museum Pedagogy (CMP) is an educational method that addresses the delivery and the development of interpretations of difficult histories. CMP is an approach to teaching about difficult histories that takes into account the ethical responses of the learner to the difficult histories, and is an approach for history workers to develop and construct ethical historical representations of oppressed, victimized, and subjugated individuals and groups. This chapter describes the theoretical foundations and methods, which I call the 5Rs, for CMP for engaging learners in learning about difficult histories. Chapter 4 presents the theoretical foundations (building blocks) and tools for developing ethical representations and interpretations for difficult histories as part of CMP.

This chapter focuses on CMP as a learning strategy that enables history workers to sensitively and gradually address visitors' anxieties and resistances to difficult histories, even when their questions seem outrageous and naive or when their resistances seem challenging, funny, sarcastic, apathetic, or painful. In the same way, CMP enables history workers to address their co-workers' resistances to difficult histories when they are training to interpret the difficult histories. In the next section, I discuss in more detail the learning process known as "loss in learning" and how the emotions associated with grief are deeply seated in learning difficult histories and are a source of learners' resistances. Understanding the psychological processes of mourning and melancholia is the underpinning for CMP, which acknowledges learners' resistances as part of the process of learning difficult histories. Through CMP, learners are supported in working through their resistances in order to pursue their engagement in interpretations of difficult histories, histories that can feel like they are just too hard to bear.

The third section will pull together these psychoanalytic concepts for working through loss through the five learning phases of difficult knowledge,[3] which are called the 5Rs: reception, resistance, repetition, reflection, and reconsideration. I will explain each of these five learning phases, which are not necessarily linear or sequential, and then provide examples and cues for history workers to use in recognizing learners' progress in grappling with the difficult histories, and eventually recognizing visitors' expressions of historical empathy. The fourth section includes a brief discussion about how the 5Rs serve history workers and other learners in the implementation of CMP.

Loss in Learning

Loss means something is missing; something that was once is now gone or changed. Loss is conditional. Loss can mean the death of a loved one, friend, or acquaintance. Loss can mean change and can mean difference. Loss can include the disappearance of an ideology, object, or a change in a relationship. The anxiety that comes with difference and change describes the feelings of loss and of losing things, of melancholic longings. And in the context of learning theory, loss in learning is consistent with Sigmund Freud's description for the work of mourning,[4] and with Anna Freud's theoretical approach to learning as internal interference,[5] and with Melanie Klein's explanation of learning as internal psychic conflict resolution.[6]

CMP requires history workers to look more closely through a Freudian lens at the mind, the internal psychic arrangement of the learner. How does learning difficult history incite feelings of loss? How does loss, as a form of change or difference, impact the learner? History workers need to take into consideration that at one level of thinking, learners are aware of their responses to a difficult history and at a deeper level learners are unaware of their unconscious connections to a difficult history. What are learners thinking and, more deeply, what are the learners feeling? To begin, if the history worker can conceptualize the visitor as a learner and the fellow history worker as a learner whose self-identities are always in a fragile state, the history worker can more sensitively address the learning scenario of a visitor or co-worker who is resistive to engaging in a difficult history exhibition, for example, and who is at risk. When history workers recognize that each visitor and history worker is a learner who uniquely identifies with a variety of relationships and multiple collective communities that shape the visitor's and history worker's understandings of the world, history workers will have a deeper appreciation of the depth of loss difficult histories can present to learners.

Using a psychoanalytic framework, history workers can better address learners' resistances and more clearly evaluate the risks difficult histories pose to learners. The learner's unconscious mind is that part of mental life of which we are unaware. It includes those impulses, ideas, wishes, and fears that occur out of sight and exert powerful influences over learners' attitudes and behaviors. Held within learners' unconscious minds are repressed reasons and memories for doing what they do, for what they are thinking and for believing what they believe. Those behaviors and thoughts are also the result of unconscious motivation.[7]

Briefly, as the description of the mind relates to learning difficult history, the learner's ego says "who I am" by keeping together the learner's concept of his or her identity. The ego drives his or her actions and responses, always striving to protect and keep the learner's identity stable. Ideas that threaten or that can jeopardize the learner's self-identity set the ego into action, telling the learner to resist, deny, or fend off that destabilizing idea, information, or thought. Learning difficult knowledge asks something intimate of the learner. It requires the learner to recognize how he or she might be implicated in the new knowledge and to recognize their attachments that organize their individual self-identity. The learner's ego is constantly protecting the learner from disruptive knowledge, knowledge that the learner unconsciously perceives as interference and as destabilizing. History workers who implement CMP begin by acknowledging that difficult history can impact the learner's internal stability as an unconscious loss to the learner's identity that can disrupt how the learner relates to the world.

Loss in learning can generate so much anxiety for the learner that an internal learning crisis can occur.[8] That is when the knowledge does not make sense to the learner or the new knowledge is in conflict with what he or she already knows to be true. A learning crisis is stressful for the learner and is also a moment when learning can happen. In the learner's unconscious mind, the learner's stable ego is faced with dissonant knowledge that is destabilizing. In a state of crisis, the learner's ego defends its position toward the new knowledge: "That is not true! I don't believe that." At the conscious level, at stake are the learner's understandings of truth and morality, and at risk is the learner's willingness to continue to learn. Here in the moment of crisis the learner faces the disruption and works to make sense of the new information, reestablishing the ego's relationship to the outside world.

Consider the scenario when a learner chooses not to face a difficult history, saying, "I don't care about that." Perhaps the history makes the learner feel insignificant or feel overwhelmed by a story that seems bigger than anything in his or her life experience. According to Britzman, analyst Alice Balint suggests that the fear of insignificance mobilizes the ego's defenses.[9] The ego defends its own narcissism in an attempt to preserve its wish to be omnipotent. Having to learn something is actually felt as an injury to narcissism, reminding the learner that the ego is not all. But when the feeling of helplessness does not go away, the insignificance returns as a threat toward the learner.[10]

The learner's desire toward the status quo, to feeling stable in his or her relationships to the world that he or she knows, and to feeling stable in how the learner knows herself or himself, is at risk with each new piece of difficult knowledge the learner encounters. The losses in learning difficult histories are the psychic events that the learner might not even be aware of but that can disturb museum-learning engagements in the form of the learner's resistance.

CMP uses the theories of loss in learning to enable history workers to support learners to work through their resistances to learning difficult history. CMP takes into consideration the mental composition of the learner's resistance to difficult history in order to sensitively address and respond to the learner's psychic resistance. Loss in learning theory requires history workers to understand how the process of grieving is a way to deal with psychic loss. It enables the learner to make sense of loss incited by learning difficult history and then continue learning. Let's take a closer look at how the learner mourns psychic loss and works through the threats posed by difficult history to his or her ego's sense of stability. The basis for the loss in learning theories includes Freud's theory of Mourning and Melancholia[11] and Melanie Klein's Object Relations theory.[12]

Freud's Mourning and Melancholia

CMP is premised on Freud's seminal work "Mourning and Melancholia," in which he explains the psychological processes of human grieving.

> [Mourning] is regularly the reaction to the loss of a loved person, or to the loss of some abstraction which has taken the place of one, such as one's country, liberty, an ideal, and so on. In some people the same influences produce melancholia instead of mourning and we consequently suspect them of a pathological disposition. . . . We rely on [loss] being overcome after a certain lapse of time, and we look upon any interference with it as useless or even harmful.[13]

In Sigmund Freud's theories of mourning and melancholia,[14] Freud found that in the healthy, though painful, process of mourning, the bereaved person labors at retrieving psychic energy from each important memory and association connected to the lost person, object, or idea. Freud calls the psychological process of mourning "working through." As mourning progresses, little by little, the reality of the loss is "worked through" and the pain diminishes. When mourning is complete, the person then feels revived and has interest and ability to connect with the outside world and has energy to invest in other relationships.[15]

Working through loss is an internal process within the negotiations of the person's ego. Moving from memory to memory, the mourner, in our example the learner, is working through the mental loss the difficult history has imposed. The learner's ego is in search of finding an internal balance among love for oneself, the effects of losing an object, and his or her changed relationship to the outside world.

Another Freudian concept is at play in the mourning process and is called "reality testing." The labor of working through is also the thoughtful evaluation of one's emotions and thoughts framed against real life. The person is considering or imagining how the loss fits into what he or she already knows. Learners in mourning, through a process called *cathexis*, invest their psychic energy called *libido* into the people, ideas, or objects that they are attached to and even love, and forge revised relationships to memories and associations connected to those relationships. This process in the context of learning and loss is in many ways a sense-making endeavor and is controlled by a drive toward preserving one's self-identity. Libido is the instinctual psychic energy derived from our basic biological urges (as for sexual pleasure or self-preservation) and that can be expressed through conscious activity. Examples of such conscious activities include conversations, writing poetry, or quiet imagining.

Freud describes the work of mourning in this way:

> Reality-testing has shown that the loved object no longer exists, and it proceeds to demand that all libido shall be withdrawn from its attachments to that object. This demand arouses understandable opposition—it is a matter of general observation that people never willingly abandon a libidinal position, not even, indeed, when a substitute is already beckoning to them. This opposition can be so intense that a turning away from reality takes place and a clinging to the object through the medium of a hallucinatory wishful psychosis. Normally, respect for reality gains the day. Nevertheless, its orders cannot be obeyed at once. They are carried out bit by bit at great expense of time and cathectic energy, and in the meantime the existence of the lost object is psychically prolonged. Each single one of the memories and expectations in which the libido is bound to the object is brought up and hyper-cathected, and detachment of the libido is accomplished in respect of it.... The fact is, however, that when the work of mourning is completed the ego becomes free and uninhibited again.[16]

Key to Freud's description of working through is the slow, repetitive process of reality testing, bit by bit, until the learner can let go of or make sense of his or her losses. The learners who are asking the same questions over again and reading the same information multiple times are working through the new knowledge. History workers who recognize that learners who are given time to work through the interference posed by a difficult history will, bit by bit, likely make sense of the difficult knowledge.

But what about the learner who is resistive and refusing to work through the new knowledge that is too much to bear? This learner is stuck and foreclosing on the learning experience. This is a melancholic learner, and the melancholic learner suffers the symptoms of mourning and suffers from an impoverished ego. Freud explains, "In mourning it is the world which has become poor and empty; in melancholia it is the ego itself."[17] Melancholia, as described by Freud, involves the inability to mourn, when the libido cannot move on to another attachment. Freud explains,

> But the free libido was not displaced on to another object; it was withdrawn into the ego. There, however, it was not employed in any unspecified way, but served to establish an identification of the ego with the abandoned object. Thus the shadow of the object fell upon the ego, and the latter could henceforth be judged by a special agency as though it were an object, the forsaken object. In this way an object-loss was transformed into an ego-loss and the conflict between the ego and the loved person into a cleavage between the critical activity of the ego and the ego as altered by identification.[18]

The melancholic learner no longer distinguishes self from the lost object and places the image of the lost object into his or her self-image. The melancholic learner asks how the historical violence or trauma causes him or her pain and might even consider how the difficult history *is* his or her personal story that causes him or her pain in that present moment. In this context, the melancholic learner imagines that the lost object is actually now a part of him or her.[19]

Julie Salverson offers an especially useful summary of the Freudian concepts of mourning and melancholia:

> In "Mourning and Melancholia," Freud (1917/1915) distinguishes between mourning, as a psychic response to loss that maintains the integrity of the other, and melancholia, as a narcissistic response that subsumes the lost other into the self. Whereas in mourning, the lost object is distinct from the self and eventually becomes replaced by something else out in the world, melancholia proceeds through identifications with what has been lost. What is lost is internalized and becomes the focus of one's own psychic pain. In a sense, the melancholic replaces the lost object with the experience of loss itself. The person lives continually with an indefinable and interminable yearning for something for which no substitute is possible.[20]

The melancholic learner cannot accept the difficult history or believes the historical trauma or oppression is his or her experience that cannot be reckoned with. The learner is stuck and resists further learning about that history. Melancholic resistance is when the learner forecloses on the learning experience.

Another central concept to Freud's theories on mourning and melancholia is Freud's concept of defense mechanisms[21] and is important to understanding and recognizing learners' resistances. The mind can protect the self through several defense mechanisms that attempt to manage internal psychic conflicts. Briefly, defense mechanisms include repression, which is the mental process of pushing conflicts back into the unconscious; sublimation, which is the process of channeling the psychic energies into socially acceptable goals such as the production of art or science; projection, which is when the ego fills the object with some of its own ambivalence; introjection, which is an extreme identification with the object taking into the ego what he or she perceived or experienced of the lost object; and splitting, which is when the ego splits into one part that takes account of reality and another that detaches the ego from reality.[22] Drawing on Melanie Klein's work, Mitchell describes splitting of the ego as stopping the bad part from contaminating the good part of the ego by disowning part of itself.[23] Observable defense mechanisms in the context of CMP are those responses from learners that indicate resistance to difficult history; for example, learners' denials or sarcastic remarks to a history recalled.

Repetition is another central Freudian concept in the process of mourning and is important to loss in learning. The bereaved, in the progression of reality testing, will reconsider multiple times how his or her loss seems. The person will ask the same question over and over—"She died? She died, really?"—as the process of reality testing unfolds. Unpleasant dreams, for example, are often repeated.[24] The process of repeating a painful event symbolically allows the learner to deeply consider the loss and how it changes the learner's relationships.[25] History workers can observe learners in mourning when learners verbally repeat a story again and again, or ask the same questions, or read a label multiple times. CMP asks history workers to actively watch for expressions from learners working through their feelings of loss.

Melanie Klein and Loss

The pioneering psychoanalyst Melanie Klein (1882–1960) focused on object relations in investigating our earliest infantile conflicts with deciphering psychotic mechanisms. Klein's object relations theoretical corpus is framed upon two Freudian tenets: unconscious thoughts are attached to language through observable activities such as play, art, talking, and dreams, giving recognizable access to particular meanings of symbols and wishes; and the formative importance of infantile sexuality.[26]

Freud first introduced the idea of object choice, which referred to a child's earliest relationships with his or her caretakers.[27] The child's caretaker, such as a parent or nanny, was an object of his or her needs and desires. The child's relationship with his or her object became internalized mental representations, or in Kleinian parlance *imago*. Klein stresses the importance of interpersonal relationships and, unlike Freud, Klein emphasizes the primacy of mother-child relationships.[28]

Key to helping history workers understand the ego's role in loss in learning is Klein's theory of the child's ego development, which is central to the person's development from infancy through adulthood. According to Mitchell, Klein utilizes Freud's notions of defense mechanisms (repression, sublimation, projection, introjection, and splitting the ego) that enable the ego to negotiate new relationships and new knowledge. In addition, Klein discovered an additional defense mechanism, projective identification, which enables "the ego to project its feelings into the object which it then identifies with, becoming like the object which the ego has already imaginatively filled with itself."[29] New knowledge and new relationships will always raise anxiety from the threat of loss due to the changing dynamics of the ego's protective attachments to her objects.[30] Defense mechanisms are enacted by the ego to cope with anxious tensions from the constant interchange between the learner's internal and external worlds, as in the introduction of new knowledge.

In her 1940 paper, "Mourning and Its Relation to Manic Depressive States," Klein links mourning to loss occurring at any age with the "depressive position." Klein describes the depressive position as a process of early reality testing and argues that this is the precedent for what will become the process of mourning later in life. Klein explains, "The most important of the methods by which the child overcomes his states of mourning is, in my view, the testing of reality; this process, however, as Freud stresses, is part of the work of mourning."[31]

According to Klein, the infantile origins of the depressive position are the child's earliest active relations to reality and to the outside world. The first object the child mourns is the mother's breast and all the plentitude, the good it has come to stand for in the infant's mind. When the good object is felt to be lost, when the breast frustrates the infant, the loss is felt as a result of his uncontrollable greed and destructive phantasies and impulses against the breast.[32]

Recognizing the disruption imposed by difficult knowledge to the learner's inner world is a key to CMP enabling history workers to address learners' resistances to difficult history. History workers can recognize that learners' engagement with new and potentially disruptive knowledge, while filled with anxiety and tension, is also a realistic and critical step in enabling learners to work through learning difficult history. Klein's theory suggests that learners work through loss by way of reality testing in acquiring knowledge; each new piece of experience has to be fit into his or her internal psychic reality. This ongoing rebuilding of the learner's inner world characterizes the successful work of mourning.[33]

History workers familiar with CMP are prepared to observe learners' responses to difficult history. While the unconscious mind is not apparent, it speaks to the outside world through verbal expressions and physical cues, such as body language. History workers using CMP are listening carefully to learners' verbal remarks and watching for physical cues to ascertain learners' level of engagement with a difficult history. History workers, while not trained psychoanalysts, indeed wear the hat of educator. Educators are tuned into their learners' needs and level of understanding, and especially to learners' responses to new knowledge. In this way, CMP asks history workers to be honing their skills at observing learners in anticipation of learners' responses to difficult histories.

The 5Rs: Reception, Resistance, Repetition, Reflection, Reconsideration

Difficult history is that body of knowledge that can be more than merely new information for learners. It can also be difficult knowledge that can challenge the ego's contained good objects that then threaten the ego and can trigger defense mechanisms against painful knowledge. The shock or disturbance the new knowledge can impose on learners can prompt resistance to learning about the history, even to the point of learners refusing to believe the history happened. History workers who understand that difficult histories can prompt loss in learning can assist learners (visitors and history workers) in the psychic process of mourning, a healthy learning process that allows for the rise of learning crises, and the working of defense mechanisms and reality testing as necessary steps for learners making sense of the difficult knowledge. In CMP, the healthy process of mourning the psychological losses felt by learners accounts for learners' tensions and anxieties. CMP helps to identify melancholic learners who are unwilling or unable to engage in learning a difficult history and who foreclose on the possibility of empathetically responding to the difficult history. The 5Rs frame the healthy process of working through psychic loss as a mourning process and help to explain the variety of reactions from those learners who are shocked and upset, or refuse and deny difficult histories.

The 5Rs of CMP help to describe the observable process of loss in learning that reverberates with the Freudian concepts of mourning and melancholia. CMP provides time for personal learning by allowing learners to work through their resistances and internal learning crises. The 5Rs of CMP can be easily remembered in a logical, linear sequence with a beginning, middle, and end: reception, resistance, repetition, reflection, and reconsideration. However, in reality, learners will not move straightforward through a linear learning progression. The learner will move in chaotic patterns, perhaps starting with resistance: "I am not going to that museum." A learner might read an article in the newspaper about genocide, reflect on that story, and then plan a visit to a museum that has an exhibit about genocide. A learner might be receptive throughout the first half of an exhibition and then midway feel resistive. Other learners might work through their resistances that emerge multiple times throughout an exhibition.

The 5Rs are all part of a nonlinear cognitive process that unfolds in unpredictable sequences over varying lengths of time, depending on the individual learner's connections and responses to the difficult histories.[34] CMP asks history workers to actively attend to learners' resistances to difficult histories and help learners to work through their individual learning crises. Through attentive observation, history workers can anticipate and recognize when learners move from one phase to another, working through their feelings of shock or disruption when faced with content the learners find challenging to accept or find too hard to comprehend.

The nonlinearity character of the 5Rs means that individual learners will start at any of the five phases and move among the phases in unpredictable sequences and spend varying amounts of time in those phases. Most learners do not move directly from reception through reconsideration. Instead, the learning is recursive and tangled with pauses, as the learner works on recalling and retracing memories and understandings.

Learners' resistances become evident through learners' verbal expressions and physical responses. History workers need to be prepared to allow for the tension-filled learning moments that difficult knowledge demands. The history workers who have little patience for learners who are struggling with a difficult history can refer to the 5Rs to sharpen their observation skills in order to support learners and to be more sensitive to the enormous variety of learners.

When resistance to difficult knowledge is misunderstood, the learners' resistances can be unfairly viewed as something other than loss in learning, perhaps viewed as prejudices or ignorance. Realize that asking those resistive visitors and fellow history workers to "Just get over it!" likely will send learners into a melancholic state and result in those learners foreclosing on the learning experience. Expressions like "That is how the history happened" and "These are the facts" will most likely not address learners' discomfort or aid them in working through their internal learning losses. History workers who use the 5Rs support the learners in crisis to work through their struggles in order to make sense of the difficult knowledge.

Reception: Who Lived Here?

Learners' audible and observable willingness to engage in an exhibit, tour, film, or program are signals of learners' receptiveness to a difficult history. The curious and attentive little girl who asked, "Daddy, is that Anne Frank?" wanted information. When the inquisitive girl asked her father, "Can you read that to me?" upon entering a new gallery, she was demonstrating her eagerness to know more. Reception is that part of the learning process when learners show that they want to engage in the interpretation being presented. Receptive learners will prepare themselves to engage in the learning experience. For example, when at the entrance of the historical slave cabin exhibit at the West Baton Rouge Museum, receptive students commonly ask, "Who lived here?" and "Was this a real slave cabin?" In many museums, learners demonstrate their receptiveness to learning about a difficult history when they pick up the gallery guide or comply with tour guides' instructions to gather in a particular space. It is genuinely hard to know each person's reasons and expectations that frame their receptiveness to learning a difficult history. The purpose for each learner's attentiveness varies greatly from general curiosity to emotional attachments, family obligations, political agendas, and so on. Wrapped into those personal reasons are threads of anticipation and intentions. In the acts of reception, learners are likely gauging their personal expectations about the learning experience that is about to unfold. Learners might ask questions about logistics or the context of the interpretation. The learner is likely considering the possibilities of the interpretation; perhaps he or she is wondering whether an exhibit about a difficult history will be relevant to him or her or perhaps too much to bear.

The National Hansen's Disease Museum in Carville, Louisiana, is located seventy miles northwest of New Orleans and thirty miles south of Baton Rouge. Carville is a small, rural town along the Mississippi River surrounded by sugarcane farms with little tourism and a population of about eight hundred. Many visitors to the museum are also visitors to the military training and medical facility, Gillis W. Long Center, which includes the museum and is operated by the Louisiana Army National Guard. The center encompasses the many buildings and facilities of the onetime Carville National Leprosarium. School groups and tourists to Louisiana who visit the museum have made a considerable drive to reach the historic site and museum, which features the difficult history that has been flippantly and regrettably called a "leper colony."[35] The nonlocal visitors' extraordinary effort to travel to the National Hansen's Disease Museum illustrates well visitors' receptiveness to a difficult history.

The majority of the visitors to the National Hansen's Disease Museum are committed to seeing this site when they arrive. The curator explained that many visitors are family members and descendants of former patients who were quarantined in Carville for life. Over five thousand patients over the course of one hundred years were condemned to live out their lives in the leprosarium. Today, many visitors are the relatives of the patients who are often searching for genealogical information or for answers about missing relatives, or looking for grave sites. Some visitors are interested in the medical history, and other visitors are merely curious about the disease and the history of leprosy. The curator explained that she calls the visitors "stakeholders" because they have ties to the National Hansen's Disease Museum and to the disease. "This history matters to the stakeholders. They have connections to the patients, the staff, the center through family ties, through work, through their ties to the region. Stakeholders include uniformed service, medical professionals, public health professionals, patients, family of staff, and [former] employees [who] are regular visitors, and those who are curious."[36]

Reception can also be seen when history workers are tasked with learning difficult histories as part of their tour-guide training. Many museums have volunteer history workers, including docents and survivors and descendants of tragedies, who deliver interpretations to visitors. Paid and unpaid history workers can demonstrate their receptiveness to a difficult history when their training course begins. For example, at an initial training session for history workers at Magnolia Mound Plantation, in Baton Rouge, Louisiana, to learn about the historical enslaved community, a paid history worker expressed her receptiveness to the new slave life history, explaining that the current tour could be modified to better reflect the number of the free and enslaved plantation residents. At the same training session, a volunteer docent exclaimed, when she was asked if she wanted to learn about the slaves who lived at Magnolia Mound Plantation between 1781 and 1865, "We need to know the history of the slaves, the stories to put flesh on the bones!"[37]

The majority of visitors can show their receptiveness to difficult history interpretations simply through the act of coming to an exhibit or public history program. They are demonstrating their willingness to engage in the history by paying admission, asking questions, and reading, looking, and listening to the interpretation content. Visitors often consider their anticipated learning experience as recreational as well as educational, and expect to see something new and interesting. History workers poised to learn about a difficult history as part of their work also have expectations about the interpretation content that they will encounter, and, in addition, have agreed to learn the stories in preparation to teach visitors and, in some historical settings, enable visitors to bear witness to a difficult history.

At the onset of a learning experience, history workers do not know how committed each visitor or co-worker is to learning about the history being presented. Also not evident is how much each individual feels he or she already knows about the subject interpreted in the venue. The quality of the learners' entrance into the learning moment and the quality of their initial attention helps to signal to the history workers the learners' reception to the learning experience. How attentive are the learners? What are they looking at, and are they facing in the direction of the presentation? What are they asking and saying?

Reception is also an opportunity for history workers to disclose to their learners (visitors or fellow history workers) the intensity of pain, cruelty, violence, or horror depicted in the forthcoming interpretation. In anticipation of visitors' reception to learning about a difficult history and history workers' reception to training to interpret a difficult history, history workers should hospitably provide warnings in introductory messages and spaces. In anticipation of the impact the difficult knowledge could have on learners, history workers should include disclosure statements about the kinds of difficult knowledge contained in the exhibit, program, and training materials. History workers can inform learners that the subject matter in the exhibit, program, or training could be upsetting or controversial.

Resistance: It Just Can't Be!

When new knowledge is perceived as dissonant or disruptive to the learner's understanding of history, or challenges the learner's self-identity or moral senses, the learner will likely repress the new knowledge and outwardly react. It is in the moments of visitors' resistance to difficult knowledge that history workers can appreciate the phrase *the unconscious speaks*. Learners' verbal expressions and body language offer cues to history workers that learners are resisting difficult knowledge and are experiencing a learning crisis. The learner might verbally refute the information, shake his or her head in disagreement, or walk away from the presentation. Learners who are experiencing loss in learning want to avoid or challenge the knowledge that they are finding disruptive or painful.

Some visitors to the National Hansen's Disease Museum, according to the curator, "have extreme reactions, especially to the graphic images of the patients. Visitors have physical reactions to the suffering like fainting or feeling squeamish. . . . Some people come and then want to leave immediately. This is not what they want to see. . . . Many family members are shocked to find their relative was quarantined and slapped with the leper label."[38] Recall the anecdote described in chapter 1 of the ten-year-old boy who came to this museum on a field trip and cried out before leaving the gallery, "I just can't stay in here!"

Resistance can be detected through expressions that can sound confrontational, like the one uttered by a history worker training at Magnolia Mound Plantation upon hearing that a slave named Charlotte was given as a wedding present to her new plantation mistress owner. The history worker said, "I would like substantial information to back that up."[39] Verbal expressions that indicate learners' resistance can sound like denials such as the one I observed in 2004, when a senior citizen viewing the interior of a slave cabin at the LSU Rural Life Museum in Baton Rouge cried out, "This is unbelievable!" Physical resistance to engaging in difficult history includes defensive actions, such as the demonstration by the teenage African American female student who refused to join her classmates on a tour of the slave cabin at Magnolia Mound Plantation and shouted loudly at the tour guide, "That's not me! I am not going in there!"[40]

Learners' spoken words that challenge the accuracy or significance of the historical information sometimes expressed as criticism, skepticism, and even sarcasm are indicative of learners' resistance. History workers who are shocked by difficult histories when they are in training, for example, will refute information or argue with trainers about the historical content. Frontline history workers who find visitors' resistance difficult to accept sometimes claim that their visitors are "not getting it" and turn to humor and jokes. History worker's humor and jokes are also forms of resistance. History workers in this scenario are unable to straightaway accept the likelihood that their visitors could question the history workers' interpretation, or that the visitors might be unfamiliar with the difficult history.

Humor can arise out of visitors' and history workers' discomfort and can function as resistance or defenses from thinking more deeply about the trauma being recalled. Simone Schweber, working as a scholar-in-residence at the U.S. Holocaust Memorial Museum in Washington, D.C., observed that humor and sarcasm can provide a release from tension for history workers who interpret difficult history on a daily basis.[41] Schweber explains that working in an awesome place inspires sarcasm out of a strange appreciation for the grandness of the museum's ambitions butting up against the complex impossibility of living in awe. A history worker, she explains, cannot "work in the field of Holocaust or genocide studies without developing a healthy dose of sarcasm/irony—or at least distance masquerading as distaste."[42]

Humor serves as a convenient coping tool for history workers who are surprised, pained, annoyed, and even frustrated by visitors' distorted, misguided, and naive responses to a difficult history. Humor is also a way for history workers to repress their discomfort in engaging visitors who are resistant to a difficult history. Consider the widely viewed satirical and comedic video series on YouTube called "Ask a Slave."[43] As Amy Tyson and Azie Mira Dungey explain in an interview about Dungey's work as a first-person historic site interpreter at George Washington's Mount Vernon, "Indeed, nestled within the satire of 'Ask a Slave' is a thread that is picked up in this interview: that living history interpretations surrounding race and slavery wage an extra emotional burden on interpreters of color who are often charged with conveying those histories for the public."[44]

Actress and museum interpreter Azie Mira Dungey launched her comedy web series "Ask a Slave" in 2013. The series has over 750,000 views of the series' first of five episodes. It is set in a game show format where visitors are asking questions of Dungey, who is in character as the fictional Lizzie Mae, a satirical version of an enslaved house servant who is dressed in period clothing. The visitors' questions are drawn from Dungey's actual experiences working as a first-person interpreter at Mount Vernon, where Dungey was once employed to portray Caroline Branham, the Washington's enslaved housemaid.

While the web series is funny, perhaps the collection of five episodes has a larger message that is, of course, not funny. Dungey uses comedy to relieve her frustrations and to highlight the paucity of historical understanding about slave life and slavery among visitors. "I never would have said most of these things that I say in the show at Mount Vernon. As Lizzie Mae, I sometimes imagine what Caroline might have wanted to say."[45] Dungey goes on to explain in the interview, "In that imagining, Lizzie Mae works to set the record straight for tourists about the ways in which their questions betray a basic ignorance about the history of slavery in the United States."[46] While many history workers find a sense of comradery in sharing like experiences from interpreting slavery and slave life to the public, the web series "Ask a Slave" also prompts history workers to consider how they might enter into those difficult conversations with visitors, the kind of tension-filled conversations recalled in the talk by the house museum interpreter at the AASLH meeting.

Learners' resistance to difficult knowledge can also indicate the learners' inability to empathize with the historical victims. Empathetic responses to difficult histories are extremely personal and are uniquely tied to the learner's relationship to the traumatic event and to those who were immediately affected. Limits of the learner's imagination might be thought of as a lack of empathy or its censorship may be within the realm of melancholia. For empathy to unfold, the learner is challenged to work through the painful learning moment. And yet, as Megan Boler explains, the learner's empathy has potential to inspire action in particular lived contexts.[47]

When the learner cannot bear to know the difficult knowledge and refuses the new information, the learning is not so much about accumulating knowledge, but rather a moment for the visitor to alter himself or herself as the internal tension develops. The tensions will likely emerge and become apparent as the learner's demonstrated resistance.[48] Resisting difficult knowledge is a learner's reaction to self-preservation, incited by his or her immediate feelings of discomfort, risk, or fear.

Learners' refusals, ambivalence, or seeming loss of interest in a difficult history can be signaled by the learners spontaneously choosing a different activity such as texting or deciding to get a drink at a water fountain, or simply by walking out of the exhibit. Verbal and physical resistance to learning difficult histories can indicate that the learners are likely contending with their personal learning crises. Resistance is an integral and normal part of learning, that healthy process of working through loss in learning. Resistance to difficult knowledge is personal and speaks through the learner's intellectual response to contemplate and question information about the historical interpretations. Resistance happens in varying degrees of internal disruption and is not necessarily an indication of the learner's lack of knowledge, but rather resistance can be a likely indication that the difficult knowledge is impacting that learner in new ways. The phenomenon of resistance can arise from anyone, from the most learned visitors and history workers to the most inexperienced.

In anticipation of learners' resistance to difficult histories, workers can consider a list of probing questions designed for educators that history workers can incorporate into training workers and in guiding visitors:

What prior knowledge or understanding is affirmed or made strange in the process of implicating oneself in one's learning? What is attended to and what is ignored? What happens when one understanding shuts out consideration of the meaning of another? How do the meanings one already holds map onto or ignore larger questions of individual and sociocultural histories?[49]

Resistance is one part of the larger learning experience when learners are faced with difficult knowledge. Resistance should not be considered a signal of an end to the learner's engagement with a difficult history. Personal learning crises are not necessarily to be avoided either. These have great potential to be learning moments. CMP acknowledges and uses learners' resistances as opportunities for teaching and encouraging learners' further engagement.

Psychoanalysis, Shoshana Felman explains, is "a process that gives access to new knowledge previously denied to consciousness, it affords what might be called a lesson in cognition (and in miscognition), an epistemological instruction."[50] Knowing and not knowing are implied by the discoveries of the unconscious. Felman encourages educators to attend to the silences and the missed and belated responses in order to begin to understand learners' learning crises. In this way, history workers can attend to learners' expressions of resistance (e.g., denials, refusals, silences), which can reveal individuals' learning crises when the new knowledge is too difficult to bear.

Felman investigated the process of teaching traumatic history to classroom students. Felman asked students to read traumatic historical accounts, including Holocaust testimonies. She was interested in revealing the qualities of estrangement inherent in the texts.[51] Felman observed her students, who endured learning crises from reading the difficult knowledge presented in the testimonies. Her students struggled to find words to express their own individual traumatic encounters with the testimonies. Felman finds that teaching takes place precisely through crisis.

If teaching does not hit upon some sort of crisis, if it does not encounter either the vulnerability or explosiveness of a (explicit or implicit) critical and unpredictable dimension, it has perhaps not truly taught: it has perhaps passed on some facts . . . that no one could therefore truly learn, read or put to use. . . . My job as teacher . . . was that of creating in the class the highest state of crises that it could withstand, without . . . compromising the students' bounds.[52]

Felman's insights are grounded in psychoanalytic notions she describes as the interminable nature of knowing, the influence of the self-reflexive and self-questioning processes in acquiring knowledge and the interplay of learners' "passions for ignorance."[53] The learner's passion for ignorance is another key concept that Felman brings to understanding resistance and loss in learning. The learner refuses to face the history, saying, "I do not want to know about this; stop the flow of information." Claudia Eppert was teaching a class of students reading Holocaust testimonies when one student stood up from his desk and threw his book against the wall, saying he would not read anymore.[54] Felman asserts that ignorance is not simply opposed to knowledge; rather, ignorance is an integral part of the structure of knowledge. "Ignorance, in other words, is not a passive state of absence, a simple lack of information: it is an active dynamic of negation, an active refusal of information."[55]

Felman's notion of the learner's passion for ignorance reminds me of Britzman's question, "What can be learned from disclaimed history?"[56] Britzman explains that feeling pain, or refusing to recognize the pain of others, may approximate trauma for the learner, and thereby thwart the possibilities for the learner to develop relationships to the historical Others by not acknowledging the incommensurability of their pain. The learner's ego is at risk in this scenario, wounding his or her own "ego boundaries that serve as defense against pain."[57] History workers can attend to learners' rising anxieties in facing their "ghosts." Felman asserts that learning from traumatic narratives necessitates crisis raised in the learning setting.[58]

The impact of learning about traumatic events can affect learners-as-witnesses who see and hear the evidence of tragedies and suffering that can also generate a "crisis of witnessing."[59] Historical interpretations bear witness to difficult histories through authentic oral histories, photographs, and artifacts. The learner burdened with receiving a testimony can be thrown into an emotional state, even so far as being traumatized by reading the testimony or by looking at shocking graphic images of atrocities. Reading exhibit labels or viewing images of difficult histories asks learners to partially know the horror that was faced by the historical witnesses and victims.

Repetition: I Need to Read That Again!

When a visitor asks his docent to repeat a portion of the tour narrative or returns to the display to reread a label multiple times, he is choosing to repeat information. When the history worker at Magnolia Mound Plantation repeatedly asked out loud, "She died? She died? Jane died?" at a training session, the history worker was asking for confirmation about the historical account of an enslaved woman who died just before being placed on the auction block. The history worker was trying to make sense of a history that she could not readily accept as true. How could Jane have been waiting to be sold at auction if she was about to die? How could she die if she was about to be sold? With each question and each rereading, the learner was working through the knowledge that was causing an internal disruption for the learner, an internal loss that was jeopardizing the learner's current understandings of slave sales as a human tragedy.

Learners' ambivalent expressions and calls for information to be repeated suggest to history workers that the learners are looking for ways to repeat content as a part of the mournful process to learn difficult knowledge. Repetition is a Freudian concept that helps to describe the process of reality testing through mourning.[60] In the context of mourning a loss in learning incited by a difficult knowledge, the learner is working through the new information bit by bit in order to make sense of the new information. The process of repeating parts of the difficult knowledge enables the learner to consider again and again the parts of a difficult history that are too hard to understand, too hard to believe, or too far afield from his or her understandings of truth. As part of the labor of mourning, the learner must work through his or her loss by repeating a story again and again, asking repetitive questions, viewing an image over and over, or reading a label multiple times. The learner is considering how the new information can be tied to his or her internal psychic reality. With each opportunity to repeat new pieces of information, the learner is thinking about how the information can make sense to him or her. The learner is retrieving images and information from memory and comparing, evaluating, and balancing those memories with the new information. Repetition allows the learner to consider more deeply the content he or she finds hard to accept. This rebuilding of the learner's inner world characterizes the successful work of mourning stirred by a difficult history.

The history worker, who could not at first make sense of the death of the slave woman about to be sold at auction, went back to reading the historical account in the training materials and asked for confirmation at the training session.[61] The exhibition *Slavery at Jefferson's Monticello: Paradox of Liberty* (January 27, 2012, through October 1, 2012), which explored slavery in America through the lens of Thomas Jefferson's enslaved plantation community, was designed to allow visitors free movement throughout the gallery spaces. Visitors could move from display to display. While there was a loosely suggested tour route in the exhibit, the self-guided visitor could return to the genealogy display multiple times after viewing the agricultural work displays or the housework displays to repeatedly read and reconfirm information. The autonomy given to visitors-as-learners to repeat information by returning to the various display cases allowed learners more opportunities to revisit information and ideas that could be more difficult to accept, unlike the strict one-way tour route at the Anne Frank House in Amsterdam, for example, where visitors cannot revisit rooms they saw earlier on the tour.

History workers who are carefully attending to learners can observe and detect when learners are seeking repetition opportunities. History workers who are using CMP will take into account when learners are repeating questions and repeatedly seeking information or confirmation about a difficult history. History workers can believe that those learners are not melancholic and are not giving up on learning the difficult history. Like the history worker who demanded "substantial information" to back up the history of a slave who was objectified as a wedding present, the history worker was asking for another opportunity to make sense of the difficult history. Those learners who are repeating information and asking questions might sound like they are refusing to engage in the difficult history interpretation, but they are much more likely working through the difficult knowledge in a sense-making, mournful learning process. The learners who leave the learning setting and resist further engagement are foreclosing on learning in that moment. Be aware that the experience of the learner coming face-to-face with an interpretation of difficult knowledge that at first shocks or repulses the learner might change from resistance to repetition, reflection, or reconsideration. That melancholic learner might reflect on the image or story that pained him and sometime later might return to the exhibit or find a book or website to try again to face the difficult history. Time is necessary for learners to work through their resistances, bit by bit, memory by memory.

Reflection: I Need Some Time.

In Washington, D.C., at the U.S. National Holocaust Memorial Museum, staff member Nancy Gillette explains that the museum galleries are designed with purposefully placed areas for visitors to separate out from the difficult history of Nazi World War II genocide to reflect, contemplate, and rest while still inside the self-guided tour route. These spaces are, in a sense, sanctuaries as places to reflect and gather one's thoughts or to physically get away from the stress of learning about genocide and racial oppression.[62]

At the Whitney Plantation just outside New Orleans in Gramercy, Louisiana, visitors are led through memorial gardens and a carefully restored church before their tour guide leads them through the restored slave cabins and the big house (the antebellum planter's residential mansion). The gardens and the church are memorial spaces designed for learners' reflection. The art-filled spaces encourage visitors to contemplate the history of the slaves whose names are inscribed on the huge monument walls. Ibrahima Seck, my group's tour guide in 2015, explained that the memorials, including the "Field of Angels," commemorate, by name, the two hundred enslaved children who died in a slave trade shipwreck, and the "Allées Gwendolyn Midlo Hall Garden" commemorates, by name, over one thousand enslaved men, women, and children whose names were documented in the south Louisiana court records. Seck asked visitors to read the names on the many walls of the memorials. He instructed visitors not to try to make sense of slavery through the many names but to see the chaos that was slavery, and not to try to remember all the names but to remember some of the names to make sense of the humanity that was violated by slavery. These instructions ask visitors to receive information about the unbelievable oppression by repeatedly reading hundreds of names in an effort to reflect on what the history of slavery in Louisiana means to each of us, quietly and individually.

Inside the National September 11 Memorial and Museum in New York City, visitors quietly walk through large open spaces in the massive corridors of the remains of the original World Trade Center that now artfully serve as history galleries on the route to the exhibits farther inside the museum. Inside a two-room gallery are the exhibits *In Memoriam* and *Rebirth at Ground Zero*, which are compulsory quiet rooms. Memorial artifacts, artwork, and photographs of the victims of 9/11 are on display. A sign outside asks visitors to respect this memorial space and remain quiet. Photographs are not allowed. Visitors silently study the portrait-filled walls and the cases with personal items that recall the personhood of some victims. Then visitors come across a set of touch screen tabletops that hold a biographical encyclopedia of what appears to hold stories about all of the victims. The biographical tables hold testimonies from survivors and relatives, and videotaped interviews, recalled memories, and oral histories that add layers of humanity to the photographic stills mounted on the walls. As visitors read, listen, click, and swipe the options on the touch screens, visitors are absorbing, wondering, and reflecting on the stories about victims in the massive database.

Farther down inside the museum on the fourth level is the historical exhibit *September 11, 2001*. To one side of this object-rich exhibition is a gallery called *Reflecting on 9/11*. This space is a collection of oral histories and written responses to the events of 9/11 that is not filled with three-dimensional objects but instead filled with testimonies, letters of support, observations, commentaries, sympathy cards, memorial ephemera, and drawings by schoolchildren. The principally reflective sentiments are from a slice of time soon after the traumatic events and document how the public collectively began to shape the memory of what soon became known as 9/11. Learners are also encouraged to reflect on the impact events of 9/11 have had on the present—about the tragedies, losses, and the subsequent changes to society. As visitors leave the concluding gallery, the exhibit text asks visitors to keep thinking about the history today and for the future. The museum's request to visitors to continue reflecting on this difficult history after their visit suggests that the history workers recognize that the story holds many hard questions and anticipate that the interpretation will affect the visitors' understandings in some way. The request to keep thinking about the history is a call for active reflection that can lead to empathy, a call to visitors to actively care about the history represented in the museum.

History workers can observe learners who are reflecting on a difficult history through the learners' conversations, comments, and their contemplative efforts to articulate what they find meaningful about a difficult history. The learner's internal drive to speak about how a difficult history makes the learner feel is a signal to the history workers that the learner is making connections between the interpretation and the learner's memories and under-standings. A middle-aged couple, in 2012, explained to me, as their tour guide at the West Baton Rouge Museum, in Port Allen, Louisiana, that they grew up in a fieldworker's cabin just like the one on exhibit at the museum. They shared with me some of their memories about poverty and living in a plantation cabin. The husband and wife reflected on the late mid-twentieth-century sugarcane worker's home and found personal connections to the exhibit and expressed their understanding about the discomforts and hardships that they personally endured, and reflected further about the people from history who lived in these types of plantation dwellings.

Learners who are reflecting might also display quiet, solitary moments, as they con-template their memories or the new ideas and thoughts prompted by a difficult history interpretation. When learners find meanings and make connections between the exhibits and the learner's personal memories or previous knowledge, positive movements are being made toward learning difficult history. History workers might hear expressions like, "I re-member when that happened!" or "This reminds me of my father's immigration story!" or "My mother told me about that!" or "How did that happen? I need to find out." Comments

Visitors quietly view a surviving staircase used by survivors as their escape route from the burning Twin Towers building in 2001. Photograph by author.

that show the learner is making connections to the difficult history, however narcissistic the comments might sound at first, indicate that the learner is contemplating the personal affects or meanings of the difficult history. When the learner is moved past resisting the difficult knowledge and is piecing together fragments of the history with his or her personal lived experiences or understandings that allow him or her to make sense of the interpretation, the learner is deciding how he or she will respond to the events, witnesses, and victims.

Learners use the reflective opportunities to discuss, question, and dwell on a history that is difficult knowledge. History workers can encourage learners to reflect on the history through dialog, and by responding to learners' questions and comments to move learners beyond resisting or passively viewing an exhibit. At first, the learner is a learner-in-crisis who is challenged to move away from feeling isolated in his or her discomfort or pain. The resistive learner who then begins the work of mourning is initially consumed with how this history "makes me feel." The passive learner likely represses the uncomfortable feelings brought on by the difficult history, saying or thinking, "This has nothing to do with me." The learner's reflective responsiveness emerges as he or she begins to develop a relationship with the history. While the learner may truly have a direct and real relationship to the victims, place, or event, or can imagine a relationship to the difficult history, the learning that is now developing is dependent on how that relationship is understood in the present. A reflective learner is thinking about how the difficult history moves the learner. How am I changed by this history? How do I understand the history through this interpretation? A reflective learner moves toward empathetically imagining how the historical event impacted the victims and society, and possibly can imagine ways the history influences the present.

The learner gradually takes on responsibility toward the difficult history by expressing that he or she cares what happened to the historical persons and that this history matters. It is a story that must be told. In these realizations, sometimes called "aha moments," the learner is moving past his or her immediate identification with the history in order to bring justice to those whose lives he or she is imagining.[63]

History workers using CMP provide learners with sufficient time to reflect on a difficult history that the learners are grappling with. Trained history workers, for example, stationed throughout an exhibit can engage learners in conversations or be available to listen to learners who are eager to share their memories and thoughts out loud. Providing opportunities for reflection and spaces to sit, read, and talk will encourage learners to reflect on the difficult history. Through dialog, learners can be encouraged to recursively reflect on their relationships to the new knowledge.[64] Opportunities to talk about their thoughts and to ask questions are important moments for learners to work through the information that they find challenging. Reflection can be entwined with expressions of repetition when the learner continues to repeat information and questions. The reflective conversations engage learners in considering what sense they can make of the new information and how they can formulate an empathetic response.

Reconsideration: How Does This Sound?

The learner who can work through his or her internal disruptions can be moved to respond to a difficult history. Reconsidering a difficult history after working through feelings of discomfort or shock does not necessarily end with closure on understanding for learners, but in many ways is an opening for the learner to respond. An ethical response to a difficult history from a learner is an active and empathetic response. The learner is moved to feel that the history matters and is moved to care about the history, and in some instances, the learner can explain why he or she cares. This ethical response is historical empathy. In this way, the historical interpretation asks learners to attempt to engage in a critical and risk-laden learning that assumes a shift of one's ego boundaries.[65]

Reconsideration is made evident when the learner has changed in some way. Revelations, resolutions, and other forms of historical empathy can be detected through learners' remarks and actions. Learners express their changed relationship to the history and their new appreciation for the meanings of the history in, sometimes, observable actions and audible comments: "I did not know this part of the story, I want to read more about it" and "How long will the exhibit be up? I will bring my son to see it." The learner might look for ways to donate to support a relevant cause or donate to the host institution, or purchase a book to learn more about the difficult history.

Some learners might offer more subtle verbal expressions as cues about how they are reconsidering a difficult history. Learners might simply say, "Oh, I see" or "I had not thought about it that way." Expressions of reconsideration can be entwined with reflective expressions. Learners might make analogies between the difficult history and another history or personal memory. For example, when visitors walk along the reflecting pool at the Oklahoma City National Memorial, some learners recall where they were on that tragic day in 1995 and share those recollections with the park ranger or members of the tour group. In thinking about his or her temporal relationship to a difficult history, the learner is working through the knowledge and reflecting on how the learner is connected to the history and what the history means to him or her. In sharing those memories with others, the learner is beginning to respond to the history, perhaps, in an attempt to recall the history or to bring his or her memory of the history into the present, as if to say, this history matters to me today.

Learners operate out of their own memories and from their own psychological relationships to those events. But which memories and which interpretations do history workers use to recall and interpret the past? When history workers attempt to grapple with competing representations of a difficult history, history workers might do so with what education theorist Marla Morris calls "the sign of a dystopic curriculum."[66] The concept of a dystopic curriculum includes a pedagogical attitude that can encourage learners' working through interpretations of difficult histories to accept the possibility of multiple perspectives. Morris suggests that in this position learners are acquiring knowledge that is self-transforming and transforms his or her relationship to the historical interpretation.

Keep in mind, however, that the idea that learners will need to find peace or resolutions in their understandings about a difficult history is not a goal for CMP. Rather, the tensions felt by learners in the experience of learning about oppression and injustice is necessary for learners to feel empathy, to demand to know more, to come to value that history, and to be moved to action. In reconsidering a difficult history, learners might recognize that the historical social issues described in the interpretation presented can inspire social justice action and education in the present.

The lead exhibit designer for the National September 11 Memorial and Museum, Tom Hennes, explains how his team worked to integrate visitors' strong, emotion-laden memories into their museum experience in order to move visitors toward reconsideration. Hennes explains,

> Making a broad range of information and narratives available, while providing a stabilizing basis for the experience, can give museum users expanded ways to encounter those aspects of 9/11 that they already identify with—and those aspects that are unfamiliar or contrary to their own experience. This offers a way for any of us to use the exhibition to open ourselves empathically to others' experience of 9/11 and to gain new perspectives on our own experience—both through the re-encounter with our memories and through the wider range of experiences represented. In that way, the museum not only enables us to honor the dead and encounter the site and history of these attacks, but also to build our capacity to engage with the complex world that is their result.[67]

A group of history workers at Magnolia Mound Plantation, through a discussion, reconsidered a historical anecdote about two enslaved sisters who lived on the plantation around 1800 to 1804.[68] One sister was sold away to a neighboring Baton Rouge plantation. After several discussions, the history workers found that this story resonated with them. The history workers reflected on how they might be able to include this slave life history in their tours. Two history workers, who at first had been skeptical about being able to expand slave life history in their tours, reconsidered how they would revise their tours and offered an interpretation that was eventually incorporated into their tour narratives.

> Docent: How would they have gotten, how often would they have gotten to see each other?
> Rose: That is exactly, that is the question. How often did they get to see each other? . . . But they are not living far apart from each other.
> Second Docent: How fortunate that they were that close. One could have been sold off [farther away].
> Rose: Even across the river to Pointe Coupee.
> Second Docent: That would have been like another world. . . . Because the chances of ever getting back across the river would have been zilch. They would have had to have passes.[69]

The history workers recognized that the history of two sisters, Venus and Juba, represented an example of how familial relationships were restricted by slavery. In this instance, the history workers pulled together information they knew about the area and about sisterly love with the slave life history. They were working through the historical pieces of information to understand the sisters' plight and subjugation. The history workers were reconsidering how they could tell a slave life story in their tours. The history workers reconsidered the story of Juba and Venus as a story about oppression by using the crippling restrictions of plantation passes and forced family separations by sale in the interpretation. Through a reflective conversation, the history workers were reconsidering that the history was important in particular ways and should be told.

When learners demand to know more, they ask questions and look for more information. These productive actions indicate that learners are engaged in the interpretation and are expressing an active historical empathy. The questions are indicative of learners' reception to the learning moment, "How many people lived in this one-room slave cabin?" and their resistive remarks that might follow, "This is too small for one family!" followed by repeating questions and asking for the information to be repeated: "I can't believe this. One entire family lived in here?" The learner moving toward reflection utters remarks like, "If one family lived here, how many people were in the family?" and "How many children were in the family?" Upon reflecting on the interpretation that one family lived in the small space and upon gathering answers to questions from a docent to explain the meanings of family and household within the historic cabin, the learner might reconsider his or her resistance and say, "Wow, this is a really uncomfortable house. Were there other living arrangements for slaves who lived at this plantation, or did all slaves live in cabins like this one?" and "Is there a book in the gift shop that describes this history?" The learner's expressions indicate that the learner has been moved by the difficult history. The learner cares and wants to know more.

Concluding Remarks

History workers who use CMP can more clearly see how, within this psychological mix, the learner's ego can place its narcissistic objects alongside those that threaten the learner's identity and understandings of the world. Through CMP, history workers are more aware of obstacles to learners' active empathetic engagement and productive ethical responses when learners are stunned, in denial, or indifferent to historical interpretations of oppression. Some historical interpretations about difficult histories do not provide learners opportunities for easy resolution. While engaging in exhibits through reading, listening, or looking in passive terms allows learners to keep their identities intact and without feelings of crisis, as demonstrated by Shoshana Felman,[70] the learners are not learning from the historical interpretation.

When learners refute full engagement with a historical interpretation, they ask, "Why does the history not comfort me?" and "Why does it not rescue me?"[71] In this moment, the learner is unable to distinguish himself or herself from the historical Other. The reading of a trauma or hearing a tour narrative about tragedy or oppression provokes a melancholic response. In the context of classroom learning, Eppert explains,

> The "reading trauma" that encompasses the encounter with Holocaust testimony is the experience of the failure of normative investments to be sustained in and through the transactional relationship between text and reader. Ideological continuities between text and reader, past and present, world and self, are breached and confronted with our own impoverishment, our subsequent grievance is for the love object that is ourselves.[72]

Through CMP, history workers ask learners to engage with difficult history interpretations that can threaten the learners' ego boundaries. The emerging learner's crisis is now a teaching moment made available through his or her refusal to respond to the historical individuals or groups. Through CMP, history workers sensitively move learners beyond passively reading, looking, and listening to difficult history interpretations that work to contain a learner's narcissistic identities. History workers need to encourage a "just mourning" by supporting learners "to take responsibility for our own response and our own learning."[73] The psychic disruptions instigated by the learner's reading-trauma are an opportunity to increase the learner's reconsideration to take responsibility for his or her response to the historical individuals and groups.

Resistive learners' denials or refusals to engage with difficult knowledge reflect learners' unmediated self-identification with the historical suffering that is bound up in the act of secondary witnessing.[74] Key to secondary witnessing is Dominick LaCapra's notion of "empathic unsettlement," in that it entails the learner as witness to distinguish himself or herself from the one who suffered. LaCapra writes,

> [I]t involves a kind of virtual experience through which one puts oneself in the other's position while recognizing the difference of that position and hence not taking the other's place. Opening oneself to empathic unsettlement is . . . a desirable affective dimension of inquiry which complements and supplements empirical research and analysis.[75]

According to Eppert, self-reflexive conversations and reflective moments enable learners to take on responsibility to separate oneself from the Other in order to respond to the Other. In beginning to respond, the learner-in-crisis is challenged to come out of feelings of isolation. According to Caruth,

> The final import of the psychoanalytic and historical analysis of trauma is to suggest that the inherent departure, within trauma, from the moment of its first occurrence, is also a means of passing out of the isolation imposed by the event: that the history of a trauma, in its inherent belatedness, can only take place through the listening of another.[76]

Responsibility unfolds from the learner's emerging responsiveness to the alienation of the historical interpretation. Hence, the work of mourning here is identifying one's limits to the historical interpretation and learning to take on responsibility toward the interpretation. The learner needs to work through a "just mourning" by going beyond his or her immediate identification with the interpretation. The learner must be able to distinguish himself or herself in order to bring justice to those whose lives he or she has imagined.[77]

These internal shifts and external responses to difficult histories involve a kind of learning to live with loss. These are key features of remembrance learning,[78] a resolute working through of traumatic experiences, initiating a discernible transformation in the learners' lives and to learn from their relationships to a difficult history. Eppert explains that in order for ethical learning moments to unfold, learners need to individually recognize and respect the differences between the past and the present, while at the same time commemorate the continuity of lived experiences into the present.[79] Eppert explains that learners engaged with remembrance learning "fundamentally alter [their] relationship with past events and modes of social interaction."[80]

CMP encourages learners to work through the traumatic history, bit by bit, to make sense of difficult history by repeating, reflecting, and reconsidering their internal disruptions, and for some learners to get beyond, saying, "That is unbelievable." The veteran soldier who had difficulties listening to the U.S. Civil War–themed lecture about a "Just War" at the West Baton Rouge Museum and the teenaged girl on a class field trip to Magnolia Mound Plantation who exclaimed, "That's not me!" and refused to enter the slave cabin exhibit were learners who expressed melancholic positions toward particular difficult histories. Each learner was faced with feelings of loss that were putting his or her self-identity into jeopardy. Each person indicated that he or she was aware of his or her particular personal relationships to the history. The historical interpretations put those understandings at risk, asking each learner to change in some way by learning the new information. The loss was felt as a disruption or interference to what the veteran and teen considered to be truths, truths that were tied to each person's self-identity. The war veteran at the lecture and the teenage student on the tour of a slave cabin exhibit were each faced with considering, "I might have to change my understanding of my relationship to the history."

Difficult history museums and historical sites can be places of mourning. These museums and sites can provide spaces for exploring loss and to exceed the learner's melancholic disposition. Britzman concludes that the learner of a difficult knowledge "must move from the desolation of the survivor to the position of analyzing her own attachments in and to the world."[81] The act of learning that addresses the learner's ego defenses requires that the learner rebuild or reorganize his or her self-identity with each piece of new knowledge. Learners who are mourning, or have mourned, are more likely to empathize and respond to the specific historical events of the Other's trauma.[82] The learner who can work through his or her internal disruptions, bit by bit, can let go of the painful objects the learner holds to be himself or herself and can be moved to reconsider the meanings of the historical trauma in the present.

Notes

1. Amy Tyson and Azie Mira Dungey, "'Ask a Slave' and Interpreting Race on Pubic History's Front Line: Interview with Azie Mira Dungey," *The Public Historian* 36, no. 1 (2014): 36–60.
2. Ibid., 46.
3. Julia Rose, "Rethinking Representations of Slave Life at Historical Plantation Museums: Towards a Commemorative Museum Pedagogy" (PhD diss., Louisiana State University, 2006).
4. Deborah P. Britzman, *Lost Subjects, Contested Objects: Toward a Psychoanalytic Inquiry of Learning* (Albany: State University of New York Press, 1998), 51.
5. Deborah P. Britzman, *After-Education: Anna Freud, Melanie Klein, and Psychoanalytic Histories of Learning* (Albany: State University of New York Press, 2003).
6. Juliet Mitchell, ed., *The Selected Melanie Klein* (New York: The Free Press, 1986).
7. Michael Kahn, *Basic Freud: Psychoanalytic Thought for the 21st Century* (New York: Basic Books, 2002), 8–9. The human mind, using a traditional Freudian map, is composed of ego, id, and superego as described by Sigmund Freud in *Beyond the Pleasure Principle* (Sigmund Freud, *Beyond the Pleasure Principle*, in *The Standard Edition of the Complete Psychological Works of Sigmund Freud*, Vol. 17, 7–64, ed. & trans. James Strachey (London: Hogarth Press, 1974, original work published in 1920). The id is the mental drive for our wants, desires, and impulses, in particular our sexual and aggressive drives. The superego works in contradiction to the id, striving to act in a socially appropriate manner, whereas the id just wants instant self-gratification. The superego controls our sense of right and wrong and guilt. It is responsible for us acting within the parameters of socially acceptable behavior. The ego mediates behavior among the ego, the

id, and the superego. The ego is concerned with consequences and avoids trouble or delays gratification. Freud explains, "The ego stands for reason and good sense while the id stands for untamed passions" (Kahn, 27). The ego manages relations with the outside world, finding balance for desires and social norms, and it is responsible for the task of repressing memories and ideas and for other modes of defense against anxiety. The ego is aware of reality and understands that behaviors have consequences.

8. Shoshana Felman, "Education and Crisis, or the Vicissitudes of Teaching," in *Testimony: Crisis of Witnessing in Literature, Psychoanalysis and History*, ed. Shoshana Felman and Dori Laub (New York: Routledge, 1992), 1–56.

9. Britzman, *Lost Subjects*, 25.

10. Ibid.

11. Sigmund Freud, "Mourning and Melancholia," in *The Standard Edition of the Complete Psychological Works of Sigmund Freud*, Vol. 14, ed. & trans. James Strachey (London: Hogarth Press, 1971, original work published in 1917), 243–58.

12. Mitchell, *The Selected Melanie Klein*.

13. Freud, "Mourning and Melancholia," 243–44.

14. Julia Rose, "Three Building Blocks for Developing Ethical Representations of Difficult Histories," *History News* 68, no. 4 (2013): Technical Leaflet #264.

15. Kahn, *Basic Freud*, 171.

16. Freud, "Mourning and Melancholia," 244–45.

17. Ibid., 246.

18. Ibid., 249.

19. Ibid., 249.

20. Julie Salverson, "Anxiety and Contact in Attending to a Play about Land Mines," in *Between Hope and Despair: Pedagogy and the Remembrance of Historical Trauma*, ed. Roger I. Simon, Sharon Rosenberg, and Claudia Eppert (Lanham, MD: Rowman & Littlefield, 2000), 63.

21. Freud, "Mourning and Melancholia."

22. J. Laplanche and J. B. Pontalis, *The Language of Psycho-Analysis*, trans. Donald Nicholson-Smith (New York: W. W. Norton and Company, 1973), 428.

23. Mitchell, *The Selected Melanie Klein*, 20.

24. See Freud, *Beyond the Pleasure Principle*.

25. Ibid., 14–16.

26. See Mitchell, *The Selected Melanie Klein*.

27. Sigmund Freud, "On Narcissism: An Introduction," in *The Standard Edition of the Complete Psychological Works of Sigmund Freud*, Vol. 14, ed. James Strachey (London: Hogarth Press, 1971, original work published in 1914), 87.

28. Melanie Klein, "Early Stages of the Oedipus Conflict," in *The Selected Melanie Klein*, ed. Juliet Mitchell (New York: The Free Press, 1986, original work published in 1928), 69.

29. Mitchell, *The Selected Melanie Klein*, 20–21; see also R. D. Hinshelwood, *A Dictionary of Kleinian Thought* (London: Free Association Books, 1991).

30. Britzman, *After-Education*, 42–44.

31. Melanie Klein, "Mourning and Its Relation to Manic-Depressive States," in *The Selected Melanie Klein*, ed. Juliet Mitchell (New York: The Free Press, 1986, original work published in 1940), 147.

32. Klein, "Mourning and Its Relation to Manic-Depressive States," 156.

33. Ibid., 167.

34. Rose, "Rethinking Representations of Slave Life at Historical Plantation Museums."
35. Personal communication with the museum's curator, 2013.
36. Personal communication with the museum's curator, 2013.
37. Rose, "Rethinking Representations of Slave Life at Historical Plantation Museums," 140.
38. Personal communication with the museum's curator, 2013.
39. Rose, "Rethinking Representations of Slave Life at Historical Plantation Museums," 200.
40. Julia Rose, "Commemorative Museum Pedagogy," in *Beyond Pedagogy: Reconsidering the Public Purpose of Museums*, ed. Brenda Trofanenko and Avner Segall (Rotterdam, The Netherlands: Sense Publishers, 2014), 118.
41. Simone Schweber, "Notes on Passing as an Insider at the US Holocaust Memorial Museum," in *Beyond Pedagogy: Reconsidering the Public Purpose of Museums*, ed. Brenda Trofanenko and Avner Segall (Rotterdam, The Netherlands: Sense Publishers, 2014), 107–13.
42. Ibid., 110.
43. Azie Mira Dungey, "Ask a Slave," YouTube, July 1, 2014, http://www.askaslave.com.
44. Tyson and Dungey, "'Ask a Slave' and Interpreting Race on Pubic History's Front Line," 38.
45. Ibid., 37.
46. Ibid., 38.
47. Megan Boler, *Feeling Power: Emotions and Education* (New York: Routledge, 1999), 156–57.
48. Alice Pitt, "Reading Resistance Analytically: On Making the Self in Women's Studies," in *Dangerous Territories: Struggles for Difference and Equality in Education*, ed. Leslie G. Roman and Linda Eyre (London: Routledge, 1997), 127; and see Rose, "Rethinking Representations of Slave Life at Historical Plantation Museums," 158–91.
49. Deborah P. Britzman and Alice Pitt, "Pedagogy in Transferential Time: Casting the Past of Learning in the Presence of Teaching," in *Action as a Living Practice*, ed. Terrence Carson and Dennis Sumara (New York: Peter Lang, 1997), 69.
50. Shoshana Felman, *Jacques Lacan and the Adventure of Insight: Psychoanalysis in Contemporary Culture* (Cambridge, MA: Harvard University Press, 1987), 76.
51. Felman, "Education and Crisis, or the Vicissitudes of Teaching," 7.
52. Ibid.," 53.
53. Ibid.
54. Claudia Eppert, "Throwing Testimony against the Wall: Reading Relations, Loss and Responsible/Responsive Learning," in *Difficult Memories: Talk in a (Post) Holocaust Era*, ed. Marla Morris and John A. Weaver (New York: Peter Lang, 2002), 45–65.
55. Felman, *Jacques Lacan and the Adventure of Insight*, 78–79.
56. Deborah P. Britzman, "If the Story Cannot End: Deferred Action, Ambivalence, and Difficult Knowledge," in *Between Hope and Despair: Pedagogy and the Remembrance of Historical Trauma*, ed. Roger I. Simon, Sharon Rosenberg, and Claudia Eppert (Lanham, MD: Rowman & Littlefield, 2000), 39.
57. Ibid., 39.
58. Felman, "Education and Crisis, or the Vicissitudes of Teaching."
59. See Shoshana Felman and Dori Laub, eds., *Testimony: Crisis of Witnessing in Literature, Psychoanalysis and History* (New York: Routledge, 1992).
60. See Freud, "Mourning and Melancholia."
61. Rose, "Rethinking Representations of Slave Life at Historical Plantation Museums," 142.
62. Personal communication, 2013.
63. See Eppert, "Throwing Testimony against the Wall," 60.

64. William E. Doll Jr., *A Post-Modern Perspective on Curriculum* (New York: Teachers College Press, 1993).

65. Roger I. Simon, Sharon Rosenberg, and Claudia Eppert, introduction to *Between Hope and Despair: Pedagogy and the Remembrance of Historical Trauma*, ed. Roger I. Simon, Sharon Rosenberg, and Claudia Eppert (Lanham, MD: Rowman & Littlefield, 2000), 8.

66. Marla Morris, *Curriculum and the Holocaust: Competing Sites of Memory and Representation* (Mahwah, NJ: Lawrence Erlbaum Associates, 2001).

67. Alice Greenwald, Michael Shulan, Tom Hennes, Jake Barton, and David Layman, "The Heart of Memory: Voices from the 9/11 Memorial Museum Formation Experience," *Museum* 93, no. 3 (2014): 34.

68. Rose, "Rethinking Representations of Slave Life at Historical Plantation Museums," 200.

69. Ibid.

70. Felman, "Education and Crisis, or the Vicissitudes of Teaching," 47–56.

71. Eppert, "Throwing Testimony against the Wall," 57.

72. Ibid., 58.

73. Ibid., 59.

74. Claudia Eppert, "Relearning Questions: Responding to the Ethical Address of Past and Present Others," in *Between Hope and Despair: Pedagogy and the Remembrance of Historical Trauma*, ed. Roger I. Simon, Sharon Rosenberg, and Claudia Eppert (Lanham, MD: Rowman & Littlefield, 2000), 213–46; and Britzman, *Lost Subjects*.

75. Dominick LaCapra, *Writing History, Writing Trauma* (Baltimore, MD: Johns Hopkins University Press, 2001), 78.

76. Cathy Caruth, *Trauma: Explorations in Memory* (Baltimore, MD: Johns Hopkins University Press, 1995), 10–11.

77. Eppert, "Throwing Testimony against the Wall," 60.

78. Eppert, "Relearning Questions."

79. Ibid.

80. Ibid., 216.

81. Britzman, *Lost Subjects*, 132.

82. Boler, *Feeling Power*.

CHAPTER 4

Response and Responsibility

Ethical Representations of Difficult Histories

Introduction

A PARADOX facing history workers to develop and implement interpretations for difficult histories is the push and pull of delivering stories that are traumatic and, at the same time, significant to learners. History workers, many of whom are public historians and educators, are tasked with finding a balance between respecting the fragility of learners' emotional responses to history and responsibly teaching the histories of human suffering. The history workers' task to decide how to remember difficult histories is an ethical issue. Social scientist Jeffery C. Alexander describes this work as an effort to separate the traumatic events from the unconscious distortions of memory.[1]

In this chapter, I use the terms *representation* and *interpretation*. It is often difficult to separate the two. Historical representations are the symbols or signifiers of a thing, person, event, or idea. Historical interpretations are explanations or descriptions of the meanings of events or ideas. Through the historical interpretations, collectivities attempt to identify the causes and effects of the traumas or the sources of historical suffering. The significance of this kind of fluid collective identity making and remaking means that the representations of the difficult histories are connected to our contemporary self-identities. In this way, history workers take on a substantial responsibility, a moral responsibility, of helping individuals and collectivities to define their solidary relationships that allow individuals and groups to share the knowledge of the suffering from history and in the present.

As discussed in earlier chapters, the knowledge of historical others' suffering is at risk of becoming our own. Alexander explains how this is an ethical dilemma.

> Is the suffering of others also our own? In thinking that it might in fact be, societies expand the circle of the we. By the same token, social groups can and then do refuse to recognize the existence of others' trauma, and because of their failure they cannot achieve a moral stance. By denying the reality of others' suffering, people not only diffuse their own responsibility for the suffering but often project the responsibility of their own suffering on these others.[2]

Learners' historical empathy for the suffering of others is a responsible response to historical interpretations of difficult histories. However, by refusing a just remembrance of historical victims, or by refusing to participate in understanding the trauma of historical Others and how the traumas are connected to the present, it restricts solidarity. This leaves contemporary victims of oppression to suffer alone and to marginalize or erase the meanings of the historical individuals' and groups' suffering.[3]

This chapter includes a Commemorative Museum Pedagogy (CMP) toolbox, offering an approach to developing ethical representations of difficult histories. The chapter is an expansion of the AASLH Technical Leaflet #264, "Three Building Blocks for Developing Ethical Representations of Difficult Histories."[4] The toolbox is designed for history workers dealing with both groups of learners, fellow history workers, or visitors. The toolbox includes three conceptual building blocks for constructing ethical representations of difficult histories. The building blocks are called the Face, the Real, and the Narrative. The techniques or tools for history workers to develop historical representations using the building blocks are detailed in this chapter. Throughout this chapter, I use the words *Face*, *Real*, *Narrative*, and *Other* as terms with unique definitions to understanding historical representations. The first three name each of the three building blocks. The fourth word, *Other*, refers to a person or group who is a marginalized or excluded subject from a difficult history. The "Other" also can refer to people from a history who were historically described as minority populations, inferior or subjugated. The "Other" can denote persons or groups who are portrayed as peripherally relevant to a historical representation. Each word is capitalized to connote that the usage is different than the words' dictionary definitions.

The push and pull history workers often feel when wanting to interpret a difficult history and the simultaneous feeling of trepidation in facing horror, or of upsetting their learners, depend on the assembly of the stuff that history workers use to tell history—the memories, artifacts, and stories. What words and phrases fairly and equitably shape the stories, and which artifacts and images can be sensitively used to signify the tragedies? Which points of view are clear and unhampered, and what selection of memories is justly positioned to recall a history? So, how do we do this justly,[5] as Claudia Eppert implores, and conscientiously,[6] as Ruth Abram describes, and ethically,[7] as Roger I. Simon demands? Representations and interpretations that encourage learners' reflective self-awareness will instigate empathetic responses that frame connections between the learner and those who suffered. CMP is an approach to develop difficult history representations that frame a moral stance to engage learners deeply enough to move learners (history workers and visitors) beyond sensing the learners' own mournful anxieties to appreciating the meaning of the suffering of others.

When readers look closely at the book cover of the historical novel *Cane River* by Lalita Tademy,[8] readers see a historical photograph. The author, a descendent of enslaved sugarcane workers, implores her readers to look closely as she explains on the audiobook recording, "The woman standing beside the oak trees staring out to the future is my great grandmother, Emily. I think she and the others who came before her would be honored to have you hear their story."[9]

Commemoration is the act of honoring the memory of someone or some community through organized, collective instruction. The key to commemorating lives lived, lost, and made tragic by extraordinary circumstances is to remember purposefully and productively. Commemoration is a kind of pedagogy that is extolled through ethical representations, and is built with the three concepts called "Faces," "Real" historical evidence, and "Narratives." The aim of commemoration is broader than preventing the tragedy from happening again. Commemorating human experiences in museums and public history venues provides present generations with opportunities to learn how particular histories are relevant today, thereby engendering courage, hope, justice, generosity, compassion, respect, and temperance in visitors and all learners. Possibilities for increasing human virtue are located at the nexus of ethics and historical representations.[10]

Road Map: Ethical Representations Honor Their Story

Difficult histories include the recollections of war, oppression, and violence. The challenge for history workers to develop ethical representations of difficult histories is finding an equitable equation for combining the three conceptual components: Faces, Real content, and Narratives. Approaches, examples, and techniques for developing ethical representations using these three components, called building blocks, are explained in the following three sections. In each building block section, there are subsections that describe techniques particular to that building block. I include brief examples from real public history learning moments to help illustrate the techniques and to clarify the conceptual basis of each building block.

When the learner decides to look at the images and artifacts that recall the history of oppression, the learner takes on the responsibility to acknowledge the historical person's pain (the "Other's pain") and consequently is compelled to respond. By acknowledging the Other's historical experience, the learner provides the world with his or her empathetic response that this history is meaningful and that the learner cares. The empathetic learner demands to know more and changes his or her understanding of the world in some way. Ethical representations result from putting together the three building blocks ("Face," "Real," "Narratives") that produce historical empathy in learners. In this way, ethical representations and interpretations of difficult histories help learners to shape their moral sensibilities and envision actions that they can take to encourage social justice in the present and for the future.[11]

Building Blocks for Developing Ethical Representations

The Face: A Philosophy

> Justice . . . is not an abstraction, a value. Justice exists in relation to a person,
> and is something done by a person. An act of injustice is condemned,
> not because the law is broken, but because a person has been hurt.
>
> —ABRAHAM HESCHEL, *THE PROPHETS*[12]

The first building block, called the "Face," comes from the French philosopher Emmanuel Lévinas. Lévinas conceived of the notion of "the face" or "the face-to-face encounter" as the ethical response to know someone who was or is human.[13] In this concept, when applied to public history venues and museums, the subject, like a co-worker or museum visitor, is responsible to acknowledge the historical Other. The "Face" calls the visitor to "give and serve" the Other by responding empathetically. This concept is helpful to building ethical representations in museums and historical sites especially because Lévinas did not literally call for a likeness of the Other's face through photographs or portraits for us to learn about the Other's history. Rather, the philosopher's concept expresses the necessity for the learner (a visitor or history worker in training, e.g.) to understand the personhood of the Other through understanding his or her human experience. Who was he, the person? Who was she, the person? Lévinas explains that knowing "the face" of the Other orders and ordains us.[14] We are ethically obligated to care what happened to people in order to appreciate history.

The work to ensure fundamental human dignity means working from an ethical imagination constituted within the fullness of a relation to another as another. The "face-to-face" disposition requires an ethical response on the history workers' part and on the part of the visitor to confront practices that diminish the dignity of the particularity of the Other.[15]

Multidimensional Representations

One tool for developing the Face is multidimensional representations of the Other. Ethical representations informed by the Face of historical Others obligates learners to acknowledge the personhood of historical individuals or groups. The Face is constructed with multiple descriptive dimensions about the Others' lived relationships to families, communities, cultures, places, and nations. One- and two-dimensional descriptions of a historical person or group use basic identifications consisting of a job title or social position; for example, "midwife" or "slave" or a person's name. Multidimensional representations demonstrate how the historical group or person is fully human through their relationships within society and to the world. Ethical representations use biographies and profiles, and ultimately require discursive constructions of a person's or a group's identity, which connects them to a complex contextual mix of their social, familial, economic, and metaphysical relationships. In this way, multidimensional representations lead learners to find connections to the historical persons' subjectivity that reveal the significance of the Other's experiences, the historical events, and to the conditions in learners' everyday lives.

Overly generalized and anonymous representations do not call the Face of historical persons into being. Such single dimensions can marginalize significant relationships across generations of historical Others and mask the diversity of an individual's experiences, expertise, and agency. Single-dimensional representations make it difficult for learners to imagine the depth of the human story being recalled. In effect, a learner's detached gaze regards the historical Other "only as someone to be seen, not someone (like us) who also sees."[16]

Consider, for example, the phrase *Holocaust victim*. In brief descriptions of the World War II genocide, learners can sweep by the complex personhood of the people, the brothers and sisters and the mothers and fathers, who perished in the Jewish ghettos and in the concentration camps. The impersonal phrase *Holocaust victim* merely accounts for a person who died in that event and succinctly marks that accounting. However, for example, referring to Anne Frank, who was a Holocaust victim and whose story is well known and elaborately recorded, brings to mind an emotional connection to the very real young girl who was a Dutch diarist, daughter, sister, friend, and a victim of the Nazi's fascist genocide.

Another example of a single-dimensional representation of a historical Other is the phrase *house slave* in the context of a tour of an antebellum plantation house. The term describes a person by a job and by the diminished social status of a slave who labored inside a big house. Without additional descriptive dimensions, the house slave from history is objectified as a part of the mechanics of a household. Even when history workers provide the historical name of a house slave on a historic site tour, history workers must critically consider if the name and job title provide enough information to describe the personhood of the enslaved house servant to move learners to reflect on her enslavement or life experience in the particular historical space.

One- and two-dimensional representations of historical Others limit learners from deeply reflecting on the stories intended to recall a difficult history. Consider the story of the enslaved carpenter listed on the 1800 slave inventory for Magnolia Mound Plantation named American Will, age thirty-six. In 2006, just over two centuries later, a docent gave a tour inside the Magnolia Mound Plantation big house in Baton Rouge, Louisiana. On the tour, the docent showed visitors an exposed section of an interior wall that revealed the *bousillage* construction and the hand-hewn cypress timbers that were assembled by slaves in 1792. The docent said that one of the carpenters who helped build the house was American Will. The visitors looked at the unique Creole building construction and then listened to the docent describe some of the Louisiana-made bedroom furniture. Where was the opportunity provided to visitors to learn about the difficult history of slavery? While the broad, sweeping description acknowledged the carpenter named American Will and his enslavement in relation to the historic house, what did visitors hear that signified the importance of remembering his life as an enslaved carpenter? Did the three descriptors (American Will, slave, carpenter) offer enough to inspire empathy for American Will? Perhaps.[17]

Multidimensional representations provide descriptions that go beyond a name and job title. Consider this description about American Will that works to describe his personhood with a multidimensional story from his life that goes beyond the memory of his forced labor to build the *bousillage* walls in the big house.

With additional layers of information, a multidimensional and a more complex view of American Will, the person, can emerge. American Will may have felt desperation for the welfare of his young family when the slave community he lived in for eight years was torn apart by the legal division of property decided by his master's attorney. American Will watched as his wife, Minta, and their five children were separated from him and forced to leave Magnolia Mound Plantation to live and labor at a cotton plantation fifty miles north of Baton Rouge. Subsequently, he ran away and headed in the direction of his family.

American Will was not only a skilled carpenter. He was also experienced in helping others run away from their sites of bondage. Since his childhood in Jamaica and through the years he spent in slavery in the American colonies, American Will had to negotiate the nuances of slavery. Even after he was traded and started his family in Baton Rouge at Magnolia Mound Plantation, he had to struggle against slavery's oppression for his family's sake. American Will had much to lose in 1803 when he fled in search of his family. He traveled north to St. Johns Plains, an area where he could be closer to his wife and children, and where he lived like a fugitive for four years. Notices were sent out to alert free men for his capture. When American Will was captured, his owners, the Duplantiers, who no longer wanted the liability of a runaway slave at Magnolia Mound Plantation, offered him for sale. The Duplantiers sold American Will to his captor, a planter in Galvezton, several miles south of Baton Rouge and even farther from his family.[18]

Expressions of responsibility emerge when learners begin to make connections among the Faces of American Will, his family, and his slaveholders, and the learners' present. Learners' questions about the oppressions and restrictions forced on family ties during slavery come to mind. Thoughts about love, loyalty, and the impact of laws on the lives of Others reverberate in the sense-making process of American Will's story. The learners' responses might move from detached observations to disbelief and dismay to assessments of the injustices revealed in the tour of the historic site. Learners will likely contemplate new questions and might be moved from indifference to considering how the injustices make the learners feel to thinking about how the historical injustices inform their understanding of the world today.[19]

Here is one of the conundrums of moving from single-dimensional representations toward multidimensional representations. While single dimensions are less descriptive and less painful for learners to encounter, as the personhood of a historical Other is more developed with multiple dimensions, the learners' encounter has the potential to be more painful and thereby increases the risk of the learners' resistance to the difficult history.

The learning experience has the potential to develop further when learners have opportunities to repeat and reflect on their biases and connections to the history and examine the social issues that surface. Ethical representations can make history workers and visitors more self-aware when they discover their connections to the historical Others. For example, the learner might have in common shared experiences such as parenthood, age, or ancestry with the historical individuals or groups. These realizations may leave learners vulnerable to feeling implicated or self-conscious and exposed. Factors of race, gender, class, sexual preference, cultural group membership, and regional identifications can combine in complementary and contradictory ways to affect the levels of learners' engagement in the public history encounters. The levels of engagement, in turn, affect the learner's predisposition to expressing empathy, resistance, or validation.[20]

Active Voice

In developing ethical representations, history workers should choose words carefully to avoid words that create a buffer between the learner and the human suffering entwined in a history. Single-dimensional representations that use collective and countable nouns tend to dissuade visitors from imagining the personhood of individuals or groups; for example, "a soldier" and "an army." While the passive voice and anonymous descriptions, without more descriptive and contextual information, make it less painful to talk about violence and oppression, they are a kind of distancing rhetoric. This can lessen learners' immediate resistances and yet more easily allow for continued engagement.

A strategy for history workers to abate objectifying human experiences is to use an active voice that demonstrates agency, while keeping in mind that the alternative passive voice tends to erase the presence of the historical individual or group. For example:

Passive sentence: The silver was polished.

Active sentence: The slave polished the silver.

Historical empathy: Charlotte, who was an enslaved house servant, watched her children as she polished the silver.

With each sentence, more information is added to humanize the story of the polished silver on display. The history about the object, "the silver," has moved toward the history about Charlotte.

History workers can critically read and listen to descriptions to know whether the historical representations are developed with either active or passive voices. By identifying the subject of the sentence, history workers can decide whether the subject is doing the action or being acted upon. In passive voice, the sentence is structured with the subject as the receiver of the action, while in active voice the sentence is structured with the subject doing the action.

Aggregate of the Anonymous

A just goal for developing ethical representations and interpretations of victims of mass tragedies is to bring visitors "face-to-face" with the historical Others. How, then, do museum workers construct a Face for thousands or millions of people who suffered? Exhibits and programs utilize tropes and sound bites that economize complex histories; for example, "six million Jews died in the Holocaust" and "51,112 soldiers died at Gettysburg." While useful, these are sweeping descriptions that avoid describing personhood and exclude many aspects of the other historical victims and agents. The complexity and overwhelming number of personal stories in mass tragedies may make ethical representations and interpretations seem impractical.

However, a kind of empirical persuasion is useful to inform learners about historical events and the extent of violence or oppression inflicted on mass populations. The "aggregate of anonymous victims" is a useful concept from Susan Sontag that speaks to the power that numbers have to help describe the scope and impact of the injustices inflicted on the multitudes of people.[21]

Statistics in some exhibits can be useful to describe the scope and impact of violence or oppression. For example, a Louisiana middle school teacher explained how she uses a football stadium as a visual metaphor for her students to imagine what a "mass of people" looks like. She asks her students to imagine the LSU Tiger Stadium in Baton Rouge filled to capacity at the beginning of the game (94,000) and how over the next two hours each section of the stadium will empty out. Then the teacher explained that she asks her students to imagine that each football fan represents a soldier who fought in the Confederate Army in the U.S. Civil War and that the total of CSA soldiers who died was 94,000. The middle school teacher reports that her students respond to this imagery and express feelings of empathy to what happened to the thousands of soldiers, who are still anonymous to the students but whom the students can more realistically imagine with the numbers and by the meaning of the mass of persons who perished.

Histories of mass populations have many layers, and interpreting several layers of experiences also brings learners closer and closer to perceiving the Faces of the historical Others who are members of a massive collectivity. Descriptions of oppressed masses can be constructed with the many sociohistorical contextual layers of relationships—the physical, economic, ideological, demographic, political, familial, and more. With each layer of information, from overviews describing the geographic setting to relationships among subgroups within communities, households, families, and individuals, learners can get closer to understanding the personhood of victims and agents. Each layer of the empirical information that makes for multidimensional representations helps learners to imagine and reflect on the variability of what happened to people affected by oppression.

History workers can effectively use biographic cameos of historical individuals and groups to further construct the Faces of victims and participants of mass traumas that bring personal experiences into finer focus. The photograph below, from the New Mexico National Guard Museum, is an example that illustrates the effectiveness of how biographic cameos can help to represent the tragedies suffered by a larger group.

In 2014, a visitor from Virginia visited the exhibit *Aggies to Recall*, which featured the stories of the twenty-six soldiers who were members of the 200th Coast Artillery, New Mexico National Guard, during World War II and were among the first to fire upon the Japanese during their initial attack on the Philippines. At the close of the hostilities in August 1945, the twenty-six soldiers featured in the exhibit perished during combat and captivity. After reading one story in particular, the Virginian called out to her group of friends on the tour, "Did you read this? This is unbelievable! He survived the horrors of the POW camp only to die on the wharf while waiting for the ship that was to take him home."

How do history workers choose the Faces to highlight from a mass trauma when there are so many stories to tell? How can the construction of one particular Face work to account for the myriad of personal stories involved in events of mass oppression or violence? History workers are pressed to ask these critical questions, including, "Does this cameo enable learners to get more intimately connected to the difficult history being recalled?" Some cameos

Visitors read the label copy "Aggies to Recall" at the New Mexico National Guard Museum, formerly called the Bataan Memorial Museum. Photograph by author.

represent the path many victims endured within and after the historical trauma represented, and other cameos represent unique or unusual experiences. Availability of historical content through research, collections, and history workers' connections and understanding of the difficult history will influence the history workers' abilities to develop the Faces in their work to construct ethical and effective representations.

Multidimensional Representations Recall Personhood to Represent the Face

- Include histories about relationships.
- Include the complexities of people's lives.
- Are site specific.
- Reference genealogical details.
- Focus cameos on individuals' stories.
- Can express a collectivity of Faces (i.e., Aggregate of the Anonymous).
- Move away from generic histories and regional generalizations.
- Move away from one- and two-dimensional representations. Go beyond a name, a job title, or position.

The Real: Responsible Authority

> Thus the presences and absences embodied in sources . . . or archives . . . are neither neutral or natural. They are created.
> —MICHEL-ROLPH TROUILLOT[22]

The Real is the second building block. Deciding whose stories to tell and what information is significant and most worthy in order to recall difficult histories is an extraordinary responsibility for history workers. Given the authority to interpret history, history workers need to reflectively ask themselves, "Can I say why I am choosing this information, and can I explain how this information will be used?" An essential method for developing the Real content for ethical representations is in the critical process of selecting the history fragments that will be used to represent human experiences.

The Real includes artifacts, images, documents, numbers, dates, and a variety of other rich empirical evidence to construct the Face and build Narratives to ethically recall difficult histories. The Real is the content that has the potential to provide validation for the history being recalled. The Real is the authentic, measured, and relevant empirical information that public history venues and museums collect, assemble, and use to recall histories. The significance of the Real stuff from the past relies on the learners' abilities to find connections to the histories. Unlike spectacles, which are entertaining and unusual, ethical representations contain information that means something for the future.

Partial Nature of the Real

Recognition of the partial nature of the Real is an important part of the process of developing ethical representations and interpretations. An effective tool for history workers is to constantly recognize that the Real is only partial. No landscape, building, or exhibit about a difficult history is large enough or complete enough to contain the extent of human suffering and sadness that they commemorate. Authentic interactions with the Real in exhibits and at historical sites ask learners to take the responsibility to contemplate how these spaces, images, objects, and descriptions represent the injustices inflected on a population. History workers need to acknowledge to themselves and to their visitors that partial perspectives in historical interpretations are inevitable. The partial nature of historical interpretations encourages history workers and visitors to discuss, reflect, and question the changing definitions of the past and understandings about the present that the Real collectively stands to represent.

The Real can help signify the suffering, the lives impacted, and the historical events. The Real brings learners closer in proximity to the suffering but can never replicate the suffering or fully account for the infinite details and emotions that were entailed in a difficult history. Writer Teju Cole explains, "[O]bjects are reservoirs of specific personal experience filled with the hours of some person's life."[23] The mute object is given voice as the historical representations fill in the story with Faces and Narratives.

History workers label objects as truths. The authentic object is intended to enable learners to equate interacting with the object-on-view with interacting face-to-face with the past—what Andrea Liss refers to as "retrospective witnessing,"[24] between truth and the visitor. Liss reflects on objects collected from Holocaust survivors in museum exhibits, explaining, "Authenticity, it is understood, guarantees the reality it can but only stand in for."[25]

The benefit of difficult history interpretations as a tool for advocating for social justice can come from the synergy of the emotional stories and the Real empirical content. Sociologist Dean MacCannell, however, explains that while the aesthetics of difficult history interpretations work to represent the events of human tragedies that can move learners to action, history workers need to keep in mind that the representations will always be incomplete.[26]

Artists, scholars, and curators who have labored to represent painful memories have given society the precious few effective symbolic representations we use to remember. They created places for us to pause and remember the suffering of the victims and to contemplate the effects of violence.[27] And yet, every such commemorative effort tries for the impossible. History workers need to acknowledge that the meaning of painful events cannot be fully contained in their symbolic representations.[28]

Representations and interpretations in museums and other public history settings are in flux, relative to time, space, and context, and are inevitably subjective. Hooper-Greenhill explains the partial nature of interpretations this way:

> "Any interpretation can never be fully completed. The discovery of true meaning of a text or a work of art is never finished: it is in fact an infinite process" (Gadamer, 1976: 124). As errors in understanding are eliminated and as new sources of knowledge emerge, so meaning is a continuing process of modification, adaptation and extension. The hermeneutic circle is never fully closed, but remains open to the possibilities of change.[29]

The partial nature of knowledge that the Real cannot wholly account for also rises from the humanness of the makers of the empirical matter. While the things from history bore witness to history, the people who made those things had to have been there in order to make the object or to take the photograph, for example. Susan Sontag explains that the simple motion of the photographer's hand "allows photographs to be both objective record and personal testimony, both a faithful copy and transcription of an actual moment of reality and an interpretation of that reality"[30] that could not be accomplished through literature or art. However, like literature and art, documentary photography can also fall into the subjective arena of truth. Sontag says, "For the photography of atrocity, people want the weight of witnessing without the taint of artistry, which is equated with insincerity of mere contrivance."[31] It is to Sontag's point of artistry that history workers must critically assess the completeness and the quality of the Real and what can be brought to learners' attention. What the history worker and visitor read into a photograph and what the photograph *should* be saying are important considerations for misreadings and misinterpretations, as well as new ideological uses for the images that will matter to learners and for future rememberings.[32] The Real used in historical representations of difficult histories can authenticate the suffering of others. While the Real appears concrete and empirical in nature, the work of history to advocate for social justice needs to remain fluid, allowing for a continuum of new information and new voices to represent injustices.

Consider the first full-scale photojournalist attempt to document war by Mathew Brady and his team of photographers. The seemingly candid presentation of the U.S. Civil War photographs, in particular those published in 1866 by Alexander Gardner, was often by design.[33] The photographs were composed and elements were arranged to achieve an aesthetic by the photographer. Mathew Brady's team rearranged and moved some of the dead soldiers at Gettysburg to compose the photograph called "The Home of a Rebel Sharpshooter, Gettysburg."[34] Staged images are one aspect of the partiality of the Real. The artistic process of framing images through the photographer's viewfinder is another, which allows the photographer to include some parts of a scene and to exclude other parts of a scene, leaving viewers to wonder if the perspective captured in the image left out compelling information just outside the frame.

Documentarian Dorothea Lange made a career of photographically recording history, mostly for U.S. governmental agencies. During the Great Depression, the Farm Security Administration (FSA) hired Lange to record rural Americans. Upon entering World War II, the War Relocation Authority (WRA) hired Lange to record the Japanese American internment project. Also a social activist, Lange quipped that the federal government first hired her to document the suffering of Americans in order to help American citizens, and then the same government hired Lange to document the suffering of American citizens that was created by the government.[35] Gordon explains that Lange used her camera to provide viewers, then and for the future, with a careful demonstration of the way prejudice can be masked by patriotism, and can lead to enormous injustice. And it is with this particular insight that history workers can critically study Lange's images in recognition of the partial nature of the Real available to represent the difficult histories of farmers during the Great Depression and Japanese Americans during World War II.

Lange's often sublime images of the Japanese internment camps offer viewers multiple levels of meaning. These can range from images showing decent housing alongside images of the same housing as indecent, to showing the irony of the schools within the camps alongside images of the college students who, by their internment, were denied their chance to attend college. Images of parents and grandparents with their children lined up to enter the food hall that are held next to Lange's images of families growing gardens can represent either the decent nutrition provided by the government or the oppression of restrictive diets and food supplies in the camps. Was the government's good care being described in showing food halls and vegetable gardens, or was the government's deprivation being illustrated through the interred families' initiative to provide for themselves within the confines of their imprisonment?

Images and artifacts from history include sometimes unknowable restrictions. The army burdened Lange in her job to photograph the Japanese internment camps by not allowing her to include the barbed wire fences and watchtowers in her photos, for example. Brady rearranged objects and people in the battlefields. The ceramic storage jugs made by a slave named Dave in North Carolina sit silently in museum showcases but only reveal the potter's thumbprints to suggest the person who made them but not the story of his enslavement. The postemancipation jailhouse on display at Whitney Plantation in Louisiana that is used to describe what the slave house might have looked like during slavery can only be a suggestion of the Real.

Historical statistics can also be biased, and oral historians can be misleading. Witnesses' testimonies can rely on blurry memories. More recently, images can be digitally manipulated. Restored historic houses lose some amount of their original patina, and unrestored historic houses, such as Drayton Hall in Charleston, South Carolina, ask visitors to imagine the furnished settings from era to era without the presence of the mansion's original furnishings. A U.S. Civil War bullet found on the hallow grounds of a battlefield tells some of the story of war but not the name of who shot the bullet or who was targeted. Pottery shards suggest the form of a vessel. The preserved wedding dress or the military uniform contain much information about its maker and how the garments were constructed but cannot alone tell the circumstances of the people who wore the garments. Furniture pieces contain much information about how the pieces were made. The wood and finishes can reveal much history about each piece. And yet researchers often need to speculate and use related references to infer deeper meanings about inanimate pieces. History workers often dig deep into the history of the Real and frequently explain that as more information comes to form new questions arise. The learner is always at some distance from completely understanding the contents of the Real materials used in historical representations.

Historical materialism naturally excludes some groups whose presence was deemed peripheral. In scripting the interpretation for the U.S. Holocaust Memorial Museum, for example, planners were compelled to decide whose memories and voices would be selected to commemorate the dead, the injured, and the humiliated. Linenthal recalls the exhibit planning process, acknowledging "any attempt to isolate victim groups' falsified history."[36] Museums and public history venues are charged with the daunting task of constructing historical interpretations with representations for histories that are essentially neverending and touch the global community. Linenthal asks, "Does a given form of universalism pay homage to human particularity?"[37] Can the voices of a few ethically represent the multitude of victims? Can history workers confidently use cameos, for example, to construct the Face of the Other who was oppressed by mass violence? The critical assessment of the partial nature of the Real is an important tool for history workers to develop ethical representations.

Brush History against the Grain

Brushing history against the grain (to borrow an iconic phrase from humanist Walter Benjamin[38]) is a critical method to select Real content for ethical representations and interpretations. Information about and from the victims, perpetrators, ancestors, descendants, and witnesses has the potential to reveal the belief systems and influences that shaped the historical events and helps relate aspects of the difficult history to present-day society. Brushing history against the grain is about approaching the information and current narrative in a critical way. To brush history against the grain, history workers can question old stories and can tell new stories, retell and reorient well-known stories, include perspectives from the margins, consider counterpoints, and provide visitors with time and resources for thoughtful review.

Brushing history against the grain is necessary because history is fluid and notions of authenticity and neutrality are organic. History workers and visitors commonly and inaccurately state that history is factual. Facts are subject to debate and interpretation. One can find counterpoints for every interpretation. For everything that is said and seen in historical representations, there is the unsaid and the not seen. History workers need to help visitors brush history against the grain and ask, "What do you think of the story?" in attempts to retrieve and give voice to the diversity of people from numerous levels of involvement in a history. Diversity is a fundamental condition of human dignity. And with each divergent perspective of the Real, new information, connections, and understandings about the meanings of a difficult history will surface for history workers and visitors.[39]

History workers can critically review their selections of Real content to represent a difficult history (i.e., brush history against the grain) by considering how the representation secures diversity and compassionate justice. History workers can listen to historical and present-day voices on the margins, or from across borders, in order to move beyond only acknowledging tolerance to move toward using the evident tensions that distinguish differences to inform and connect learners to a difficult history.

Brushing history against the grain for sociologist Antoinette T. Jackson was "a lightning bolt moment."[40] In a 2008 news story, Jackson saw how the genealogical connections of a public figure were instrumental in focusing public attention on the legacy of slavery. In this scenario, the Real content representing a difficult history about First Lady Michelle Obama's genealogical ties to South Carolina plantation slavery moved Jackson to ask, "What makes [First Lady] Michelle Obama's roots and this moment of public reckoning with slavery from the vantage point of a descendent [of slaves] different from all other moments and all other conversations?"[41] The news headlines raised productive tensions for Jackson, bringing the reality and relevancy of American slavery into our lives in 2008. Michelle Obama's connections to a former antebellum plantation disrupted the memory of slavery as past and brought that past into the present. As quoted in the *Daily Telegraph*, Michelle Obama said, "My past involves uncovering the shame while digging out the pride, so that other folks feel comfortable about embracing the beauty and tangled nature of the history of this country."[42]

Compassionate justice is from the side of empathy and not always found on the side of the law.[43] The Real can support representations with compassionate justice when history workers critically question not merely how the Real might be able to call out evil or admonish the oppressors or agents of suffering, but can include an analysis of the relationships between the oppressed and the imposing power. To critically view and imagine difficult histories as complex interdisciplinary events, history workers can bring into focus the networks and relations of power, oppression, resistance, and agency. Brushing history against the grain can mean looking for and questioning the ideological pathos and institutional social dynamics that supported and enabled the oppression, in addition to locating and representing the events of subjugation, exclusion, and persecution.

The Maryland Historical Society and the Contemporary Museum in Baltimore invited artist activist Fred Wilson to create a monumental exhibit using the historical society's collection to express his vision of how museum objects are used to write and rewrite Maryland's social history. Wilson's resulting exhibition, *Mining the Museum*, which ran from April 1992 through February 1993, addressed the challenge by exploring how one museum had ignored the histories of people of color.[44] The project invited innovation to "subvert the dominant paradigm," to use a phrase from anthropologist Miles Richardson.[45]

Wilson used the exhibit *Mining the Museum* to consider how deconstructing the museum apparatus can transform a museum into a space for ongoing cultural debate.[46] Participating museum educator Lisa G. Corrin explains that the experiment was part of a social history movement in American museums to publicly purge its past and embrace "owning up to the social inequities it reinforced through its unself-critical practices."[47]

Based on her museum's learning experience in developing and opening *Mining the Museum*, Corrin explains the tightly interwoven ties among collections, interpretations, and exhibitions:

> While updating labels and dioramas or historicizing the museum is no doubt valuable, are these changes enough? Museums must consider the infrastructure and value systems that generated prejudicial practices to begin with and use the self-study to change daily practices in programs, management, and governance. The "new museology" or critical museum history, argues that we cannot separate the exhibition from the museum or from the method from the meaning of the institution.[48]

The Maryland Historical Society's experimental exhibit used unique assemblies of the Real artifacts to brush history against the grain. The exhibit demanded that learners consider recognizable artifacts through a different lens. For example, Wilson placed wrought iron slave shackles in the same case as a silver tea set to associate the metalsmith crafts in a new light. Wilson placed a KKK hood inside a fancy wicker baby carriage to rupture legacies of family values.

CNN television news anchor Don Lemon took a heritage tour to Ghana with his mother, Katherine Clark, in 2014. The family had learned that they descended from eighteenth-century West African slaves through a DNA analysis and were in search of their genealogical history. The trip was focused on a guided tour of the Ghana slave castle, which CNN recorded and broadcasted that fall.[49] The Portuguese-built castle was once an export prison that held African slaves bound for the Americas.

Coming face-to-face with the history of their ancestors' captivity in the dark, damp cellars of the ancient castlelike prison where thousands of people were chained, starved, and mistreated was hard for the mother and son tourists. Lemon and Clark cried, hugged, and stood speechless in the Real spaces of the historic site *Ghana's Doors of No Return*. Observing the Real, Lemon touched a wall with chains that once restrained slaves from moving and commented on the visceral connection he felt through the artifacts. The scene was wrought with grief and emotion.

Brushing history against the grain goes even deeper into the complexity of the history, beyond the instance of Lemon's and Clark's emotional and intellectual realizations that brought the mother and son to that moment. Who could survive these circumstances, and who could impose such cruelty? History workers developing ethical representations of this part of history can go further and ask, "What were the dynamics of the relationships among the victims and oppressors that empowered the systems of oppression?" History workers are encouraged to analytically look at the laws, social obligations, and powers that limited the possibilities for justice and freedom over time. Peeling back the layers of memory can reveal important historical junctions that, if left forgotten, could otherwise impede just remembering. Brushing history against the grain can facilitate the reintegration of silenced or marginalized memory back into current collective consciousness.

History workers can study and select Real content that can reveal connections among the slaves who passed through the Ghana slave castle, the European monarchal political system, and the emerging sixteenth-century global economy. While the Ghana castle tour represents the horrible suffering of people enslaved, it also speaks about the royal crowns of Europe and the growing merchant class on three continents. An interpretation that goes with and against the grains of memory, from the slave castle that represents the plight of the enslaved in colonial West Africa to the palaces and castles of the monarchies in Lisbon, London, Paris, and Amsterdam and back to Ghana and the Americas, points to multiple connections for learners to explain how this difficult history was possible.

Exhibits and programs are mediated learning experiences, and the Real content of ethical representations depend, in part, upon the history workers' self-regulated moral controls. While history workers need to recognize their obligations to their organizations and visitors, and to the historical Others, they still need to be able to reconcile their personal views and preferences. To start recursive examinations of a selection of Real content, history workers and visitors can consider if the stories reproduce unjust social relations—for example, racism or sexism—and if the stories legitimatize the exclusion of groups or knowledge. History workers can question the forms of authority telling the stories, and can develop interpretations that encourage visitors to ask questions as well. Counter narratives can be found for nearly every interpretation. Ethical representations within this stance depend on such committed and organizational discipline. Thus, when selecting components of the Real, history workers can brush history against the grain in an effort to systematically reflect on their obligations and personal moral controls.

Benjamin's prophetic advice, to brush history against the grain, suggests that history workers further challenge the social order's cyclical nature and spin in a counter direction to begin to unwind society's powerful networks and institutions to reveal the history workers' own complacencies and positions of authority to themselves.

Assessing the Real

Gauging the effects of the Real in ethical representations requires vetted scholarship and evaluation. History workers can employ outside historians, other professionals, and descendants of the difficult history, for example, to review exhibit drafts and help provide diverse perspectives for the representations. Seeking peer reviews or publishing history research that will be used as the basis for exhibits, films, performances, and other public history formats is an excellent avenue to ensure the Real selected for particular representations speaks with authority. Historical representations invariably reflect their creators and the present moment. Objects alone are dumb, despite the historic authenticity of the object itself. Crew and Sims explain, "Authenticity is not about factuality or reality. It is about authority. Objects have no authority; people do. It is people on the exhibition team who must make a judgment about the past."[50]

History workers with professional training are familiar with using primary sources and the current accepted professional research techniques to confirm information and provide supporting references. For example, genealogists will look for at least two references to confirm lineage. While public history presentations are often set within the parameters of informal education and do not commonly share all the scholarly tools used with visitors, such as citations, best practices to develop historical representations and interpretations must be backed by scholarship and vetted sources. History workers' expertise is an important tool in the construction of the representations and interpretations for difficult histories. The history worker's knowledge, relationships, and position in his or her community and society guide him or her in identifying and selecting the Real. The corroborative powers of the Real materials that history workers use to represent and interpret a difficult history create an informative, vetted, and responsible context for the Real to enrich the history worker's argument.

Through visitor studies, history workers can unpack how an assembly of Real content representing a difficult history effectively speaks to learners as authentic, useful, and otherwise. Visitor studies analyst Conny Graft emphasizes that history workers can use visitor evaluation research in the process of developing responsible and meaningful representations for current and potential visitors by asking for feedback and collecting responses to historical interpretations from diverse audiences.[51]

Attachments to one's personal identity have a profound effect on visitors' and history workers' expectations and experiences interacting with the Real content used to represent a difficult history. Visitors' feedback can further inform history workers about the effects, perceptions, and impact of the historical representations. Visitor evaluations can help history workers design more effective interpretation strategies to hone the multiple dimensions of the representations of the Faces of the historical Others, clarify the significance of the Real content, and refine the tone of the Narratives.

Shocking Content

Difficult histories are shocking, and the power to shock learners can range from productive to unproductive and from supportive to harmful. The Real can contain representations of horrific events. Often, emotionally charged images have the potency to arouse astonishment, fear, and thoughtfulness. Shock can be a reaction to the immoral world and can provoke learners to ask questions and critique representations. Shock can pique and sustain learner engagement in order to learn about difficult histories.

The risks of using shocking materials include offending, frightening, or emotionally hurting learners. Learners can be dismayed or overwhelmed and foreclose on continuing their learning about a difficult history. The shocking content can be too much to bear or seem too disconnected from the learners' understandings. When visitors give up and express that "there is nothing we can do," apathy can set in. When history workers and visitors become habituated to images of oppression, the overabundance of images dulls their senses. Passive empathy or indifference will impede history workers' and visitors' abilities to care about the difficult histories. Shock can wear off, and learners can become complacent.

How much shocking or graphic content is too much to bear? Consider, for example, an exhibit of extreme barbarity in James Allen's *Without Sanctuary* that featured a gruesome early twentieth-century photography collection of lynchings in the American South. The exhibit of sepia-toned souvenir photographs tested many twenty-first-century viewers' tolerance for shocking images. Articles, books, blogs, and conversations were set in motion to grapple with the meanings of the violent history.[52] Audiences and critics both applauded Allen's exhibit and admonished Allen for bringing in the racist history from the margins, and for asking the public to remember and reconsider what the difficult history means today. The ongoing intensity of public responses, even years after the exhibit opened, illustrates the power of the voices that speak from the Real content from difficult histories. Allen's exhibit also illustrates the challenge, the kind of challenge that history workers have called "the tough stuff," in determining the fitting use of shocking material.

History workers should use a critical process for selecting shocking content by asking themselves,

- "Why does this story need to be told now?"
- "Who are you telling the story to?"
- "How does this story relate to the human condition today?"
- "What is the purpose and the expected outcome of telling the story?"

These questions must be weighed against the risks of learners showing signs of foreclosure or indifference.

History workers need to be prepared to address learners' responses to difficult histories and consider the risks. Training history workers to support learners who are upset or uneasy is in the best interest of the institution's personnel, the organization itself, and the visitors. For example, the Anoka County Historical Society in Minnesota held the exhibit *Vietnam: Veterans' Experience* from 2005 to 2010. The historical society worked closely with the Veteran's Administration to train the site's history workers to recognize signs of visitors' distress and how to address visitors' emotional reactions.

Also, sensitively preparing visitors to learn about difficult histories is an ethical practice for museums and public history venues. Exhibits and programs should include warnings and orientations that explain the extent of shocking materials used in the historical representations, especially if the content includes adult themes, indecent activity, hard language, intense or persistent violence, nudity, or other elements that illustrate immorality. History workers must be aware and vigilantly sensitive to learners' well-being. This is more than a courtesy—it is responsible practice.

Questions to Brush History against the Grain

1. How are experiences to be understood? (Is the point of view from the victors, the oppressed, or witnesses, or in the moment or looking back?)
2. What information will reorient learners' perspectives?
3. How does this information enable or constrain personal and social possibilities?
4. What is my view of the historical Others or the event? Can I find other views?
5. How did the oppressive forms of power in the history manifest themselves, and what traces of the historical oppression appear today?
6. To what responsibilities to the difficult history am I, a history worker, held answerable, and to what responsibilities are visitors held accountable?

Narratives Tie the Face and the Real Together

[I]n dialogue, the intention is not to advocate but to inquire; not to argue but to explore; not to convince but to discover.

—LOUISE DIAMOND[53]

Visitors ask, "What happened to people?" Composing Narratives is the third building block for developing ethical representations to answer that basic question. Curators, educators, exhibit designers, and docents all contribute to the development of Narratives. Curators write label content, educators write tour narratives, exhibit designers place the artifacts, and docents tell the stories. An array of narratives converges from these contributors (who collectively are responsible for articulating the multiple voices from the past) and from the voices of the visitors, the community, and the museum or historic site. The institution ultimately is responsible for equitably telling the stories that recall difficult histories.

Narratives help to develop the Face by describing personhood and act to tie together the components of the Real. Narratives explain how the experiences of the historical Others were the results of ideologies and organized actions in a historical context. Narratives in exhibits and programs ask visitors to consider the circumstances and limitations of the lives of the historical Others, the injustices of such limitations, and how learners can empathetically respond.

Narratives for ethical representations contain four key components:

1. stories about subjects and Others
2. recognition of the partiality and biases of the representations
3. purposeful interpretation that demonstrates the relevance and significance of how the history matters
4. opportunities for learners to converse, contemplate, and express ideas

Storytelling

Components of storytelling are inherent in the dissemination of historical Narratives. Narratives are stories and descriptions of events that are read, seen, and heard through a variety of presentation formats. Narrators deal with continuity over time to tell stories. Unlike informational archives that deal with units of time like a record, historical Narratives describe the lives of persons and the changes in places, organizations, and nations that impact people.

Ethical representations and interpretations use Narratives about the past that can reveal, with varying degrees of clarity and certitude, the history workers' position and the learners' perspectives that are tied to the present. The Narrative includes stories that are structured in the active tense and are filled with historical references, remembrance language, tensions, hopeful purposes, educational intentions, sensitivity, unanswered questions, and likely include colloquialisms and temporal memes. Like a story, the historical Narrative is composed of a beginning, middle, and end, offering insights and viewpoints but not always conclusions.

Narratives are carefully composed responses to learners' demands for information. History workers in a variety of professional roles ultimately are charged with the educational mission to address learners' interests and questions. When visitors enter a preserved slave cabin from Allendale Plantation at the West Baton Rouge Museum in Louisiana, they commonly ask, "Who lived here?" Indeed, it is reasonable for visitors to want to know about the people that made the sparsely furnished cabin a home. At this receptive juncture, the history workers are obliged to respond to visitors' questions and to tell the history of slavery at Allendale through ethical representations.

The cypress two-room cabin from the sugar plantation called Allendale Plantation is imbued with richer meanings when the Narrative given by the tour guide describes the personhood of the slaves that made this place a home. The historical Others are, perhaps at first, defined by their enslavement when visitors learn that the dwelling was a "slave cabin." The inhabitants were slaves, and also they were a family that included a mother, father, likely another adult, and at least two children. With added layers of information, the space now describes more than plantation quarter architecture; it is also about the site of a family's enslavement. The Faces of the historical residents emerge in the Narrative as real people, not as characters from fiction or vague memory, when the visitors learn about the cabin's residents, Valery and Lavinia and their sons. Valery Trahan and Lavinia Ballard were married but separated when Valery went to war as the enslaved valet to his Confederate master, Henry Watkins Allen, in 1861. Lavinia was a fieldworker who stayed on the plantation despite the Union troops' encampment there. Valery returned to the destroyed Allendale Plantation after the war as a free man and married Lavinia again, but this time in the eyes of the law at the parish courthouse in 1891. Lavinia could receive Valery's veteran pension.

There are great possibilities for using storytelling for ethical representations. However, the insights, viewpoints, and conclusions that are communicated through storytelling can be told from narrow and biased perspectives. The biases in the stories' telling, however subtle or unintentional, raise the risk of raising learners' anxieties and disregarding historical Others, for example, by intentionally, naively, or obliviously excluding voices from the past.

Well-planned Narratives are carefully selected stories that do more than inform learners. Narratives clarify meanings and provoke and reveal connections among historical events and people to explain how and why the history matters.[54] An approach for using storytelling in Narratives that brush history against the grain is to tell new stories or to retell well-known stories that include voices and perspectives from the margins and provide learners with time and resources for thoughtful review.

Empathetic Unsettlement:[55] Tensions

The emerging Faces of historical Others and the brushed history of the Real content tied together through Narratives will likely expose new ideas and perspectives about historical claims to truth. Tensions will surface as each visitor and history worker grapples with the new, difficult knowledge that disrupts one's understandings of morality or with new knowledge that runs counter to the dominant Narratives they learned in school or from familiar and well-regarded sources. The kind of tension elicited by a representation or an interpretation of a difficult history is also a tool for raising the learner's attentiveness to the oppression and empathy for the victims.

Spoken and written Narratives can provide powerful lines of inquiry and suggest alternative perspectives to help learners find meanings and to support learners' work through painful knowledge. History workers can use Narratives to anticipate and respond to learners' rising tensions and to address learners' discomfort and confusion. When learners exclaim, "That is awful!" or "I cannot believe that!" Narratives, as part of CMP, need to offer learners interactions and information to enable them to reflect on their resistances and tensions.

Effective ethical representations, however, do not ease all of the learners' tensions and do not resolve all of the learners' conflicts in learning about difficult histories. Rather, Narratives can raise tensions and identify conflicts. Narratives can make the moral tensions visible and problematic. For example, sociologist Dean MacCannell considers the tensions raised by the paradox of the good that visitors gain by visiting Auschwitz in the way the historic site symbolizes the dignity of its victims in the face of unspeakable cruelty, while simultaneously considering the way the site symbolizes the evil of their Nazi oppressors.[56]

History workers should acknowledge the tensions raised by Narratives and not attempt to fully resolve them. Narratives should express differences, varying viewpoints, and disagreements without overstating or overromanticizing the Real. In shaping Narratives and in listening to Narratives, learners might feel increasingly uncomfortable as they make connections and feel implicated or dismayed. Through Narratives, history workers can acknowledge the tensions, disagreements, and controversial points of view, but should not expect learners to find resolution or comfort by believing, "Oh, that issue is in the past and does not affect me now."

Asking learners to accept their unsettlement that arises from the tension is an important aspect of "just remembrance." The unsettlement felt by learners also provides learners with the energy to think more critically about the difficult history. Narratives in ethical representations can help to explain how the difficult history included injustice, and that particular social issues are still unresolved and relevant. Unsettlement gives learners reasons to continue to reflect on the difficult history beyond their museum visit and perhaps to use their experience to influence change.[57]

Narratives are not intended to moralize, accuse, or scold people from the past or in the present. Indignation would put history workers and visitors in defensive positions, making the Narrative less about empathy and more about power. Nor should Narratives simplify the outcomes of difficult histories suggesting harmonious ends. Narratives that attempt to resolve tensions can instill complacency in learners toward the difficult history, thereby allowing learners to hold on to notions of happy endings. Narratives that attempt to pacify tensions for learners can misguide learners into believing the issues of oppression and violence no longer need to be considered or addressed.

Narratives about difficult histories often include recollections of controversy, which can lead to raised tensions within and among history workers and visitors. The Narratives can be powerful statements to demonstrate that difficult histories matter now. Ethical representations of difficult histories have the power to awaken a passion in learners by asking them to look at history from multiple viewpoints, viewpoints that can reveal the struggles for a more just and compassionate moral order. Brushing history against the grain through ethical representations can raise learners' tensions by offering fresh or conflicting viewpoints. Roger I. Simon argues,

> Such images assert a truth that threatens to dissolve barriers erected to keep identities safely within the bounds of the existing social order. After the historical fragments were blown free of codifying structures that entrapped them, it was necessary to catch them up again in new sets of discursive relations. The elements of the past were to be rescued and redeemed, drawn together in new constellations that connected with the present. The intent is not to collapse past and present but hold them together in a mutually referential tension.[58]

Tensions are part of what make some histories difficult. Avoiding and nullifying controversy is not an optimal practice. Controversial topics in museums and at historical sites can be valuable tools to generate public engagement and to initiate discussions about critical issues. Tensions that are raised through difficult history representations and interpretations promote problem solving and critical thinking. Indeed, the call from within the museum profession since the last quarter of the twentieth century to expand museum practice to include dialogs with visitors resonates with the increasing number of exhibits and programs about difficult histories in museums and historic sites worldwide.

An example of a controversial exhibition that generated tensions and encouraged conversations opened in late October 2010 and was titled *Hide/Seek: Difference and Desire in American Portraiture*. The exhibition, which straddled the fields of art and history, was assembled by the Smithsonian Institution National Portrait Gallery as the first major survey to examine the influence of sexual difference upon modern American portraiture. The exhibit traced how art reflects society's evolving attitudes toward sexuality, desire, and romantic attachment. Through both the history of the portrayal of gays and lesbians in American art and the artistic expressions of gay and lesbian artists through portraits, the exhibit, as its title suggests, "explored the power of the portrait to reveal and conceal."[59]

Hide/Seek included 105 works of art (101 images and four videos). The exhibit became the subject of controversy when one of the videos, "A Fire in My Belly" by David Wojnarowicz, was called out as "anti-Christian." American political leaders threatened the Smithsonian Institution's funding. The head of the Smithsonian ordered the director of the National Portrait Gallery to remove the video from the exhibit. According to museum ethicist Sally Yerkovich, while the director's action sparked international attention, it also prompted screenings of the censored film across the United States and in the United Kingdom and other parts of Europe.[60]

Museums put themselves at risk of raising tensions and public disapproval when they take on the challenge of interpreting controversial subjects. Controversial representations raise the stakes for institutional accountability and responsibility. As in the case of the *Hide/Seek* exhibition, the history workers' and their institution's authority and accountability were put into question. The risk of criticism from visitors, communities, the media, scholars, or advocacy groups can put history workers in a defensive position. The criticism can jeopardize the history workers' and the institutions' reputations or funding base and, perhaps even more threatening, controversy puts the museums' authoritative position at risk. Sally

Yerkovich explains that controversial exhibitions while raising tensions can also raise important issues. The exhibit *Hide/Seek* prompted an international conversation and stirred consciousness-raising dialogs.

Narratives describing difficult histories can elicit unintended controversies, raising tensions that can work against the history workers' plans to commemorate the past. Consider how the original *Enola Gay* exhibit from 1995 offers today's history workers a well-examined, controversial exhibition as an illustration of how an exhibit initially missed the voices of the exhibit's stakeholders and neglected balancing multiple viewpoints. The tone of the original script was dogmatic rather than conditional.[61]

Now consider the exhibit at the Oklahoma City Memorial and Museum described by Edward Linenthal.[62] In the first few weeks after the bombing, suggestions on how to memorialize the human losses and suffering came pouring into the mayor's and the governor's offices. There was widespread concern, however, that the memorial would be tied to one influential stakeholder's view that would trump the larger community's convictions. Controversy began to boil when rumors spread that the city had already decided on a memorial design. Linenthal reports, however, that the exhibit and memorial planners in Oklahoma City demonstrated a studied and inclusive process that included multiple voices and maintained public engagement and an ongoing dialog with stakeholders not just to avoid controversies, but more to build a memorial and a historical interpretation that would be long lasting and relevant to diverse audiences.

The pressing questions on how to interpret the tragedy came from those who suffered personal losses, and from survivors, civic groups, religious groups, and citizens from within the city and beyond. Oklahoma City mayor Norick believed that "we couldn't have all these different memorial agendas; the city needed to take control of this."[63] The mayor appointed attorney Robert Johnson to serve as chairman of the Oklahoma City Murrah Federal Building Memorial Task Force. "Johnson realized that the credibility of the project rested on the privileged place of voices of family members and survivors, and this commitment became the bedrock on which the entire process rested."[64] The task force believed that the common thread for a successful memorial project was to collect community input and participation to avoid resentments from or exclusions of stakeholders.

The comparison of the *Enola Gay* exhibit and the Oklahoma City Memorial and Museum planning demonstrates the importance of multivocality in historical representations and underscores the need for front-end evaluations to anticipate public reception and the potential impact of the interpretation. History workers need to research much more than historiography in their work to develop historical representations for difficult histories. The role and possible reactions of stakeholders (including visitors, patrons, supporters, victims, witnesses, and the affiliated communities) in the life of historical representations must be accounted for in commemorative interpretation planning. History workers are compelled to critically deliberate on how suitable their responses are to the controversies that will likely arise. Formative evaluations and focus group testing is especially useful in the planning stages for exhibitions and programs to enable history workers to better identify and address controversial topics and the possibility of unanticipated community and visitor responses.

Interpretations that make use of ethical representations use Narratives to make new comparisons, draw parallels, describe relationships, and raise questions. The new tensions and new conclusions and determinations include empathy, hope, and imaginative envisioning. In the healthy process of working through a difficult history, Narratives offer learners new phrasing, new points of view and questions, arguments, excitement, disappointments, and expanded understandings that can lead to tensions that inspire dialogs and conversations during and after the historic site or museum visit.

Comfortable Entrances

Ethical representations and interpretations are fluid and can be developed and presented in sensitive and gradual ways. The tension, shock, and intensity of the Real and the emotional conditions described by the Face can make difficult histories even more difficult to represent, interpret, present, and receive. The use of comfortable entrances includes Narratives that steadily move from single-dimensional representations toward multidimensional representations of historical persons or groups that more fully commemorate oppressed populations and recall the oppressors in order to gradually and sensitively develop their Faces. The risk of resistance to the difficult history can increase as the description of the Other's personhood becomes more developed and learners begin making more personal connections and meanings about the life of the Other.

Comfortable entrances can be well-known phrases, objects, or spaces in a historic site or museum that are less intimidating and more familiar than new phrases or new images that are at a higher risk of upsetting the learner's status quo. Comfortable entrances often include the familiar descriptions of particular histories that the learners are more likely to receive before they encounter more complex and potentially upsetting content of ethical representations. Some comfortable entrances used by history workers at well-established institutions are the habitually used descriptions, and the well-known artifacts and spaces traditionally associated with the historical themes at that site. Comfortable entrances include the familiar memes that are readily shared and received. Such traditions and habits, however, are at risk of complacent acceptance by history workers and visitors as such Narratives are often attached to the iconic meanings of a historic site or artifact. CMP requires history workers to regularly and rigorously examine traditional narratives, symbols, and phrases. While history workers can use the well-known memes as comfortable entrances that might more immediately meet learners' expectations, the history workers must also recognize that the comfortable entrances are not the ending but the beginning of a longer journey that serves the aims of social justice education and can inspire empathy for just remembering. Comfortable entrances serve as introductions or vehicles to segue into tougher components of a difficult history.

In the case of an antebellum plantation house tour in 2005 at Magnolia Mound Plantation, where slave life history was first being elevated and expanded, the history workers (volunteer and paid docents) were more likely to incorporate the new slave life stories into their house tour narratives if they could individually identify an artifact, phrase, or a physical space where they were comfortable in order to then introduce the new slave life stories.[65] In this way, the history workers verbally moved from single dimensions toward the more anxiety-filled multidimensional Faces of the enslaved population. When the history workers found that they could guide their visitors through the big house and choose familiar rooms and artifacts to prompt the new slave life stories, the history workers were more comfortable expanding their Narratives to further include slave life stories. The history workers started with the traditions afforded by the comfortable entrances within the well-rehearsed tour route and then expanded their Narratives to include the relationships among the planter family, the slaves, and the big house spaces. In this way and over time, the history workers expanded their Narratives to include multidimensional slave life histories and new historical viewpoints.

For example, a history worker at Magnolia Mound Plantation brought visitors into the parlor in the big house and used a comfortable entrance describing how the planter family used the room and highlighted some of the decorations. Then the history worker (who was once reluctant to change her tour) introduced Charlotte into the tour Narrative, an enslaved house servant who lived and labored on the plantation, and explained the duties Charlotte had in keeping the parlor. Moving toward describing Charlotte's personhood, the history worker briefly described how Charlotte came to the plantation as a wedding present to the newly married slaveholders. The comfortable entrance into interpreting slavery history for this history worker was the work-life connection Charlotte had to the parlor setting. Charlotte's work-life story enabled the history worker to talk about slavery and to further develop a Face for Charlotte by including a tragedy Charlotte suffered as a mother in 1803. The history worker continued her tour Narrative, explaining that Charlotte was sold with only one of her two daughters, Rosette, at eight years old, to New Orleans. Two months later, the Magnolia Mound Plantation planter sold Charlotte's other daughter, Frosina, thirteen years old, to another Baton Rouge plantation.[66]

The expanded Narrative raises more questions about slavery, motherhood, and plantation life than the traditional tour that only spoke about the decorative arts in the parlor and how the planter family used the social household space. The objectification of Charlotte as a wedding present sheds light on the oppressive reality that slaves were deemed as property. The sad fate of Charlotte's family raises learners' tensions about parenthood and leaves many questions about Charlotte's family's fate unanswered. Learners must be able to move beyond the comfortable entrances in Narratives in order to allow for the tensions that are necessary for ethical representations.

Hope

Ethical representations of past horrors—for example, slavery and genocide—are possible because of the promise of a better future. Every visit to an exhibit or program about a difficult history is an occasion for social affirmation, renewal, and questions that lead to changes in individual and communal values. History workers accept the responsibility to commemorate difficult histories because they believe their work will make a positive difference. The history worker and visitor take a hopeful stance when he or she can respond to the exhibit or program by saying, "I care."[67]

Commemoration is the act of collective instruction.[68] Instruction is a hopeful endeavor with aims at effecting change in the future. The benefits for exhibits and programs about difficult histories for the viewing public are improving human character and social relations. To that end, ethical representations in exhibits and programs, at their best, are informative, enlightening, and stereotype dispelling. The representations should be compelling influences that lead to action and understanding. The hopeful intent for developing ethical representations is aimed at securing fundamental human dignity and engaging learners in good will and envisioning a better future. Part of building ethical representations is a process of history workers being pragmatically self-aware. Such attempts are largely projects of hope in constructing pathways to envision how the past is tied to our present and future.

Including expressions of hope in Narratives is not an ubiquitous call to free society from all discrimination and oppression. Nor do hopeful messages or conclusions in Narratives need to articulate expectations for swift transformations or universal peace. Rather, the pedagogical work of developing ethical representations fundamentally demonstrates to learners why they should care about society, which is a crucial first step for empathy and social justice education.

Language about hopefulness could sound like advice, warnings, counseling, or optimism for the future. Couched in social justice education, however, Narratives that work toward representing difficult histories are hopeful commitments to learners promising learners that the history matters. Narratives cannot guarantee solace or reconciliation. Instead, Narratives for ethical representations of difficult histories offer productive tensions, descriptions, questions, and prompts to learners to reconsider how the history can inform the present. The Narratives should avoid trite examples or a romanticized aesthetic. The Narratives cannot end with storybook conclusions, "The End." Unlike a cinematic movie or a storybook, narratives representing difficult histories cannot conclude with wishful thinking that whatever follows the difficult history will be "fine." Instead, hopefulness entwined in interpreting difficult histories is shared in the guise of social action, reflective contemplation, and concern for others.

The Anne Frank House includes themes of hopefulness in productive and historical representations. Anne Frank's father, Otto Frank, survived World War II, and after the war his personal resolve was to fulfill his daughter's wish to publish her diary. Anne Frank's diary was first published in 1947, and thereafter it was published in sixty-seven languages. The published diary has been read by millions of people around the world. Otto Frank's vision, inspired by his daughter, was to teach the difficult history of his family's persecution in order to educate the global community about the horrors of hate and genocide. Hopefulness in representing difficult histories is directed at the future. Hope in this context is the aspirational vision learners take on in reflecting on difficult history, a feeling that can range from optimism and expectations to resolutions and the ability to envision changes in the present and for the future.

Just Imagine

Through written labels, audio programs, and presentations, history workers can encourage learners to "just imagine" the historical settings of oppression or the decisions historical Others faced. Historical representations and interpretations ask learners to imagine how the Face, the Real content, and the Narrative work together to describe that which is nearly indescribable. Memory is only partial, and yet the historical representations are attempting to recall what happened. Some learners prefer to consider the difficult knowledge internally, and other learners appreciate the opportunity to talk with other people. An active imagination enables visitors to piece together ideas from the Narrative and the Real content to come to personal understandings and raise new questions. Narratives that include questions are also asking learners to use their imaginations as well as to retrieve memories and prior knowledge. Eventually, the content moves learners from imagining "what it was like" and "how this makes me feel" to imagining how the historical injustices can inform their possible actions and decisions in the present and the future.

History workers can use Narratives to encourage learners to brush history against the grain, especially with Narratives that use a biopic lens in the telling. Narratives can provide accounts that can help learners imagine the setting of the historical event from the victim's point of view, and from the points of view from witnesses, bystanders, perpetrators, accomplices, or even descendants. Such telling that brings several viewpoints to the learning encounter can move learners to imagine the circumstances and agents' responses, thereby stirring learners' empathy to imagine the possible ties the history might have to the present.

Narratives should keep the familiar strange in order to maintain tensions in learning difficult histories and to encourage learners' imaginations. New, fresh, or revealing Narratives can encourage learners to continue to wonder and contemplate the history. Narratives should include unresolved questions to allow learners to consider how the questions could be answered. This requires sometimes using contradictory descriptions that are necessary for discursive constructions of subjectivity; for example, father/slaveholder, settler/traitor, or queen/tyrant. These tensions are only made available through critical research, questioning multiple relationships, and listening to a variety of voices.[69] Encouraging learners to imagine another way of understanding a difficult history or by listening to the history from different voices, or from different political, economic, or geographic angles, can increase the possibilities for meanings.

Courage

History workers who interpret difficult histories accept the responsibility to develop ethical representations with enough confidence and courage to believe that their work to commemorate the difficult histories will make a positive difference. Courage as a tool encourages history workers to take the risks of facing the difficult histories, of facing the resistances from learners. Courage is also needed by visitors who need to remain committed to learning about the difficult history despite the pain or anxiety the histories cause the visitors. Both kinds of learners, visitors and history workers, use courage to support their commitments to invest resources, energy, time, and thought into finding meanings in the difficult histories. Learners' willingness to develop ethical representations and to learn about the difficult histories requires courage in the face of the many risks that can arise, as discussed in chapter 2.

Considering the benefits of representing difficult histories, also discussed in chapter 2, history workers should not be discouraged when co-workers and visitors resist learning about a difficult history. Prepared and confident history workers can look to developing history learning experiences and recognize that those learning moments have the potential to halt or to develop further when learners reflect on their biases and connections to the history and examine the social issues that surface. Historical representations with multiple dimensions can make learners, at times, feel implicated, and at other times feel more self-aware when they discover their connections to the historical Others. Such realizations can leave learners vulnerable to feeling self-conscious and exposed. Factors of race, gender, class, sexual preference, ethno-cultural group membership, and regional identifications combine in complementary and contradictory ways to affect levels of engagement, fostering feelings of exclusion, agreement, or empathy.[70] Narratives that offer relevant definitions of a moral culture provide learners with encouragement that their feelings about society's moral social fabric have not been dissolved. Apprehensive learners use courage to press forward in reconsidering how their new knowledge might serve society.

Allowing learners to discuss and consider the human stories of loss and achievement demands that the history workers realize the risks of raising learners' solemn or angry exchanges and other forms of learners' resistance. History workers' determination to help learners work through their losses in learning demands that the history workers encourage learners to imagine alternatives to the oppression in order to build and renew communal relationships, discourage violence in the future, influence present-day politics, and to teach about love and hate.

Learners who engage in dialogs about difficult histories open many possible experiential outcomes. Outcomes can range from learners' intimate realizations and reconsiderations to indignant resistance or foreclosure on further engagement in learning about a difficult history. History workers' belief in the significance of the difficult history and their commitment and courage are essential to their work in developing Narratives for representations of difficult history.

Dialog

Dialog is an open process of communication based on mutual respect in which visitors and history workers focus on listening to, talking about, and working through painful and sometimes unbelievable stories and images. Ethical representations and interpretations can use Narratives that include planned dialogs and facilitated conversations in order to engage learners in thoughtful interactions with difficult histories. Briefly, dialogs are between two parties typically focused on a single idea or thread, and conversations are among several parties about several ideas and can go in multiple directions. Dialogs and conversations can include a series of encounters for learners with multiple opportunities to read, view, listen, and converse about the difficult history. These are also important learning opportunities for learners to work through their resistances to the difficult knowledge, the moments where history workers should be watching for the 5Rs to unfold. History workers trained to engage learners in sensitive dialogs about difficult histories provide learners with opportunities to repeat, reflect, and reconsider the difficult knowledge that can be hard to accept or understand.[71]

Cliveden, a historic plantation house museum in Philadelphia, interprets the history of the Chew family, the enslaved Cliveden community, and the site's role in the American Revolution. The site's history workers engage their visitors in facilitated conversations that embrace the tensions and contradictions woven into the difficult history of eighteenth-century colonial slavery. The environment the history workers designed for the site's interpretation provides an atmosphere where visitors are made to feel respected and safe and thereby encourages them to express themselves during their visit.[72] The facilitated conversation is part of a visitors' program called "Cliveden Conversations," which is a socially interactive conversational exchange among a trained history worker and a group of visitors "that allows strangers to discuss history in ways that can feel empowering."[73] The strategy for the planned conversations is to enhance visitors' comfort when they are talking with strangers (fellow visitors and history workers) about slavery and plantation life. The facilitated conversation is designed to move visitors toward working through some of their personal resistances to the difficult history.

Strategies to create safe and respectful spaces for dialog in public history venues such as guided tours include personal introductions among the tour group members. The history worker, the docent or tour guide, for example, introduces himself or herself and asks the visitors in the group to also introduce themselves. Some history workers simplify the introductory portion of this approach by asking group members, "Where are you from?" The personal introduction allows everyone in the group to feel included and to feel connected to the group, which can often be an assembly of strangers. Introductions can help visitors to relax and be more willing later in the tour to ask questions and engage in conversations.

Jewish persecution is interpreted at the Corrie ten Boom House in Haarlem, The Netherlands.[74] Corrie ten Boom and her family hid Jews in their small three-story house above a watch store to help many Jews escape from Nazi persecution. Before the tour begins at the Corrie ten Boom House, visitors sit in the original period living room in a circle. The docent begins her presentation with a short welcome and asks the visitors to introduce themselves by name and the city where they live. Arranging the group of learners in a circle, or another formation where learners can see one another, helps to facilitate conversational exchanges.

> At Cliveden, trained facilitators, some who are professional psychologists, get people out of their own viewpoints to consider those of others. It sounds simple, but the basic act of having a person introduce himself or herself to a stranger began the dialogue and made it easier to engage in discussions of history. And surveys from participants say that the hardest part of the process was getting over the anxiety of social introduction to a stranger of another race or background.[75]

Another strategy to generate facilitated conversations among learners is activity-based programs. For example, at Cliveden, visitors are asked to work in pairs or in small groups to develop a historical timeline in order to encourage conversations and opportunities for learners to hear alternative viewpoints and to incorporate a collection of historical perspectives.[76] At the East Tennessee Historical Society in Knoxville, docents engage students in a hands-on activity called "Objects over Time," in which students arrange a collection of historical artifacts in chronological order and, as a group, are encouraged to discuss the connections among various sequences of historical events. At the West Baton Rouge Museum in Port Allen, Louisiana, tour guides engage students and adult visitors in taking the voter registration literacy test that was administered to black Louisiana citizens in the first half of the twentieth century. Upon completing the test, the tour guide reviews the answers with visitors, who then discuss how they did on the test and what their thoughts are about the once lawful obstacle to enfranchisement.

Visitors on an intimate tour of the historic space in a private home where Jews hid during the Nazi occupation. Corrie ten Boom House Museum, Haarlem, The Netherlands. Photograph by author.

The history workers at these sites found that learners are more likely to participate in discussions about difficult histories and find a common vocabulary to expand upon the new ideas through facilitated conversations. In regard to historical interpretations about the difficult history of slavery, David Young, executive director at Cliveden, found that facilitated conversations with visitors and history workers increased visitors' respect for new ideas and different points of view. He found that the facilitated conversations that include a welcoming tone tend to encourage more inclusive narratives that then lead to more powerful ethical representations.[77] It is a tough challenge for history workers to allow their learners to feel measured degrees of pain and discomfort. Planned dialogs and facilitated conversations can carefully make use of the raised tensions and provide opportunities for conversations that encourage visitors to discuss the difficult history and express empathy.

Not all conversations or exchanges are planned, however. History workers should be prepared for visitors to spontaneously comment or ask questions. And sometimes learners say very little or nothing at all. At the National September 11 Memorial and Museum, on the day I visited in November 2014 with hundreds of other visitors, the galleries were remarkably quiet and devoid of conversations. It is reasonable for history workers to say to visitors, "There is nothing wrong with standing back and thinking." While there are no guarantees for reflection or reconsideration, many historic sites and museums with prepared history workers are well suited to provide meditative opportunities and spaces for learners to look longer or to take refuge from looking.

Tours and programs should include opportunities for discussions and questions. History workers need to be able to engage learners in talking about the difficult history and how to respond to learners' comments and questions, especially how to maintain a safe and respectful atmosphere for everyone on the tour or in the history learning experience. Spontaneous dialogs can be sensitively and politely managed by history workers who themselves are prepared to guide discussions with visitors on relevant historical and current subjects, to allow learners to work through the 5Rs, and to keep the tour or program on schedule and on topic. A good foundation for productive discussions is a relaxed atmosphere and an understanding among learners that their ideas and questions are important and will be considered.

Learners need to feel comfortable in order for discussions to happen and for learners to be able to ask their questions. History workers need to establish a relaxed atmosphere at the start of the tour or program. History workers need to warm up their audiences in order to relax learners and to establish a rapport of trust. History workers can begin building a relationship with learners in their welcome. The history worker can open by introducing himself or herself and other relevant personnel, and if the format allows, can ask the learners to introduce themselves. The history worker can ask questions about the learners' comfort or needs regarding the forthcoming presentation or discussion. History workers might offer a big-picture description of the historical interpretation and clarify key concepts in a friendly and knowledgeable tone at the onset. History workers should have prepared discussion questions and planned comfortable entrances for the tour or program. Friendly gestures and making eye contact with learners are important mechanisms for building trust. History workers can validate learners' questions by thanking them for their questions or by expanding on the questions asked. By responding to learners' positive and negative comments and questions, history workers can indicate that they heard the remarks and can also use the remarks as part of the dialog to sensitively guide the interpretation toward the history workers' interpretational aims.

Moderated group discussions and facilitated conversations, or even a one-on-one discussion with a learner about a difficult history, can be an important part of the learning process. To prepare and encourage learners to participate in conversations and dialogs, history workers can explain the structure of the forthcoming tour or program, the planned time frame, the level of trauma or the degree of shocking content that will be presented, and that learners' questions are welcome. History workers can acknowledge to learners that the presentation or discussion about a difficult history might offer them new ways to think about the difficult history. Learners need to feel that they will be listened to and that what they have to say will be sincerely responded to. History workers need to demonstrate from the onset of the presentation that they can be sensitive and responsive to learners in order to establish trust. A technique toward this end is to acknowledge and thank learners for their verbal contributions throughout the visit or program.

Timing is another important aspect for productive dialogs and conversations. Give learners time to respond to questions and the history presented. A few seconds can feel like many minutes when history workers are waiting for a response from learners. Learners also need time to formulate questions and answers, and to make sense of new information. Sometimes history workers can plan pauses for the tour route or in the program. History workers should also welcome spontaneous dialogs. History workers can also use prepared questions to prompt discussions among the group members. History workers can invite learners to look for something specific in the exhibit or read something in particular to prompt questions and discussions. Remind learners that a variety of interpretations and personal experiences might come to mind and ask, "What do you think about this?" To maintain a respectful learning environment, history workers can encourage learners' responses by offering, "Let's consider several ways we might determine . . ." or "There are several ways this story can be told."

Learners' anxieties about offering wrong answers can be reduced when history workers ask open-ended questions and explain to learners that the questions can have many valid answers. The safe learning environment is enhanced when history workers are open to learners' expressions of personal feelings, perceptions, and sharing of life experiences. History workers can reward visitors for their contributions to the dialog by looking attentive, asking follow-up questions, offering sources for additional information, or by highlighting that what was said was of value to the group discussion.

History workers need to be prepared to lead and to moderate conversations that have the potential to turn tense, controversial, hostile, or defensive. These can happen when the learners are likely feeling resistant to the difficult history. History workers need to be patient and refrain from insisting that resistant learners "just get over it" or quickly accept the difficult knowledge. History workers should limit their use of cutoff phrases such as "Thank you for your comment but we need to move on." When questions and comments go off topic or turn controversial or adversarial, history workers need the discretion to politely acknowledge those remarks and offer, "Thank you for sharing your thoughts; here is another way to consider this point." This moment could be an opening to offer repetitive opportunities for the learners to work through difficult knowledge.

Some learners are very vocal and have many spontaneous comments and questions. These burning questions are often the common, well-known hot issues related to specific difficult histories and often generate strong yet predictable reactions and controversy. These questions could also signal that the learner is searching for opportunities to repeat and reflect on information. The new information could be running counter to how the learners understood the history and are experiencing a loss in learning. History workers can be prepared with well-researched and expanded responses, given the predictability of some of the burning questions from learners. Other techniques to channel the abundant energy and tension of the more zealous or resistant learners is to ask them to write down or remember their additional questions and comments and explain when a good time will be to talk in depth about the topics raised. The history workers should sincerely thank the zealous learner for his or her interest without patronizing him or her. Be prepared to offer further reading references and websites and offer directions within the museum or historic site where the learner can find more information on the topic he or she is focused on working through.

Learners' voices can be part of the Narrative by acknowledging or incorporating their questions, shared stories, and comments. Spaces designed for learners to share their responses about the exhibit or program encourage learners to share, reflect, and reconsider the meanings of the difficult history. Ideas for learner participation are well considered by Nina Simon in her book, *The Participatory Museum.*[78] Writing surfaces on walls and tabletops and videorecorded and digitized media assemblies are inviting exhibit components for learners to share their observations and feelings about a difficult history and the interpretation approach at the site. Empathetic remarks often appear in these public journal settings. The captured and then shared visitor responses can enrich and validate learners' understandings of a difficult history.

Nine Storytelling Components in the Narratives for Ethical Representations

1. Narratives use words to describe Faces, the Real, context, and conflicts.
2. Narratives are interactive with a variety of ways to engage visitors—listening, reading, viewing, entering spaces, handling objects, engaging in dialogs, and responding.
3. Narratives set a purposeful tone and embrace tensions to explain why the history matters.
4. Narratives are gestures of hope, courage, and commemoration.
5. Narratives are organized stories that can use comfortable entrances and make complex connections.
6. Narratives encourage the active imagination of learners.
7. Narratives encourage learners to respond to the difficult history with active empathy.
8. Narratives are paced and allow for ensuing discussions focused on the topic.
9. Narratives are respectful and sensitive to learners' experiences and provide appreciative and safe environments in which learners can respond.

Conclusion: Response and Responsibility

History workers have the responsibility to commemorate difficult histories through ethical representations built with the Faces of historical Others, Real content from history, and sensitive Narratives. Using this framework to recall difficult histories respects all people, past and present, as persons. Visitors have the responsibility to learn and to empathetically respond to the difficult history, and ultimately to find connections between the histories and the conditions that exist now and possibly into the future.

A kind of courage emerges from history workers and visitors who are compelled to develop and respond to the ethical representations. All responses, regardless of their magnitude, are valid, even when learners recognize that their immediate responses and actions, however subtle, have not yet changed the world. Valiant responses from history workers and visitors begin when they acknowledge their fear or pain and become accountable for learning about the difficult history. When history workers can help visitors and fellow workers develop a sense of belonging to a moral culture, the power of hope and courage stemming from communal membership allows learners to reconsider how they can respond and imagine ways they might bring justice to others.

The implicit purpose for ethical representations is to remind adults and inform children that violence, oppression, and trauma are what human beings are capable of doing. Demonstrating empathy about difficult histories better enables learners to make informed contributions to society. Public history sites and museums take the risks to represent difficult history to awaken a kind of passion in learners, a desire with a particular urgency, by challenging the taken-for-granted historical truths and revealing the struggles for a more just and compassionate moral order. Developing ethical representations engages history workers in addressing the challenges of prompting this passion in learners and developing the knowledge needed to direct and sustain learners' responses to difficult histories.

Notes

1. Jeffery C. Alexander, "Toward a Theory of Cultural Trauma," in *Cultural Trauma and Collective Identity*, ed. Jeffery C. Alexander, Ron Eyerman, Bernhard Giesen, Neil J. Smelser, and Piotr Sztompka (Berkeley: University of California Press, 2004), 8.
2. Ibid., 1.
3. Ibid.
4. Julia Rose, "Three Building Blocks for Developing Ethical Representations of Difficult Histories," *History News* 68, no. 4 (2013): Technical Leaflet #264.
5. Claudia Eppert, "Relearning Questions: Responding to the Ethical Address of Past and Present Others," in *Between Hope and Despair: Pedagogy and the Remembrance of Historical Trauma*, ed. Roger I. Simon, Sharon Rosenberg, and Claudia Eppert (Lanham, MD: Rowman & Littlefield, 2000), 213–46.
6. Ruth J. Abram, "Harnessing the Power of History," in *Museums, Society, Inequality*, ed. Richard Sandell (New York: Routledge, 2002), 125–41.
7. Roger I. Simon, *Teaching against the Grain* (New York: Bergin & Garvey, 1992).
8. Lalita Tademy, *Cane River* (New York: Warner Books, 2005).
9. Lalita Tademy, *Cane River* audiobook narrated by Shari Belafonte and Edwina Moore (New York: Hachette Book Group, 2005).
10. See also Dean MacCannell, *The Ethics of Sightseeing* (Berkeley: University of California Press, 2011), ix.
11. Deborah P. Britzman, *Lost Subjects, Contested Objects: Toward a Psychoanalytic Inquiry of Learning* (Albany: State University of New York Press, 1998); Elizabeth Ellsworth, *Teaching Positions: Difference, Pedagogy, and the Power of Address* (New York: Teachers College Press, 1997); Claudia Eppert, "Throwing Testimony against the Wall: Reading Relations, Loss and Responsible/Responsive Learning," in *Difficult Memories: Talk in a (Post) Holocaust Era*, ed. Marla Morris and John A. Weaver (New York: Peter Lang, 2002), 45–65; Simon, *Teaching against the Grain*; Freeman Tilden, *Interpreting Our Heritage*, 4th ed. (Chapel Hill: The University of North Carolina Press, 2008).
12. Quoted in Simon, *Teaching against the Grain*, viii.
13. Emmanuel Lévinas, *Ethics and Infinity: Conversations with Philippe Nemo*, trans. Richard A. Cohen (Pittsburgh, PA: Duquesne University Press, 1985).
14. Ibid.
15. Simon, *Teaching against the Grain*.
16. Susan Sontag, *Regarding the Pain of Others* (New York: Farrar, Straus and Giroux, 2003), 72.
17. In 2015, tour guides at this historical plantation site provided a multidimensional description of American Will that goes beyond the earlier tour narrative.
18. Julia Rose, "Rethinking Representations of Slave Life at Historical Plantation Museums: Towards a Commemorative Museum Pedagogy" (PhD diss., Louisiana State University, 2006).

19. See Simon, *Teaching against the Grain*; and Richard Sandell, ed., *Museums, Society, Inequality* (New York: Routledge, 2002).

20. Rose, "Rethinking Representations of Slave Life at Historical Plantation Museums," 204, 221.

21. Sontag, *Regarding the Pain of Others*, 61.

22. Michel-Rolph Trouillot, *Silencing the Past: Power and the Production of History* (Boston, MA: Beacon Press, 1995), 45.

23. Teju Cole, "Object Lesson," *New York Times*, March 25, 2015, http://www.nytimes.com/2015/03/22/magazine/object-lesson.html, 4.

24. Andrea Liss, *Trespassing through Shadows: Memory, Photography and the Holocaust* (Minneapolis: University of Minnesota Press, 1998), 69.

25. Ibid., 82.

26. MacCannell, *The Ethics of Sightseeing*.

27. See James E. Young, *The Texture of Memory: Holocaust Memorials and Meaning* (New Haven, CT: Yale University Press, 1993).

28. MacCannell, *The Ethics of Sightseeing*, 177.

29. Eilean Hooper-Greenhill, ed., *The Educational Role of the Museum*, 2nd ed. (London: Routledge, 2002), 13.

30. Sontag, *Regarding the Pain of Others*, 26.

31. Ibid.

32. Ibid., 29.

33. Ibid., 53.

34. Ibid., 54.

35. Linda Gordon, "Dorothea Lange Photographs the Japanese American Internment," in *Impounded: Dorothea Lange and the Censored Images of Japanese American Internment*, ed. Linda Gordon and Gary Y. Okihiro (New York: W. W. Norton & Company, 2006), 19.

36. Edward T. Linenthal, *Preserving Memory: The Struggle to Create America's Holocaust Museum* (New York: Penguin Group, 1995), 33.

37. Ibid.

38. Walter Benjamin, *Walter Benjamin Illuminations: Essays and Reflections*, ed. Hannah Arendt (New York: Schocken Books, 1968).

39. Simon, *Teaching against the Grain*, 23–25.

40. Antoinette T. Jackson, *Speaking for the Enslaved* (Walnut Creek, CA: Left Coast Press, 2012), 52.

41. Ibid., 49.

42. Ibid., 57.

43. Simon, *Teaching against the Grain*, 25.

44. Lisa G. Corrin, ed., *Mining the Museum: An Installation by Fred Wilson* (New York: The New Press, 1994), 8.

45. Personal communication, September 2004.

46. Corrin, *Mining the Museum*, 8.

47. Ibid., 2.

48. Ibid., 3; and see Peter Vergo, ed., *The New Museology* (London: Reaktion Books, 1989).

49. Don Lemon, "Don Lemon's 'Roots,'" October 10, 2014, CNN, http://www.cnn.com/2014/10/10/world/gallery/roots-don-lemon/.

50. Spencer R. Crew and James E. Sims, "Locating Authenticity: Fragments of a Dialogue," in *Exhibiting Cultures: The Poetics and Politics of Museum Display*, ed. Ivan Karp and Steven D. Lavine (Washington, DC: Smithsonian Institution, 1991), 163.

51. Conny Graft, "Visitors Are Ready, Are We?" in *Interpreting Slavery at Museums and Historic Sites*, ed. Kristin Gallas and James DeWolf Perry (Lanham, MD: Rowman & Littlefield, 2015), 73–75.

52. James Allen, *Without Sanctuary: Lynching Photography in America* (Santa Fe, NM: Twin Palms, 2000).

53. Bettye Pruitt and Philip Thomas, "Institute for Multi-Track Diplomacy," in *Democratic Dialogue—A Handbook for Practitioners* (Washington, DC: General Secretariat for the Organization of American States, 2007), 20, http://www.idea.int/publications/democratic_dialogue/upload/Full_file_low.pdf.

54. See Tilden, *Interpreting Our Heritage*.

55. The term is discussed by Dominick LaCapra, *Writing History, Writing Trauma* (Baltimore, MD: Johns Hopkins University Press, 2001).

56. MacCannell, *The Ethics of Sightseeing*, 50.

57. Eppert, "Throwing Testimony against the Wall," 50.

58. Simon, *Teaching against the Grain*, 144.

59. Sally Yerkovich, "Reflections upon *Hide/Seek*," Unpublished paper presented at the Annual Conference of the International Committee on Museums of Archaeology and History and the International Association of Museums of History (Helsinki, 2011), 1.

60. Ibid.

61. Harris Shettel, "Exhibit Controversy: Can It Be Avoided? Can We Help?" *Journal of Visitor Studies* 17, no. 2 (1997): 268–75.

62. Edward T. Linenthal, *The Unfinished Bombing: Oklahoma City in American Memory* (New York: Oxford University Press, 2001).

63. Ibid., 176.

64. Ibid.

65. Rose, "Rethinking Representations of Slave Life at Historical Plantation Museums."

66. Ibid., 429.

67. MacCannell, *The Ethics of Sightseeing*, 59.

68. Sontag, *Regarding the Pain of Others*, 85.

69. Simon, *Teaching against the Grain*, 59–60.

70. Ibid., 67.

71. Julia Rose, "Interpreting Difficult Knowledge," *History News* 66, no. 3 (2011): Technical Leaflet #255.

72. David W. Young, "Expanding Interpretation at Historic Sites: When Change Brings Conflict," in *Interpreting African American History and Culture at Museums and Historic Sites*, ed. Max van Balgooy (Lanham, MD: Rowman & Littlefield, 2015), 43.

73. Ibid.

74. See Corrie ten Boom with John and Elizabeth Sherrill, *The Hiding Place: The Triumphant True Story of Corrie ten Boom* (New York: Bantam Books, 1974).

75. Young, "Expanding Interpretation at Historic Sites," 43.

76. Ibid., 42.

77. Ibid., 44.

78. Nina Simon, *The Participatory Museum* (San Francisco, CA: Museum 2.0, 2010).

CHAPTER 5

Expanding and Elevating Slave Life History Interpretations and Uncovering Commemorative Museum Pedagogy

Introduction

"THERE ISN'T any." That was the direct and plain response I received when I asked the then director of Magnolia Mound Plantation (MMP) in 1999 for historical information about the enslaved community that once lived and labored at the antebellum sugar and cotton plantation just outside downtown Baton Rouge, Louisiana. I was newly hired as the curator of education at the American Alliance of Museums (AAM)–accredited historical site museum, and my first interpretation assignment was to develop a tour of the historical slave cabin that had been moved from Cherie Quarters on Riverlake Plantation in Pointe Coupee Parish to MMP. The two-room cypress cabin was carefully moved and reconstructed under the attentive supervision of a consulting architectural historian. The raised Creole-style cabin, complete with a central double hearth, was placed on the farthest edge of the site, away from the big house, to represent the onetime slave quarter that housed the enslaved families and individuals from roughly 1786 to 1865.

After much work with my colleagues in education at MMP and a year spent piloting school programs to interpret the slave cabin exhibit with hundreds of visiting students between 2000 and 2003, I decided to work full-time on the question about who actually lived in the MMP slave quarter. The existing educational programs at MMP about slave life generically recalled slave life without the names and "Faces" of the enslaved families and individuals who once lived and labored there. Walk-in visitors could request a guided tour of the slave cabin after they finished a tour of the big house. Essentially, when I began the exploration of slave life representations at MMP, the site interpretation was segregated. The stories told on the tour in the MMP big house were about the planter family's lives, and the slave cabin interpretation was about an anonymous population that labored in sugarcane and cotton fields and lived in an area on the plantation referred to as the slave quarter. However, there were a few instances of integrated free and enslaved historical spaces. For example, the open-hearth kitchen building was used to tell an integrated story, where the lives of the enslaved cooks and the planter's wife, referred to as the plantation mistress, intersected.

An interpretation approach of including in the tour an equal number of stories and an equal amount of time devoted to the free and the enslaved historical residents brings up key questions about the effectiveness of a separate but balanced interpretation strategy. An alternative approach to the separate interpretations is an integrated narrative, or biopic narrative, where historical interpretations simultaneously include perspectives of plantation life from both free and enslaved residents. Lonnie Bunch, historian and the director of the National African American History Museum in Washington, D.C., explains that integrating mainstream history museums can mean adding black interpretative elements to mainstream museums, but it does not mean those stories will be truly integrated. In the context of his work at the Valentine Museum in Richmond, Virginia, Bunch concludes,

> Museums must realize that . . . [a museum does not] simply [develop] segregated presentations about groups that are traditionally underrepresented in our cultural institutions. . . . It is incumbent on [museums] to work towards a new exhibition paradigm—one in which exhibitions transcend "*separate but equal*" presentations [my emphasis]. It is essential for museums to create a new synthesis that allows visitors to see how diverse ethnic and racial groups in this society struggled and interacted with each other. This interaction, often violent and often contested, shaped and changed each group and the whole society. Creating such a synthesis and presenting it honestly—warts and all—is not easily accomplished. But it is a goal worthy of the effort.[1]

Eichstedt and Small documented this pattern of racially segregated tours at historical plantation site museums throughout the Southeast.[2] At the end of the twentieth century, Colonial Williamsburg once found it more palatable to keep African American history separate from the mainstream stories of the white founding fathers.[3] More recently in the early 2000s, I observed many tours at Louisiana historical sites, including MMP, which offer segregated tours and exhibits that interpret free and enslaved histories.

Given this backdrop, I wondered, with MMP's interest in expanding slave life representations, what were the obstacles preventing rapid progress toward integration of the tour? I was interested in researching history workers' resistances to elevating and expanding the representations of slave life at MMP in hopes of taking steps to encourage and ensure more inclusive and ethical historical representations of planation slave life. This was a pedagogical challenge, and I was prepared to examine history workers' resistances and responses to expanded slavery history through an educational psychoanalytic lens. Slavery was indeed difficult knowledge for the MMP history workers and others to learn.

In 2003, I was a volunteer docent at MMP, and the administration agreed to allow me to conduct an in-depth study at their historical plantation site museum. The in-depth study followed my initial piloting of school tours and programs. I recognized early on that, in order to ethically interpret the history of slave life at MMP, much original research needed to be done. I went about researching and documenting the history of the MMP enslaved community.[4] My research focused on the enslaved communities that lived at MMP from the time the plantation was established in 1786 up to the end of the U.S. Civil War. In that roughly eighty-year period, over three hundred slaves had lived at MMP. This research resulted in a history report that I shared with the administration and history workers at MMP.[5]

In this chapter, I use the MMP case study of expanding and elevating slave life representations in an integrated tour to describe the evolution of CMP, and to illustrate how history workers as learners engage in learning a difficult history. The case study focuses on how individual history workers responded to the expansion of slave life in the interpretations that challenged the Eurocentric perspective that had been laid over the historical landscape for nearly forty years.

A national phenomenon of historical sites looking to transition from a more exclusive planter-focused interpretation to an integrated interpretation has proliferated since the 1980s. It has been complicated by the history workers' anxieties about learning the difficult history of slavery and their role in engaging the visiting public with the difficult history. Institutionally speaking, MMP's efforts to transition the interpretation to expanded slave life representations in 2003 to 2005 was further complicated by the history workers' loyalties to the established tour and to the iconic meanings long emphasized at MMP. I found a consistency in the kinds of responses and resistances to expanding slave life representations from the MMP history workers as other researchers have found among history workers charged with interpreting slave life at many other historic sites and museums.[6]

After attending and presenting at many workshops, public history sites, and museum conferences across the United States and in Canada, I can report that thousands of history workers have been actively and determinedly revising their site's interpretations to include or feature their site's difficult history, many of which are historical sites where slavery and racial subjugation were once imposed. I cannot yet report that all is reconciled and that difficult histories are ubiquitously and justly recalled. I can, however, say that more and more history workers are becoming increasingly aware and sensitive to the need to represent historical injustices and are partnering with social justice agencies and other history workers to investigate, document, and interpret difficult histories and to inspire active historical empathy for audiences worldwide.

In 2015, at the annual conference for the AAM in Atlanta, Georgia, for example, multiple sessions, workshops, and learning tracks were focused on social justice education and advocacy for civil and human rights through museum work. The wave of support and commitment to "empathetic museums," as described by museologist Gretchen Jennings during her panel session at the AAM meeting, indicates that history workers and other museum workers are seeking program strategies and pedagogical approaches to engage learners in learning about, and empathizing with, the victims of oppression from the past and in the present. As I described in chapter 1, the movement has been mounting for decades.

Between 2003 and 2015, through the generous efforts made by the administration at MMP and the volunteer docents and paid tour guides, I was able to document how history-workers-as-learners both desired and resisted learning the difficult history of slavery at this historical plantation site museum. In 2005, I used my research on slave life at MMP (i.e., the history report) to work with a group of history workers to develop a revised integrated tour narrative with expanded representations of the enslaved families and individuals. After my 2005 study, in the years between 2006 and 2014, I held three training workshops for volunteer docents and paid tour guides at MMP that were focused on interpreting the enslaved population on the tours, and spoke with staff and volunteers to follow subsequent changes to the MMP site interpretation. In 2015, ten years after the revised tour project began, I revisited MMP and spoke with history workers and visitors about the slave life representations at MMP in order to better understand the dynamics of CMP over an extended time period. The ten-year view revealed the ongoing commitment of the MMP history workers to expand and elevate the history of slave life in the site's interpretation and the power of the learners' reception and resistance.

Road Map

In this chapter, I describe how a group of MMP history workers engaged in learning the difficult history of slavery in order to expand and elevate slave life representations on their tours. Their experience led to the development and formalization of CMP and offers future history workers a valuable example of how expanding slavery history and other difficult histories can radically change the iconic meanings of well-established historical sites. The challenge asked the MMP history workers to change the stories that they had been using to interpret the plantation site for the public for nearly forty years, and to rearrange their personal understandings of what the historical plantation site represented. The charge to rethink the historical representations of slavery at MMP necessitated that the history workers and the institution's supporters rearrange the narratives that tied together their collective memories with the well-known stories and their personal identifications with Louisiana plantation history to now include the new historical slave life data and to address their resistances to the difficult history of slavery. Describing the origins and evolution of CMP will help readers better understand CMP and will help illustrate the impact of collective memory, personal identities, and resistance to difficult histories on learners' engagement, learning, and subsequently, on the content included in historical interpretations.

In the next section, "Institutional Commitment to Slave Life Interpretation," I describe the guiding questions that shaped the 2005 study and the social framework that the study was set against. My mission for the study was pedagogical. In my search to better understand how history workers grappled with changes to include plantation slavery, I also visited private and other public historical plantation sites and read critics' reports. I was observing an inconsistent pattern of plantation slave life representations.[7] Many of these historical plantation sites overwhelmingly privileged the memory of the white planter families, while representing a generic recollection of the enslaved populations. Consequently, I was left asking, How can history workers be moved to expand their interpretations to teach the site-specific slavery histories of plantation life?

In the third and fourth sections, "Brief History of Slavery Interpretation at MMP" and "The History Report: Baseline History of Slavery at MMP," I provide a summary of the slavery interpretation at the historical site museum followed by a brief timeline for the history of Magnolia Mound Plantation. The baseline history about the plantation and the site as a museum will help readers track the examples of the changes proposed for the historical tour narrative by the history workers in the study.

In the fifth section, which is called "Overview of the 2005 Study," I briefly lay out the components and results from the 2005 study. I describe the history workers who were participants in the study while keeping their identities anonymous. These history workers generously gave their time to participate. I briefly describe the history workers' experiences in learning the newly introduced difficult history of slavery at MMP. The results of the study include the history workers' responses and how the history workers' reactions subsequently helped to shape CMP. Their unfiltered responses revealed the 5Rs in the data and helped me to identify the three building blocks for ethical representations. I describe the coding process I used in the study and explain how the data showed a unique set of parameters that shaped the phrasing and attributes distinct to the MMP history workers who were charged with interpreting plantation slavery.

While there are many commonalities among the learners' responses to the difficult histories in general, researchers should keep in mind that each difficult history—mass oppressions, violence, and traumas—will undoubtedly include different and distinctive resistances and responses from learners (history workers and visitors) as they engage in their site's specific histories. In this section, I include a description of the specific types of learners' resistances that emerged from my study at MMP and that are common to history workers who were focused on learning and interpreting slavery history. The characteristics of the resistances to slave life history from this study offer other history workers a useful repertoire of recognizable resistances and responses that history workers can acknowledge in order to assist resistant learners. The study reported here is not intended to serve as a how-to guide to transition a site interpretation from a planter focus to an integrated focus. That kind of an interpretation overhaul is a different kind of endeavor that requires fundamental philosophical modifications to the entire historical site enterprise.[8] This case study was concentrated on investigating how history workers as learners engaged in learning and interpreting slavery history.

In the sixth and final section, I describe the ongoing evolution of slave life interpretation at MMP today. I revisited MMP as a visitor ten years after my study in 2015 and observed several tours, spoke with several tour guides, and reviewed the tour guide training manual. The ten years that followed the study reveal an interesting progression of revisions to the tour narrative and training as subsequent generations of docents and tour guides came through MMP.

Institutional Commitment to Slave Life Interpretation

Interest in the interpretation of slave life history at MMP has been evident at least as early as the 1980s. The Friends of Magnolia Mound Plantation produced a long-range site plan in the 1980s with multiple blueprints that included out buildings and workspaces where enslaved laborers once lived and toiled. Subsequently, the historical open-hearth kitchen building, weaving room, and cash crop and kitchen gardens were installed and used to represent workspaces of the enslaved workers. Likely, the watershed moment at MMP to more fully expand the historical plantation site's interpretation to represent the enslaved community came in 1993, when a slave cabin from Pointe Coupee Parish was installed on the MMP grounds. Two years later, MMP served as the first venue for the national traveling exhibition *Back of the Big House: The Cultural Landscape of Plantation Slavery* in 1995.[9] Elevated representations of slave life at MMP continued to emerge incrementally.

In south Louisiana, other historical sites and museums have also been slowly adding or expanding their interpretations specifically to include slave dwellings and slave life stories. Between 1990 and 2015, I found thirty-three Louisiana museums and historical plantations that either have or have added slave life representations to their exhibits. Such dynamics can be seen, for example, at West Baton Rouge Museum, Oakley Plantation at Audubon State Historic Site, Destrehan Plantation, Laura Plantation, Evergreen Plantation, Oak Alley, and Hermann-Grima & Gallier Historic House.[10]

Among the many examples of sites in Louisiana that are expanding their slave life interpretations are Evergreen Plantation in Edgard, Louisiana,[11] and Oak Alley Plantation in Vacherie, Louisiana. In the late 1990s, these historical sites went about restoring and reproducing original slave quarter cabins and researched and developed representations of each of the enslaved communities. Evergreen conducted archeological digs and invested in extensive research to recognize the history of the lives spent in the slave quarters. At Oak Alley Plantation, the administration first installed a permanent historic marker that recognized the location of the slave quarters, while still providing their traditional "hoop skirt" tours of the big house that focused on the planter family. Since then, Oak Alley Plantation has made much progress in documenting the enslaved population and has partnered with researchers at Tulane University to develop an interpretation plan and constructed reproduction slave cabins that are furnished with slave life exhibits.

In addition to the late twentieth-century and early twenty-first-century expansion of slave life representations at individual sites and museums, in 2009, the Louisiana Department for Culture, Recreation and Tourism developed a web-based African American Heritage Trail titled "A Story Like No Other."[12] The statewide heritage trail is designed for tourists, students, and researchers to locate sites to visit that tell the history of free and enslaved African Americans. The expanded representations of slave life and slavery history in the region are clear evidence of the public history communities' growing commitment to increasingly interpret the difficult history of slavery.

Brief History of Slavery Interpretation at MMP

The following brief review of slavery interpretation efforts at MMP provides a context for the responses from the history workers who were engaged in the 2005 study. My study used

MMP as a case study to develop a workable pedagogy about how history workers received new slave life information and how they went about using the information to revise the site's traditional European American interpretation of plantation life. The resulting pedagogy, subsequently titled CMP, aims to be a responsible and sensitive learning strategy to engage learners with difficult histories. CMP is based on the results of the MMP history workers' responses to learning and interpreting newly found MMP slave life histories. I wanted to know what kinds of negotiations would unfold between the history workers' personal attachments and loyalties to the longstanding interpretation and the newly documented historical record about the MMP enslaved community. For the history workers, at stake was the loss of the iconic meanings of MMP, and potentially a loss to the museum's patron community. Also at stake were the missed opportunities for a just remembrance of the historical enslaved community and social justice education.

The slave cabin exhibit was added to the grounds at MMP in 1993 in the interest of historical accuracy, commercial seduction, and to address the growing public demand for more inclusive representations of the historical population. The Creole-style big house at MMP was originally built in 1791, and was initially built by a planter and his slaves. Roughly ten years later, another owner had the house expanded, and slaves under the direction of a Creole architect did the work. The big house survived the ravages of the Civil War but eventually deteriorated due to the neglect resulting from hard economic times. The big house was saved from the wrecking ball in 1966 and was meticulously restored and furnished in the first decade the museum was open for public tours from 1975 to 1985.

The big house tour and the collection of the big house furnishings were built upon the well-documented genealogies of the Duplantiers, the planter family that owned the plantation from 1802 to 1841. A group of local historians and active historic preservationists led by Lois Bannon published *Magnolia Mound: A Louisiana River Plantation*,[13] which chronicles the history of the big house and the French and French American planter families who owned MMP. This book, and Catherine Clinton's *The Plantation Mistress: Woman's World in the Old South*[14] and Eugene D. Genovese's *Roll, Jordan, Roll: The World the Slaves Made*,[15] were used to train the docent corps at MMP starting in the late 1970s through the 1990s. The docent program was popular with volunteers from the Junior League of Baton Rouge. The female corps of well-educated and dedicated volunteers wore their own period dresses to lead tours, and demonstrated cooking in the open-hearth kitchen building.

The MMP history workers had long envisioned a slave cabin exhibit on the grounds with fenced yards for chickens and pigeons, and a wash building, kitchen garden, kitchen building, overseer's house, *pigeonnier*, cash crop garden, and weaving, carpentry, and blacksmith shops. The site conducted an archeological investigation in partnership with Louisiana State University to research, design, and build the historic open-hearth kitchen building and kitchen garden. By the time the slave cabin was installed, the site already had added the *pigeonnier*, kitchen building and garden, the cash crop garden, the overseer's house, and the weaving, carpentry, and blacksmith shops. Each historical exhibit space had informative interpretations and enjoyed tremendous support from volunteer weavers, gardeners, cooks, and docents. The interpretation focus for the tour of the big house was on the planter family and French Creole and Louisiana decorative arts. The interpretation focus was augmented by the outbuildings and gardens that referenced how the enslaved men, women, and children worked to support the lives of the planter family.

The history workers at MMP chose to portray the white southern plantation mistress as a hardworking household manager[16] to counter the legacy of the Southern belle and to counter the stereotype of the "useless" white woman as the epitome of femininity.[17] This was in response to second-wave feminism,[18] which had gained momentum in the 1980s. Surrounded by growing criticisms directed at the plethora of historical plantation museums for their racially biased interpretations, and following decades of maturing social history and feminism, the MMP history workers (paid and volunteer) maintained on their tours the representations of the husband and wife plantation owners as the industrious plantation mistress who was the household slave manager and the honorable plantation master who was a businessman and war hero. Together, the master and mistress of MMP were represented as slaveholders of an anonymous and Faceless enslaved population.[19]

While the MMP workers were open to a nonstandard interpretation (i.e., the feminist view), they were also limited or constrained by the European American privileged perspective that shaped the institutional mission and tour narrative. This was still evident in the MMP tour narrative in 2005 through the rhetorical accounting of the plantation mistress who managed slaves in the big house and who kept the keys to the spice box that the enslaved cook needed daily, all in support of the planter's agricultural business enterprise. The history workers' loyalty to a patriarchal legacy was the colonizing ideology that helped to perpetuate history workers' and visitors' understandings of race, gender, class, and, more broadly, an early-twentieth-century memory of the New South, which historically was based on a white southern heritage narrative.[20] The history workers' attachments perpetuated and preserved these meanings for MMP as a symbol of French Creole Louisiana sugar plantation life, which consequently acted to marginalize the memory of historical black enslaved families and individuals.

The anonymous representations of the enslaved women, men, and children were generic references used to support a refined heroic story about the planter's family in the MMP big house. The planter's ancestry, and his first and second wives' roots from the wealthy upper class in France and from the Creole upper class in Louisiana and Alabama, were carefully explained to visitors. Visitors were also told about the significance of the planter's successful involvement in the American Revolution and his personal encounters with the Marquis de Lafayette. The tour narrative used stories about the planter's family, referring to the master and the mistress and their progeny, to fill the period rooms with stories about what colonial and antebellum sugar plantation life was like for the wealthy planter class. The tour traced the floor plan of the big house using the fine collection of furnishings and meticulously appointed decorations that were selected to reflect information about the planter family. This was the situation as late as the 1990s to the early 2000s when I was planning the 2005 study to examine the effects of expanding the slave life interpretations at MMP.

When I was first asked to develop the interpretation for the slave cabin exhibit in 1999, the pressing questions that came to my mind were, Who were the slaves and How can the history workers learn to interpret the difficult history of slavery that had not been part of the big house tour? At this early stage of my work at MMP, the more subtle, although prevailing, interest in extending the historical plantation's interpretation to include representations of slaves was to augment the plantation social hierarchy that held the white planter family at the apex of the social structure, above the social ranks of an overseer and tradesmen and slaves. With the planter focus in place, how, then, could the stories of the enslaved community be elevated? Would the history of the MMP slave community be sanctioned to the slave cabin exhibit, kitchen building, and weaving room, for example? In fact, that was the trajectory in place in 1999. The administration decided to keep the tour of the big house exclusively about the planter family with slaves shown in supporting roles to the lifestyle of the planter family. At that moment, a lone historical document dated 1786 was in place in the planter's office in the big house that listed the slaves purchased by the original owner of MMP. The list of slaves was used by the docents and tour guides to describe how the planter conducted business in the big house.

At that time, the administration supported a separate tour to interpret slavery called "Beyond the Big House," which was offered to all visitors and school groups after they had finished a tour of the big house, and also to visitors who specifically had made advanced reservations for the "Beyond the Big House" tour. The MMP slave cabin stood to commemorate the historical enslaved population, yet it also specifically encapsulated the African American families and individuals into an anonymous group of people without their real names and personal histories. The slave cabin was a commodity, a cultural property,[21] another object to see at the museum. These are some of the circumstances that dictated how slavery was interpreted at MMP before 2005.

The administrative history workers at MMP were aware of some of the difficulties that expanded slavery representations would impose on the tours and on the frontline history workers, who were the tour guides and docents. Interpreting slavery at MMP was always important, but indeed uncomfortable for the history workers. An informative example comes from an interview I conducted with a retired MMP director in 1999. The retired director explained to me that her plan in 1993 was to add the Cherie Quarters slave cabin to the grounds at MMP in order to represent a household of an enslaved family in the MMP slave quarter. To that end, the retired director worked with an exhibit team to collect period furnishings that included a rope bed and a mattress. The retired director described how the exhibit team developed a furnishing plan for the slave dwelling with reservations. Her description indicated that the exhibit team was still ambivalent about recalling plantation life. She was worried about "flack" the exhibit might receive from the public, who might contest the presence of a slave cabin on city-owned grounds as "too unpleasant of a memory."[22]

An indication that the retired director and the exhibit planners were concerned about the risks and had fears of controversy was confirmed when the exhibit team decided it was "too harsh" for visitors to view the more oppressive cabin interior with only moss-filled pallets used by slaves to sleep on the cabin floor. The retired director recalled the exhibit planners' discussions about how to represent the quality of life of the slaves. Would their choice for bedding in the cabin, for example, indicate the enslaved family was well provided for, or would the bedding selected for the exhibit describe the restrictions slavery imposed on the household in the cabin? The exhibit team chose to use a period wood-framed bed with a moss-filled mattress in the exhibit. The planning process that the retired director recalled suggests that these history workers were grappling with the tensions they felt by the difficult history of slavery.

In the context of assessing slave life interpretations at historical plantation museums, Eichstedt and Small explain,

> Some people believe that ignoring the past or whitewashing it (literally) will allow healing to occur; that we can get on with a just world by simply looking forward from today; that there need be no account of the past, no dredging up of old skeletons, no probing of old wounds. We fundamentally challenge this assertion. We believe that without a full and open discussion of the past, its relation to contemporary inequalities and oppressions, and considerations of how to respond to these historical and contemporary inequalities, true healing cannot take place. Sites that pride themselves as providing history to the masses have an important role to play in this process—either as maintainers of oppressive patterns or as teachers for a just future.[23]

How, then, do history workers at historical plantations go about expanding slave life representations to include fuller descriptions of humanity? What can we make of the need to heal wounds and examine buried skeletons? What are the obstacles to interpreting expanded representations of the historical enslaved individuals whose stories tell about how they impacted the history of Louisiana?

While critics have recognized that ethnocentric practices and institutional ideologies perpetuate exclusionary interpretations at historical plantations,[24] educational psychoanalytic theories have enabled me to look more closely at the omissions and exclusions of slave life histories at MMP on a more individual level. As I discussed in chapter 3, Deborah Britzman explains learning difficult knowledge is a kind of "interference" in the learner's internal world.[25] I considered the possibility that new slave life histories introduced to the MMP history workers might disrupt the history workers' individual understandings of plantation history and challenge the history workers' attachments and loyalties to the traditional European American–focused meanings that had long been associated with MMP. The theoretical scholarship within educational psychoanalytic corpus that addresses questions about how learners engage in reading historical narratives of difficult histories was an approach that seemed to be on target with this predicament. What happens when stories are too much for the learner to bear? Claudia Eppert,[26] Simon and Eppert,[27] Ellsworth,[28] and others offered insights into this kind of difficult learning, also described in chapter 3. These theoretical insights were critical in my analysis of the MMP history workers' responses to the new slave life histories that I had asked them to consider using on their tours. When I delved deeper into my query, I explored whether the history workers found the newly introduced slave life histories dissonant to how they understood MMP plantation life, and if so, I examined how the history workers could work through the disparities.

I set about answering these three key questions to understand the learning processes at play when the difficult history of slave life was introduced and used to revise the interpretation of the big house at MMP:

1. How have the history workers represented slave life?
2. What happens when the history workers grapple with the difficult knowledge that slave life representations present?

3. What pedagogical strategies can be developed to sustain the history workers in working through their resistances to learning and in expanding historical representations of plantation slave life?

The History Report: Baseline History of Slavery at MMP

The first step before the 2005 study could be implemented was to research the enslaved community at MMP from the time the plantation was established to the end of the U.S. Civil War. The baseline history I documented was shaped, in large part, by the sequence of European American ownership of MMP, which was instrumental to tracing the history of over three hundred slaves that were affiliated with the plantation. The records revealed that the many families and personal histories of the enslaved persons from MMP were kept in depositories in Louisiana, and in online resources. To find the information specifically about the individual slaves, it was vital to have an accurate and detailed genealogical history of the slaveholding planter families because the information I sought was largely organized by the names of those slaveholding families. The names and histories of the enslaved individuals and families who lived at MMP, or were affiliated with the planter families, were most often found through records organized in the sequence of the MMP owners: Hillin (1786–1791), Joyce (1792–1802), Duplantier (1802–1841), and Hall (1849–1869).

With the planter families' records as the basis, I found the multidimensional descriptions of many of the enslaved individuals and families. I used civil and criminal court records, online databases, census data, church records, family records, wills, succession records, conveyances, ship manifests, and secondary resources. The resources were held at LSU Hill Memorial Library's special collections in Baton Rouge, Department of the Archives at the Catholic Diocese of Baton Rouge, East Baton Rouge Parish Public Library, Louisiana State Library, and the Alabama and Louisiana State Archives.

The resulting document was called the "history report," which included the family histories and personal histories of the slaves and their relationships to slaveholders, the plantation, Baton Rouge, and Louisiana. The history report detailed the genealogies and family stories of the slave community at MMP from the slave ships and slave markets to the births, deaths, marriages, slave sales, and records of illegal defiance.[29] In addition, I created a database of the persons enslaved at MMP and the former slaves who continued to be linked to MMP through the end of the nineteenth century. The history report also looked at the economic, political, familial, religious, and agricultural parameters that shaped the lives of the plantation community. The history report provided the basis for accurately revising the original tour narrative at MMP in order to expand and elevate the slave life representations.

The first enslaved population at Magnolia Mound Plantation included six West African adults and one child (Thomas, John, Lucia and her daughter, Catherine, Jenny, and Anna), who survived the Middle Passage and then were sold at the New Orleans slave market in the late eighteenth century. The plantation was established in 1786 with a Spanish land grant to Scotsman James Hillin. Hillin; his wife, Jane Stanley Hillin; their five children; and the six enslaved Africans from the Senegal-Gambia region started a plantation on roughly 950 acres on the east bank of the Mississippi River in Baton Rouge.

Around 1791–1792, Hillin sold the plantation, without the enslaved individuals, to John Joyce. Joyce brought a new group of enslaved families and individuals, roughly fifty enslaved people, to MMP. Joyce owned MMP with business partner John Turnbull. By 1798, both men had died, leaving their business, property, and slaves to be divided between their widows. Fifty-four of the enslaved men, women, and children at MMP were claimed by the widow Constance Joyce and her two children in 1800, all of whom were living at MMP at the time.

In 1802, when Constance Joyce married Armand Duplantier, the slaves from three different plantations were combined and brought to live and labor at MMP. Due to financial reasons, around 1803 and again in 1814, the Duplantiers aggressively sold many of the MMP-held slaves, severing many of the enslaved families and drastically disrupting the lives of the slaves they sold and held.

By the 1820s, the enslaved community had stabilized and the Duplantiers added more slaves from the New Orleans slave market to the enslaved MMP community. This enslaved community at MMP most often ranged from fifty to sixty-five residents, and included multiple generations of families living together at MMP for at least another twenty years, until at least the time of Constance Duplantier's death in 1841. Some of the original enslaved MMP community members continued to be held at MMP through George Hall's ownership, the fourth plantation owner, until the end of the Civil War.

The complicated historical twists and changes in legal ownership of MMP, and the major movements of groups of slaves among MMP and other plantations owned by the planters' relatives, suggest that many of the enslaved individuals and free individuals affiliated with MMP had long-term relationships over multiple generations.

Some of the enslaved families that were more thoroughly documented in the history report included Quashee's family, John and Celia's family, Abram's family, American Will's family, Charlotte's family, and Josephine's family. During the Duplantier's ownership of MMP, the big house was the residence of the planter family, and the enslaved families lived in approximately fourteen to sixteen cabins in the slave quarter behind the big house. Less than ten people lived in the big house, and around fifty people lived in the slave quarter, and an overseer, who was most often a single man, lived in a small overseer's house near the slave quarter.

Two family cameos below provide examples of multidimensional representations developed from the available records of two of the families that lived, labored, and experienced forced and permanent separations. Quashee's family and John and Celia's family stories are two of the family cameos included in the history report. These stories help to illustrate the depth of the information discoverable from careful investigation of the historical records.

Quashee's Family Story

Baton Rouge was a small Spanish colonial town at the end of the eighteenth century when forty-four-year-old Quashee and his thirty-four-year-old wife, Take, had their first child, Juba, in 1784. Juba was born in Louisiana as a slave. Her parents were captives from West Africa who survived the Middle Passage and were sold into slavery to a businessman, John Joyce. Joyce brought the family to Baton Rouge to cultivate cotton and indigo on his plantation on the east bank of Mississippi River just south of Baton Rouge. Joyce brought as many as fifty-four enslaved individuals to his new River Road property, most of whom were in young families like Quashee's family. Juba was eight years old when she came to live as a slave at Magnolia Mound Plantation with her parents and her newborn sister, Venus.

Quashee and Take were forced to work in Joyce's fields. By the time their eldest daughter was seven or eight years old, she worked alongside her parents in the fields. The baby girl, Venus, likely was swaddled to her mother's back while Take labored in the fields, only allowed to stop to nurse her infant daughter. The family of four lived in one room of a two-room cabin set in the slave quarter between the big house and a swamp. Quashee and Take were likely able to grow fruits and vegetables and were allowed to raise chickens in the small plot outside their cabin to supplement their meager diet of rationed cornmeal and pork. They were also allowed to sell any surplus from their garden in the Baton Rouge market on Sundays and could keep the cash to buy supplemental clothing or supplies for their family. Slaves received clothing once or twice a year, which was distributed by the overseer. Slaves' clothing rations were inexpensive and of poor quality. Quashee rarely saw his master, Joyce, who lived in Mobile, Alabama, while the MMP overseer controlled the daily lives of Quashee's family.

After Quashee's family had been living at MMP for six years, Joyce suddenly died at sea. Baton Rouge planters and businessmen hovered over Quashee's community inventorying all the buildings, livestock, and slaves at MMP. Quashee, his wife, and two children were counted, examined, and listed on a court record in 1800. New French-speaking owners appeared at MMP in 1802 and moved into the big house facing the river. They were Armand and Constance Duplantier and their young and teenaged children. Juba was a young woman and Venus was eight years old by then, and the sisters were told to work in the big house to serve the new planter family. Quashee, Take, and other slaves continued to work in the cotton, indigo, and corn fields. Now they saw a master regularly, and the slaveholder ordered the enslaved workers to gin cotton and bundle indigo wood that was to be shipped to New Orleans on its way to Europe.

The Duplantiers were planning to move to France and sold many of Quashee's slave quarter neighbors to planters in Baton Rouge, New Orleans, and other places in Louisiana. The Duplantiers severed Quashee's family in 1804. The Duplantiers sold Quashee and Take (and possibly eleven-year-old Venus) to a French physician who lived in Port Allen across the Mississippi River. Juba was separated from her family and from the community she had grown up with at MMP. Juba was sold alone as a house servant to a German man who owned Mount Hope Plantation, which was five miles from MMP. Constance Joyce Duplantier asked the courts to let her keep twelve-year-old Venus at MMP. If Venus was not sold with her parents, but stayed at MMP, then it would have been possible for Venus and Juba to visit each other by walking on Highland Road that connected to the two plantations. Venus could have only left MMP with permission from the Duplantiers, who, by law, could write a pass that would have allowed Venus to leave MMP and travel the five miles on Highland Road to see Juba.

Juba remained at Mount Hope Plantation. In her lifetime, Juba likely had to learn several languages: Kwa from her parents, French from her first owners, Spanish and English to buy and sell goods at the Baton Rouge market, and German from her owners at Mount Hope Plantation. Baton Rouge grew around Juba, who witnessed the small town's transition from a colonial fort to an American town.[30]

John and Celia's Family Story

John and Celia came to live and labor as slaves at MMP when their new master was assembling a slave population to cultivate his cash crops of cotton and indigo. Their master, John Joyce, who lived in Mobile, Alabama, was heavily invested in land in Louisiana and traded slaves and cattle throughout the Gulf Coast region. Joyce purchased slaves for his new Baton Rouge plantation where only a small fraction of his landholdings had been cleared for crops by the slaves held by the previous plantation owner. Joyce used slave labor to establish larger fields and to build his plantation big house, slave quarters, cotton gin, and outbuildings. The plantation stood on the River Road along the Mississippi River. Joyce used slaves to build and maintain the required levees to hold back the seasonal floodwaters.

Enslaved husband and wife, John and Celia lived in one room of a two-room cabin in the slave quarter closer to the swamplands at MMP behind but still in view of the big house. The slave quarter likely had fourteen to sixteen cypress cabins, which housed fifty-four enslaved men, women, and children, most of whom lived in family households in the quarter. John was originally from Congo, Africa, and had survived the arduous and dangerous Middle Passage. Celia was born a slave in Jamaica. Celia and John were purchased by John Joyce at the New Orleans slave market and were brought to MMP around 1792.

Two years after they arrived at MMP, John and Celia had their first child, a son named Jacob. John and Celia likely labored in the MMP fields cultivating the planter's indigo, cotton, and corn. Soon after, the couple had another son, Neptune. Each day, their young sons might have remained in the slave quarter under the care of an older enslaved woman who could no longer labor in the fields. Even though Celia had to work, she might have carried the youngest boy into the fields in order to nurse him. The family survived on a daily ration of pork and corn. The evenings were the only time available when they could tend to their small garden to grow foodstuffs, tend chickens, and fish in the nearby swamp.

After John and Celia established their family and had been living at MMP for six years, they learned that their master, John Joyce, died at sea. Soon after, John, Celia, and their two young sons were counted, examined, and listed on a court record in 1800. Jacob was six years old and Neptune was fourteen months. Two years after the succession inventory was completed, John and Celia had their third son, Coachi. Life and work at MMP changed under the new owners, Armand and Constance Duplantier, who chose to live in the summers at MMP and in New Orleans in the winters. In 1804, John, Celia, and Coachi were claimed by the plantation's mistress, Constance Joyce Duplantier. Her minor children, Josephine and William Joyce, claimed Neptune and Jacob as their property. The Duplantiers decided to sell John and Celia's family. Because the Duplantiers were planning to move to France, the slaveholders began aggressively selling members of the MMP slave community. John and Celia's family was severed apart. The Black Code, the laws governing slavery in Louisiana, stated that children under ten years old could not be separated from their natural mothers by sale. Despite the law, ten-year-old Jacob and four-year-old Neptune were sold to a planter in Baton Rouge. Celia and Coachi were sold to another slaveholder in Baton Rouge. John was sold to a plantation just south of MMP. The five family members were likely never reunited.[31]

Overview of the 2005 Study

In January 2005, the director and curator of education at MMP agreed to allow me to conduct the study at their historical plantation site museum. They explained that they were interested in expanding the site's slave life interpretation. The study unfolded over the next nine months. The study focused on the responses from a group of four history workers who were asked to use the newly introduced history of the MMP enslaved population (based on the history report) in order to expand the slave life representations in their tours of the plantation big house.

The 2005 study was an action research study. The action research study required the history workers to be active stakeholders in the process of shaping a revised tour of the big house. The history workers agreed that their goal was to draft a tour narrative of the big house that covered the period between 1786 and 1841, and that included expanded representations of the enslaved residents. Action research is a qualitative research strategy that is team based, with its efforts focused on improving the quality of the performance of an educational organization.[32] The research is designed and conducted by the same practitioners who utilize data to improve their own practice. I selected an action research approach to examine how the history workers would respond to using the newly compiled history report to expand their representations of plantation slave life, while simultaneously offering the history workers the opportunity to be invested in the revised narrative.

At the time of the 2005 study, the guided tour through the big house and the nearby kitchen building described plantation life through Louisiana decorative arts, Creole architecture, and the genealogy and lifestyle of the Duplantier planter family. The tour included descriptions of historical household customs, foodways, colonial Louisiana, means for educating the planter family children, the role of the Catholic religion on family life and life in the colony, and general references to slavery. After the forty-five-minute guided tour, visitors were invited to walk the grounds to view the outbuildings, including visiting the slave cabin on their own.

Plantation slave life history was also interpreted in a program called "A Day in the Life of a Slave" for school groups. Slavery was also interpreted for school groups and for the general public each February as part of Black History Month, with a professional dramatic first-person performance based on different themes drawn from American slavery history.

The study concentrated on the plantation big house and kitchen building because the regular tour associated with the big house and kitchen building was most frequently offered and had little mention of the details of slave life. The regular tour was given to drop-in visitors, most of whom were tourists, and to school groups on field trips. I reflected on Lonnie Bunch's call to elevate African American history by integrating museum interpretations and by moving away from "separate but equal" tours.[33] My original intent was to interpret the MMP landscape as a whole, which would have included the slave cabin exhibit. It became apparent to me that targeting the entire MMP landscape was too broad, and could run the risk of the study not addressing the most central source for MMP's planter-centric interpretation—namely, the regular tour in the big house and kitchen building. The team members would have faced a different kind of challenge in expanding the "Beyond the Big House" tour in the slave cabin than being faced with expanding the regular tour of the big house and kitchen building with historical slave life representations.

Selecting the study participants was a crucial step in the study. It was important to identify history workers at MMP who believed that expanding slave life representations for the site interpretation was a worthwhile endeavor—an endeavor that they were willing to invest time and energy into in order to develop a new tour narrative. At the time of the study, MMP employed five professional staff, eleven paid staff, and approximately twenty-five volunteers. The museum director and curator of education recommended candidates for inclusion on the action research team. The selection of history workers needed to reflect the widest variation of experiences, including their length of employment at MMP, type of position (volunteer or paid), an interest in slave life history at MMP, and some responsibility for interpretation at MMP. Based on these criteria, I invited four history workers to participate on the action research team: one volunteer docent, one part-time employee, and two full-time employees. I considered myself the fifth team member, having been a former employee and docent. Ultimately, the action research team included one man and four women. Our range of affiliation with MMP varied from less than a year to multiple decades. Three team members were native to Louisiana, two were fluent in French, and two had ancestral ties to France. The MMP history workers who were not formally participating in the action research study were given an orientation and overview of the ongoing study. The five-member team did not include

Rear view of Magnolia Mound Plantation big house from the kitchen building and garden. Photograph by author.

Slave cabin exhibit at Magnolia Mound Plantation, Baton Rouge, Louisiana. Photograph by author.

any African American history workers. In an attempt to partially address this shortcoming to include present-day African American voices in the project, I arranged for two outside scholars, who are African American, to critique the new tour narrative, which was a critical step in the study. One scholar was a history professor and the other scholar was a sociology professor, and both had expertise in American slavery history.

The MMP administration and history workers generously agreed to allow me to observe the museum's operations as a participant observer and to use the museum to conduct meetings and interviews. I was fortunate to receive permission to carry out the study at the museum with an understanding that MMP would receive no monetary benefits or other tangible benefits from the study other than access to the results of the study and the research from the history report.

The Study Unfolded

I described to the team members that their participation would include allowing me to observe their tours and to interview each team member about their tours, that they would be required to read the history report about the MMP slave community; and that they would participate in team meetings to develop a revised tour narrative based on the newly uncovered slavery history. The revised tour was referred to by the team as "the new tour." The team understood that developing a new tour would take three drafts to complete. I also shared some of the recent criticisms of plantation museums[34] with the team members to help convey the urgency of their work to revise the tour at MMP.

I completed the docent training program that was in place at the beginning of the study period in order to work from the same interpretational baseline as my fellow team members. In the second phase of the study, I observed the team members as they led tours, and I conducted post-tour interviews with each team member about the current tour and the possibilities for future revisions to the slave life representations in the tour. In the third phase of the study, I asked the team members to read the history report about the MMP enslaved community and to highlight stories and to select information in the history report that they would like to use in order to expand the tour of the big house with MMP slave life history. The team met twice to discuss how to expand representations of slave life for the tour by basing their suggestions on the new data in the history report. Some team members informally discussed their ideas for revising the tour narrative outside of the team meetings. During team meetings, I collected their comments and suggestions in written notes and from taped recordings. The team members were assured of their anonymity. After compiling their suggestions for the new tour, I used their suggestions to draft a revised version of the tour for the big house. After the team read the new tour, I edited it to include the team members' comments and referred to this version as the second draft of the new tour. Then the two outside scholars reviewed the second draft of the new tour narrative. I used the scholars' comments to draft a third version of the new tour narrative. The third tour narrative followed the same tour route and same time frame as the original tour. However, the third tour narrative now included stories about the slaves and the planter family in each room on the tour. The slaves were described in multiple dimensions, including their names, job titles, family ties, and their relationships to the enslaved and free plantation population. The stories were relevant to rooms on the tour and to local, regional, and, at times, national and international events, for example, the slave trade, slave rebellions, the French Revolution, and Louisiana statehood.

Due to the events of hurricanes Katrina and Rita in 2005, MMP was closed for several weeks. Our action research team adapted and agreed to read the third version of the new tour individually rather than meet at MMP for a third team discussion. Each team member met with me for a one-on-one interview to share his or her thoughts about the third version of the new tour.

The last phase in the study was for team members to pilot the third version of the tour. One team member felt he was too new to the museum and had not learned the tour well enough to pilot the tour. Another team member would not pilot the tour, saying she was not pleased with the third version of the tour. She no longer wanted to support the project to add expanded representations of slave life to the big house tour, although she did agree to be interviewed about the new tour. Only two team members agreed to try out the third version of the new tour narrative in the MMP big house by leading fellow team members on a pilot tour. I conducted post-tour interviews with each of the two team members. They spoke about how they felt about giving the new tour with the expanded slave life histories.

The results from the study formed the basis for me to formulate CMP, a sensitive pedagogical approach that addresses how learners grapple with difficult histories in museums and public history venues that is based on educational psychoanalytic theories on loss in learning. The goal of collecting history workers' responses to adding slave life to the existing tour enabled me to identify some of their personal understandings about historical plantation life and their emotional responses to the difficult history. For designing CMP, the most important data I collected was the team members' verbal responses to learning and to interpreting the newly introduced slave life history. The study focused on the history workers' responses to essentially three texts: the then present tour narrative, the history report, and the new tour narrative with expanded representations of slave life. The ethnographic strategies for data collection and analysis included observation field notes, tape recordings, transcripts, and collected responses from the team members in field notes. Their individual and group responses helped to identify and develop an approach that could move learners past objectifying the historical enslaved characters in one-dimensional representations and more toward subjectifying the enslaved individuals with multidimensional representations to more fully and ethically recall the subjugated population from the margins.

Findings

The synthesis of my findings brought forth a clear working hypothesis that framed the broader discussion and results:

> Team members who engage in learning and using new information about slave life at their historical site suffer and mourn losses that "difficult knowledge" can incite, disrupting the traditional meanings and team members' personal attachments to the historical site.

I analyzed the roughly five hundred pages of transcripts obtained from the action research using the constant comparative method.[35] My analysis was grounded in the educational psychoanalytic theories, especially related to mourning and melancholia and loss in learning described in chapter 3. My qualitative study called for an inductive analysis. I analyzed the clusters of data using the constant comparative method, which is a rigorous way of grouping ethnographic data and finding patterns and relationships. Once I established a baseline from my initial tour observations and docent training, I then analyzed the transcripts and field notes of team members' responses to the six data-generating activities: tour observations, post-tour conversations, team meetings, informal interviews, outside scholars' reviews, and pilot tours. The variety of data I collected in individual and group formats provided a range of perspectives.

The code words I used were desire; traditions and habits; planter focus; attachments and loyalties; one-dimensional and multidimensional representations; forty-five-minute rule; not enough time; group dynamics; risks and fears; ambivalence; scholarly evidence; passion for ignorance; difficult knowledge; balance and basic facts; foreclosure; learning crisis; comfortable entrances; and fitting in.

Looking closely at the team members' verbal responses was the key to understanding the team members' changing relationships to the difficult history of slave life, especially as the slave life information was expanded and developed with the Faces, the Real content, and the Narratives.

I organized the data in clusters labeled by propositional statements. The propositional statements describe the broad themes I found in the coded data. Below are examples of some of the more provocative propositional statements from the study at MMP organized by the five themes, which eventually became known as the 5Rs in CMP (described in more detail in chapter 3). This selection of statements is also useful to history workers who are working with personnel who are resistant to interpreting slave life history. Understanding the variety of history workers' responses to learning and interpreting slave life helps history workers assist learners to work through their resistances and feelings of loss in order to empathetically and ethically represent slavery history for the learning public.

History workers who, for example, are training frontline interpretation personnel can make use of these codes and similar codes to assess where in the learning process the trainees are in working through a difficult history. The 5Rs help to distinguish history workers' ambivalence or commitments to interpreting difficult history.

Theme 1. Reception

    a. Team members expressed enthusiasm about learning new slave life history to make the MMP tour narrative "more real" and to "put flesh on the bone." (desire)

    b. Team members were loyal to the traditional tour narrative and were reluctant to change the planter-focused tour when adding new slave life history to the tour narrative. (traditions and habits)

    c. Team members engaged in slave life history to support the site's traditional planter-focused tour. (planter focus)

d. Team members expressed interest in slave life stories that supported team members' attachments and loyalties to French Creole heritage interpreted at MMP and the Duplantier family. (attachments and loyalties)

e. Team members used generic stories and terms to describe slave life, and were interested in additional information about historical slaves' names and jobs. (one-dimensional and multidimensional representations)

Theme 2. Resistance

a. Team members used the forty-five-minute time frame for their tours as a restrictive guideline. When the traditional tour was at risk of changing from an exclusive story about the planter to an integrated story with free and enslaved residents, the "forty-five minutes" became a steadfast rule. (forty-five-minute rule)

b. Team members solicited other team members to support their distrust and questioned the accuracy of the history report. (group dynamics)

c. Team members expressed concerns about offending visitors if they changed the planter focus of the regular tour. (risks and fears)

d. Team members expressed enthusiasm for new information on slave life but then had various reasons for rejecting the new information. (ambivalence)

e. Team members were skeptical or rejected new stories about enslaved families or slave life that were generated from newly introduced historical records. (scholarly evidence)

f. Team members offered reasons why they did not have time or access to resources to learn about slave life at MMP. "Anna and I don't have five hours to spend in the library."[36] (passion for ignorance)

g. Team members openly refused information that challenged their deeply felt personal attachments and loyalties to French Creole heritage interpreted at MMP and to the Duplantier family. (attachments and loyalties)

h. Team members said that if more enslaved individuals were included in the tour then the regular tour would become a "slave tour." (balance)

i. Team members argued that the meanings of the big house were based on the legal ownership of MMP and the interpretation on the regular tour had to focus on the legal owner's stories. (basic facts)

j. Team members preferred to increase slave life representations at MMP by expanding the "slave tour" and keeping the regular tour exclusively about the planter family. (separate slave tour)

k. Team members who could not reconcile the disruptions the new slave life stories presented to the regular tour or to their personal attachments and loyalties refused to engage in the project of expanding slave life representations at the museum. (foreclosure)

Theme 3. Repetition

a. Team members reread the history report and the new tour narrative, or repeated slave life information out loud that they refused to accept as believable or as historical and/or as significant. "Joan died. She died? Joan died."[37] (learning crisis)

b. Team members were loyal to the traditional tour narrative and were reluctant to change the planter-focused tour when adding new slave life history to the tour narrative. (traditions and habits)

c. Team members stated many times that the big house was the home to the Duplantier family and that the tour should be about the big house. (basic facts)

d. Team members, when faced with new information, openly repeated their deeply felt personal attachments and loyalties to French Creole heritage as interpreted at MMP and to the Duplantier family. (attachments and loyalties)

Theme 4. Reflection

a. Team members spoke with each other about the study, the contents of the history report, and the new tour narrative outside of the organized study activities to share ideas and gather support for their individual views on slave life history content. (group dynamics)

b. Team members discussed their difficult knowledge, adding, bit by bit, pieces of new information. (learning crisis).

c. Team members oscillated in their commitment and hesitation to expanding slave life representations. "I don't know . . . you know."[38] (ambivalence)

Theme 5. Reconsideration

a. Team members were more likely to incorporate slave life stories into their tour narratives if they could individually identify a physical space, artifact, or noncontroversial topic or phrase to introduce the stories. (comfortable entrances)

b. Some team members continued to use generic references and jobs to represent slaves, while other team members began to incorporate more historical and personhood stories about slave life into their tours. (one-dimensional and multidimensional representations)

c. Team members were more likely or able to use newly introduced slave life information and multidimensional representations of slave life after much time had passed and when they had opportunities to repeat and reflect on the slave life information by reading or through conversation. (working through)

d. Team members found agreeable ways to use new slave life information without making radical changes to the regular tour narrative. (fitting in)

Slave life had not been a traditional part of the meanings of MMP's interpretation. Team members were faced with painful histories that raised learning crises for the individual team members. At the end of the study, two team members with personal attachments to French Louisiana plantation history foreclosed on further engagement with the difficult knowledge slave life presented. The other two team members were able to work through the difficult knowledge slave life presented and were willing to add expanded slave life stories to the regular tour.

In summary, I identified six specific ways team members engaged in learning difficult knowledge about slave life at MMP; six ways team members engaged in learning to live with loss.

1. The 5Rs appear in unpredictable sequences and can reoccur.
2. The 5Rs take varying amounts of time, weeks and months.
3. Sometimes learning comes to a halt and learners foreclose on engaging with new slave life histories.
4. Comfortable entrances are mechanisms that help learners to work through difficult knowledge. Comfortable entrances are physical places and verbal expressions that enable history workers to move closer to shaping and using more multidimensional representations of slave life on their tours.
5. One-dimensional precedes multidimensional representations of enslaved individuals and families in a gradual, transformative learning process.
6. Fitting in is a method of adding slave life information bit by bit to the present tour without radically changing the tour and without overwhelming the learner's status quo, but sustains the planter-centric interpretation longer.

I formalized and generalized these findings into the CMP approach, which is applicable to many museums and historical sites that interpret difficult histories. In retrospect, team members were initially receptive to new information about MMP's enslaved community, and then showed various combinations of resistance, repetition, reflection, and reconsideration as the history workers recognized how the slave life representations changed the regular tour narrative. The new information posed disruptions to the traditional interpretation of MMP and to team members' personal attachments to plantation heritage. A team member might have refused information and repressed that which was too much to bear, as his or her ego wished to ignore or forget that which he or she could not stand to know. Slave life stories from the history report had to be mourned; the difficult history had to be worked through "bit by bit" by the individual team members.

Responses Demonstrate the 5Rs

Team members were immediately interested and receptive to one-dimensional representations of enslaved individuals as a means for enhancing the regular tour. Team members expressed their desire for the new historical information that would help make their interpretations "more real." For example, the team member I call Anna said, "and if we can have a name of a slave we can link with speaking of the slave code, the Black Code, and it would be more realistic because we use the name of a slave that was actually here."[39] The idea that historically accurate slave names would make the tour more real appealed to the team. The team member I call Gwenn exclaimed, "I would love to know the names, who the house servants were, because those were the ones the family would have been most concerned with."[40] Generic slave life stories were tolerable for team members and afforded team members a level of comfort or complacency in interpreting slave life. The team member I call

Karen was aware that the current tour included a repertoire of stories about slave life that she had learned from the docent training manual and from observing other MMP museum workers lead tours.

I go through the first two rooms and in the girls room, well in the master bedroom we talked about the slave entrance, and then the tiers of slaves, we talked about the bath tub and filling up the water, them [slaves] sleeping on the floor in the girls bedroom. In the dining room the job of the slave boy pulling the punkah. Talking about the spices in the relationship between the mistress and the cook. And the mistress and the health of the slaves. We talked about [it] also in the salon, I talked about demonstrating what would have gone on when the men were sitting around the table talking about farming and planting but also slave rebellions and things that were going on in slavery issues.[41]

These generic references to slave life were familiar stories that provided team members with "comfortable entrances" to incorporate some of the new historical slave life information into their representations of individual slaves into their tours. All of the team members referred to the "bath story" in the master bedroom as a good place to refer to house slaves on the tour. The bath story is a good example of data I coded as "traditions and habits." In my analysis, I found that traditions and habits were comfortable entrances for team members who used the slavery history to support the planter-focused tour. Stories, like the family bath story, were based on conjecture and made references to a nameless slave who filled and then emptied the tub full of water or chopped the firewood to heat the bathwater. The names of house servants included in the history report were welcomed additions to expanding the bath story, which was already part of the tour.

One-dimensional representations did not challenge or disrupt the traditional interpretive focus on the planter family's history and afforded team members comfortable entrances into discussing slave life on their tours. However, the multidimensional representations of the MMP enslaved community from the history report, and those used in the new tour narratives, changed the interpretation, bringing the enslaved individuals into focus, and provided Faces for the enslaved families and individuals.

The introduction of the difficult knowledge about MMP slave life seemed to instigate a rise of team members' ego defenses. As the task to add slave life to the tour continued, the team members were required to work through the new knowledge that each team member found difficult. The museum director supported the project to expand the slave life representations on the big house tour, which helped to keep the project going forward. Learning the difficult knowledge meant that the team members were compelled to reorganize their understandings with each new piece of knowledge, to continue to resist the new knowledge, or to find parts of the new knowledge that he or she could bear to use in the existing tour that did not immediately and significantly disrupt the status quo. The team members' individual ego defense mechanisms, for example, refusals and denials, worked to stabilize the individual team member's internal psychic status quo. The name American Will, for example, was a single-dimensional representation of the historically documented enslaved carpenter that was readily accepted by the team for the revised new tour. And the name of a house servant, for example, Charlotte, did not jeopardize the team members' individual internal status quo. However, when stories about American Will and his wife's African origins and their subsequent family separation, and Charlotte's family separation and her personal story of being objectified as a wedding gift, were suggested for the tour, three out of the four team members initially resisted these multidimensional representations. At a team meeting, two team members declared, "That is not what the tour is about" and summoned the forty-five-minute rule. At that moment, two of the four team members felt certain that there was not enough time in the tour to mention more than the name of a slave on the tour.

At the first team meeting, the team members emphasized stories that highlighted the planter family's relationship to France, which seemed to support the four team members' attachments to the interpretation long told at MMP. The team members I call Anna and Gwenn agreed that the tour should also include stories about Armand Duplantier's friendship with General Lafayette during the American Revolutionary War. Anna pointed out her attachments to Armand Duplantier, announcing, "It is important that we have to explain General Lafayette, to explain the status of Armand Duplantier. He was not a nobody."[42]

Stories that reminded team members of the Duplantier's slaveholding status posed difficulties for some team members. Each team member's ego was engaged in defending itself from interference that the history report, and then the new tour narrative, imposed on the individual team members. The team members' resistive responses were acts of self-preservation to the internal challenges posed by the history report and the changes in the new tour. The new information disrupted what team members knew was "true" about MMP, and what was "right" in the social order and within the security of his or her ego.[43]

It was a struggle for each team member to shift the interpretation focus seen through a singular lens of the planter family to a much more layered history that included multiple perspectives of plantation life seen through experiences of slaves. For example, clearing more land meant more financial risk was invested to increase income for the planter family, but also meant longer hours away from family and added work for the enslaved families. The team discussions included many examples of team members' expressions of resistance to expanding slave life representations. For example, they expressed their need to be loyal to the longstanding tour narrative and to the iconic meanings of MMP as the home of a well-regarded French planter, Armand Duplantier. Two of the team members' understandings about Armand Duplantier's character were jeopardized by the slave life stories.

Team members' anxious emotions were raised by the newly revealed information in the history report that showed Armand Duplantier struggled financially and dabbled in the slave trade. These stories were difficult knowledge for Anna: "The Code and the situation of bankruptcy that is where I disagree with [the research] completely. And I refuse to analyze it like that"[44] and "[The research] interprets Armand as a bad guy."[45]

I explained to Anna that our use of the history of the bankruptcy story and the other legal battles Armand faced was a means for tracing the stories of the enslaved residents at MMP and not to judge Armand Duplantier. I said to Anna, "The reason why that is important to us in terms of the slaves' lives, it impacted the slaves [who] were a part of these transactions."[46] When I assured Anna that our intentions for revising the tour were not to harm MMP, but to enrich the interpretation for broader audiences, Anna was more willing to engage with the history report during the meeting. I found that these negative stories about Armand Duplantier were difficult knowledge for Anna. Anna candidly explained, "So that is why I am afraid."[47]

The expanded representations about slave life were readily resisted by three of the team members as too long and too distracting to the stories about the Duplantier family, and were better suited in a separate tour. The multidimensional representations tended to overwhelm the planter-focused tour, disrupting the memory of a harmonious planter family and a complacent plantation community.

Some of the team members' reception to adding slave life representations to the regular tour of the big house was buoyed by a belief that the regular tour would essentially stay the same and that the slave life information would be added to the standing tour. At first, portions of the tour were not edited out to make time for new histories about the slaves who labored in the big house or on the plantation. When the slave life information replaced standing portions of the tour or lengthened the narrative on a stop on the tour, some of the team members expressed concern and resistance. The forty-five-minute rule, for example, was invoked as a guiding restriction that was given by a higher authority than the tour guides and docents, and was heavily called upon at the beginning of the study to resist expanding the tour to include expanded slave life representations. Even though the director at the beginning of the study and the subsequent director during the study supported changing the tour, and allowed editing out portions of the tour to make room for new information, the team found the task difficult.

Team members expressed fear, ambivalence, dismay, refusals, and denials, which appeared as verbal expressions found in the clusters of data I identified as resistance. Over several months during the study, team members worked through their relationships to the changing historical narrative and to the changing selection of historical individuals being included on the tour. In several instances, team members demonstrated new or increased empathy and productive ethical responses toward historical individuals in the form of reconsidering the multidimensional representations of slave life.

Consider the anxious resistance expressed by the team member whom I call Gwenn. During the second team meeting, Gwenn made references to some of her ties to Louisiana plantation history in her resistant responses that indicated that the slave life history was difficult for Gwenn to use in the tour. The team was interested in the history of twin brothers, Harry and Dick, who were enslaved at MMP. Gwenn thought their story would enrich the regular tour because she had personal information about some of the chores given to young slave boys on Louisiana plantations. Gwenn explained that her interest in Harry and Dick came from her direct relationship to Louisiana plantation heritage.

> I guess it was partly because some of the slave plantation's populations and their descendants had stayed on my mother's family plantation. And it was traditional that the man in the family had two little black boys who were his errand runners.[48]

When it came time to craft the passages for the tour about the twin brothers, Harry and Dick, Gwenn found the descriptions of the brothers' parents and three sisters too hard to use in the tour. The stories were overwhelming. Their African-born father, a carpenter, died at MMP, and their mother remarried and was sold away with their three younger sisters, leaving the boys without family at MMP. While the stories were condensed to a single sentence, as written above, Gwenn found it too disruptive to the tour. Gwenn expressed her resistance to the multidimensional representations of slave life when she explained that learning the kinship ties of the enslaved family was too confusing. Gwenn had reflected on including enslaved brothers Harry and Dick in the new tour narrative.

> Oh, I like Harry and Dick. . . . Because Harry and Dick as being probably in the same age group with the boys who tended to be their own personal slaves. And whether they were their slaves per se or whether they just happen to be here, those kids would have played together. The other, ah, I think is too involved. The carpenters yes, Harry and Dick, but to go into the wives and all is too much. It gets confusing.[49]

Gwenn did not want to interpret Harry and Dick as sons who lost their parents. In the same discussion, a team member I call David argued that if the team has the information about Harry and Dick's parents, Fanny and Abram, it should be included in the tour narrative. Gwenn replied that all that was necessary were their names and to say that Harry and Dick were playmates to the planter's sons.[50] The single dimensions were tolerable for Gwenn, while David preferred adding more dimensions to develop the Faces of the enslaved brothers. The team members' negotiations of the way slave life would be represented in the revised tour narrative included many examples of resistance to multidimensional representations, although over the months, different team members opted to reconsider Harry and Dick's history and included their family story in the new tour narrative.

Gwenn demonstrated that her self-identity appeared in jeopardy after she read the third version of the new tour narrative. From my analysis, I found that Gwenn remained loyal to the regular MMP tour and expressed that she was experiencing loss. Gwenn felt that the Duplantier family members were lost in the new tour narrative, which caused her observable pain and grief.

Gwenn explained that the new tour narrative did not reflect her vision for the proposed tour: "I will preface this on saying you can approach this in several different ways and my approach for my purposes and your approach for your purposes would be diametrically opposite."[51] Gwenn continued to explain that while the new tour narrative was "excellent for showing both ways of life" it did not address Gwenn's goals for the regular tour of the big house.

"So that for me the story of the family who owned the house, the house being what we [history workers] are expected to interpret, I find them lost in the process."[52] Gwenn refused to learn the new tour narrative for her pilot tour. However, admirably, on her pilot tour, Gwenn willingly read aloud the third version of the new tour narrative, which was a melancholic response. The slave life stories likely imposed on Gwenn's understandings of what was most meaningful about MMP. Gwenn had foreclosed on the project of expanding the slave life representations on the regular tour of the big house by not using anything more than the names of select slaves from the history report.

Engaging in the history report in passive terms and with one-dimensional representations allowed team members to keep their identities intact, and to hold on to the traditional meanings of MMP without feelings of crisis as seen in Gwenn's experience. However, according to Felman, without crisis, the learner is not learning from the text.[53] As shown by Eppert[54] and Felman, and as was demonstrated in this study, repetitive and reflective assessment of the text could begin to move learners toward working through their individual learning crises.

In contrast to Gwenn, who was a melancholic learner, was the team member whom I call Karen. Karen was mournful in the way she worked through the history that she found difficult to learn and use for the tour. At the first team meeting, Karen agreed with two other team members that they had to stick to the forty-five-minute rule that would limit how much more could be said about slave life on the tour. At the second team meeting, Karen could not grasp the story of Charlotte, the mother of two young girls, who was once used as a wedding gift to the planter's wife. Karen first repeated Charlotte's name and job as an enslaved house servant and her family status as a mother multiple times. Months later, Karen was able to tell the story of Charlotte being used as a wedding gift and opted to use the words *objectification* and *dehumanization*, words that Karen had refused to accept earlier in the study. Karen was working through the difficult knowledge. Karen had to separate her pain in learning about Charlotte's suffering from Karen's suffering that she was experiencing in learning about Charlotte's life story. Karen was able to elevate Charlotte as more than a house servant, to a person with a Face who was humiliated and oppressed. At first, Charlotte's name and job title were less painful for Karen to talk about, and only later was Karen able to reconcile the tour narrative with the suffering that Charlotte had endured.

Karen expressed empathy for Charlotte's family, demonstrating that the Other's pain was especially meaningful to her when Karen explained that the way her parents raised her and her siblings was very important to Karen. Karen was upset by the slave life histories, especially after reading about enslaved families' forced separations. She repeatedly referred to the *Code Noir* that forbade the separation of young children from their mothers and questioned the possibility that the code was not followed. Karen also repeated the stories and focused on the horrors of the enslaved family separations, which she explained she could not imagine. Karen was working through her "relationship" to a historical enslaved mother who grieved. For Karen, to empathize with an enslaved mother's losses, she had to first mourn her own internal psychic losses so she could retell the enslaved mother's stories on the tour. Karen's learning experience recalls Eppert's description of a "just mourning,"[55] the pedagogical project encouraged through self-reflexive moments and reflective conversations when learners take on responsibility to separate herself or himself from the Other in order to respond to the Other. At the conclusion of the study, Karen had reconsidered the difficult history of Charlotte's enslavement. Karen gave a pilot tour that successfully integrated the histories of ethically represented free and enslaved MMP populations, including Charlotte's family story.

In recognizing the historical characters' subjectivity, MMP team members were at times faced with the responsibility to bear witness to the Other's loss; losses recalled in the traumatic stories of enslavement and stories of losses affecting the planter family. On occasion, each team member independently expressed empathy for the historical characters. Team members' interpretations of plantation life were complex recollections of remembering and forgetting, of knowing and not knowing how life was lived on plantations in freedom and in bondage. The two team members with direct French ancestry may have been faced with traumatic histories that posed dual conundrums. First, those team members were faced with their responsibility to respect their French and French American ancestors in how the team members described French Louisiana plantation life on their tours. Second, they, like all the team members, were faced with the newly introduced responsibility to feel empathy for the historical enslaved population that they had not yet fully recognized.

The team members' emerging understanding of the history of slave life at MMP necessitated three psychological events. The team member could distinguish herself or himself from the historical characters in an empathetic relationship, which resisted narcissistic identifications with the represented suffering. Second, each team member in time, and with reflection, could form a meaningful relationship to the historical Others that acknowledged the team member's inability to fully understand the historical traumatic events. Third, each team member had to allow the meanings of MMP to change by rearranging his or her understandings and psychic relationships to Louisiana plantation history.

The team members' resistances were not a failure to respond to the historical individuals. The team members' resistances were more likely aligned to avoid pain in the process of bringing losses to consciousness. The new tour narrative was not fun or empowering for the team members; rather, the tour with expanded representations of slave life recalled the enslaved population's oppression that had previously been eluded to in MMP's interpretation of plantation life. The experience of learning the difficult history at MMP for the team members, to varying degrees, was informative yet also disruptive, humbling, hard, and, at times, painful.

Observations Ten Years after the Study

In ten years, from 2005 when the MMP history workers received the history report to 2015, the slave life representations have been continuing to expand at MMP. In 2015, I went on several tours at MMP, spoke with some visitors who completed tours, spoke with staff, and reviewed the tour guide training manual. I found that the history workers had continued to reconsider the difficult history of plantation slave life and had been expanding how slave life is represented at MMP. The role that slave life history plays on tours in 2015 in explaining the history of MMP has been considerably augmented. In 2005, the average number of times slave life was heard mentioned on the big house tour was six on eleven stops. And in 2015, the average number of times slave life was heard mentioned by tour guides and docents was twenty times on eleven stops. While the tour remains forty-five minutes and the tour route is about the same as it was in 2005, the required tour narrative in the tour training manual for the big house and kitchen included a sevenfold increase in references to slave life than was included in the tour before 2005. Significant changes can be found, especially in the new "tour script" that was implemented in 2009 to train tour guides and docents.

While the number of times slave life is mentioned has significantly increased, the slave life representations are still largely single dimensional. Most of the slave life mentions are historical names of slaves, accurate job titles of enslaved individuals, and the use of the words *slave*, *slaves*, and *enslaved*. The tour script does use multidimensional representations in some instances. For example, the tour script recalls stories about American Will and Charlotte, and describes how slaves were educated and how the Catholic religion was imposed on the slaves for marriage and other rites of passage. In general, however, the Faces of the enslaved population are still peripheral. The inclusion of slavery in the historical plantation tour at MMP in 2015 approaches what Eichstedt and Small have described at other southern plantation sites as "relative incorporation."[56]

Institutional commitment for expanding slave life representations has been maintained over the ten-year period. Since the study at MMP concluded in December 2005, each subsequent director became familiar with the history of slavery and slave life at MMP. Each director held training workshops using content from the history report and worked on finding a variety of ways for frontline history workers to expand slave life representations throughout the tour of the big house and kitchen building. The three directors supported revised versions of the tour narrative and saw that slave life and references to the historical enslaved families and individuals were included in each room on the tour of the big house and in the kitchen building.

The training materials from 2009 included a revised tour based on the third tour narrative that was prepared by the action research team in 2005. History workers at MMP continue to access research about slave life at MMP, including information from a collection of early nineteenth-century letters written by Armand Duplantier to his family in France that became available at Louisiana State University after 2008. The history workers also worked on a revised furnishing plan for the slave cabin exhibit in order to more accurately represent family life as was lived in the MMP slave quarter.

The work to expand and elevate the historical representations of slave life at MMP, after ten years, demonstrates how deeply complicated the individual workers' resistance is to interpreting slave life. While the museum's mission supports the predominance of the planter-focused narrative, there is room for elevating the historical presence of the enslaved community. In 2015, an online description explained that "Magnolia Mound's mission is to illustrate and interpret the lifestyle of the French Creoles who formed the fascinating culture, which still influences and pervades life in southern Louisiana."[57] The 2009 tour guide manual explains that the mission at MMP is

> to preserve, collect and interpret the historic house and site, through education, and demonstration of early plantation life in south Louisiana. This will be done through interpreting MMP's architecture, collections and through education that represents the experiences of family life and social history [related] to the culture of 19th century Baton Rouge and the larger community.[58]

Museum director Katherine Kane at the Harriet Beecher Stowe Center in Hartford, Connecticut, explains that transforming the interpretation to include slavery at historic sites, where slavery had not been an interpretation theme before, involves changing the institution's culture and reshaping the organization's values and mission to align with the historical content.[59]

For ten years (2005–2015), history workers have been interpreting MMP with an increasingly renewed commitment to increase slave life representations. However, at the individual level, the range of history workers' personal commitment has been highly variable. I have documented, as late as 2014, a history worker who had refused to represent slavery on her tour to the other extreme of a tour guide, who, in 2015, exclaimed, "I like to talk about slavery in every room in the big house."

Thus, interpreting the difficult history of plantation slavery at MMP continues to expand as the individual history workers continue to grapple with the difficult history. Over the years, as new history workers arrive at MMP, the meanings of the historical plantation, which more often include slave life, are evolving. Learning the difficult history of slavery and the difficult task of changing the meanings of MMP from a harmonious European American and French Creole planter family interpretation to a more complicated integrated story of free and enslaved residents is ongoing.

While a gap remains between the historical interpretations about the enslaved and the free plantation residents, intersections are coming into focus at multiple junctures in MMP's tour narrative. The points of intersection in the narrative have the potential to inspire historical empathy and make connections to social justice issues in the present day. History workers can interpret the site-specific histories of the families and individuals, making connections among the families' relationships to work life and home life, to enslavement and freedom, to mercy and oppression, and to capitalism and community. The integrated stories and multidimensional representations could illustrate the social tensions and the decisions made by the planter family and by the enslaved residents, which were the decisions that wrote the course of their lives at this place.

The research done with MMP history workers revealed the need for an approach like CMP. CMP is a pedagogical strategy that accounts for history workers' resistances and learning crises in order to expand and elevate historical interpretations of slave life and other difficult histories. The MMP case study illustrates how critical it is to sensitively address the complexity of history workers' resistances and responses. CMP encourages history workers to learn and interpret difficult histories in order to develop ethical representations that, while painful to engage, tell meaningful stories that tackle important social issues, inspire historical empathy, and support social justice education.

Notes

1. Lonnie G. Bunch, "Fueled by Passion: The Valentine Museum and Its Richmond History Project," in *Ideas and Images: Developing Interpretive History Exhibits*, ed. Kenneth L. Ames, Barbara Franco, and L. Thomas Frye (Nashville, TN: American State and Local History Association, 1992), 283–312.

2. Jennifer L. Eichstedt and Stephen Small, *Representations of Slavery: Race and Ideology in Southern Plantation Museums* (Washington, DC: Smithsonian Institution Press, 2002).

3. Eric Gable, "Maintaining Boundaries or 'Mainstreaming' Black History in a White Museum," in *Theorizing Museums*, ed. Sharon MacDonald and Gordon Fyfe (Oxford, UK: Blackwell, 1996), 177–202.

4. Julia Rose, "Rethinking Representations of Slave Life at Historical Plantation Museums: Towards a Commemorative Museum Pedagogy" (PhD diss., Louisiana State University, 2006), 20.

5. Ibid., 365–41.

6. See, for example, Eichstedt and Small, *Representations of Slavery*; Paul A. Shackel, *Memory in Black and White: Race, Commemoration, and the Post-Bellum Landscape* (Walnut Creek, CA:

Altamira Press, 2003); Max van Balgooy, ed., *Interpreting African American History and Culture at Museums and Historic Sites* (Lanham, MD: Rowman & Littlefield, 2015).

7. Julia Rose, "Melancholia to Mourning: Commemorative Representations of Slave Dwellings at South Louisiana Historical Plantations," *Journal of Curriculum Theorizing* 31, no. 3 (2005): 61–78; Julia Rose, "Preserving Southern Feminism: The Veiled Nexus of Race, Class and Gender at Louisiana Historical Plantation Home Sites," *Taboo: The Journal of Culture and Education* 8, no. 1 (2004): 57–75; and Julia Rose, "Collective Memories and the Changing Representations of American Slavery," *Journal of Museum Education* 29, nos. 2 & 3 (2004): 26–31.

8. Katherine D. Kane, "Institutional Change at Northern Historic Sites: Telling Slavery's Story in the Land of Abolition," in *Interpreting Slavery at Museums and Historic Sites*, ed. Kristin Gallas and James DeWolfe Perry (Lanham, MD: Rowman & Littlefield, 2015), 47–60.

9. See John Michael Vlach, *Back of the Big House: The Architecture of Plantation Slavery* (Chapel Hill: University of North Carolina Press, 1993).

10. Additional museums and historical sites that specifically interpret slavery as part of their mission that opened since 1990 include the African American River Road Museum in Donaldson, Louisiana, and Whitney Plantation in Gramercy, Louisiana.

11. Mary Ann Sternberg, "Sustaining Evergreen: Preserving a 250-Year-Old Sugar Plantation," *Preservation: The National Trust for Historic Preservation* 65, no. 2 (2013): 19–25.

12. Louisiana Department of Culture, Recreation and Tourism, "A Story Like No Other: African American Heritage Trail," May 1, 2015, http://www.astorylikenoother.com.

13. Lois Bannon, Martha Yancy Carr, and Gwen Edwards, *Magnolia Mound: A Louisiana River Plantation* (Baton Rouge, LA: Pelican, 1984).

14. Catherine Clinton, *The Plantation Mistress: Woman's World in the Old South* (New York: Pantheon Books, 1982).

15. Eugene D. Genovese, *Roll, Jordan, Roll: The World the Slaves Made* (New York: Vintage Books, 1972).

16. See Clinton, *The Plantation Mistress*.

17. See Drew G. Faust, *Mothers of Invention: Women of the Slaveholding South in the American Civil War* (New York: Random House, 1996); and William Pinar, *The Gender of Racial Politics and Violence in America: Lynching, Prison Rape, and the Crisis of Masculinity* (New York: Peter Lang, 2001).

18. Chris Weedon, *Feminism, Theory and the Politics of Difference* (Oxford, UK: Blackwell Publishers, 2000).

19. Rose, "Preserving Southern Feminism."

20. See David W. Blight, *Race and Reunion: The Civil War in American Memory* (Cambridge, MA: Harvard University Press, 2001); Michael Kammen, *Mystic Chords of Memory: The Transformation of Tradition in American Culture* (New York: Alfred A. Knopf, 1991); Drew G. Faust, *The Creation of Confederate Nationalism: Ideology and Identity in the Civil War South* (Baton Rouge: Louisiana State University Press, 1988).

21. Henry A. Giroux, *Postmodernism, Feminism, and Cultural Politics: Redrawing Educational Boundaries* (Albany: State University of New York Press, 1991).

22. Rose, "Rethinking Representations of Slave Life at Historical Plantation Museums," 20.

23. Eichstedt and Small, *Representations of Slavery*, 270.

24. Ibid.

25. Deborah P. Britzman, *Lost Subjects, Contested Objects: Toward a Psychoanalytic Inquiry of Learning* (Albany: State University of New York Press, 1998).

26. Claudia Eppert, "Relearning Questions: Responding to the Ethical Address of Past and Present Others," in *Between Hope and Despair: Pedagogy and the Remembrance of Historical Trauma*, ed. Roger I. Simon, Sharon Rosenberg, and Claudia Eppert (Lanham, MD: Rowman & Littlefield, 2000), 213–46; Claudia Eppert, "Throwing Testimony against the Wall: Reading Relations, Loss, and Responsible/Responsive Learning," in *Difficult Memories: Talk in a (Post) Holocaust Era*, ed. Marla Morris and John Weaver (New York: Peter Lang, 2002), 45–65; Claudia Eppert, "Entertaining History: (Un)Heroic Identifications, Apt Pupils, and an Ethical Imagination," *New German Critique* 86 (Spring–Summer 2002): 71–102; and Claudia Eppert, "Histories Re-imagined, Forgotten and Forgiven: Student Responses to Toni Morrison's *Beloved*," *Changing English* 10, no. 2 (2003): 185–94.

27. Roger I. Simon and Claudia Eppert, "Remembering Obligation: Pedagogy and the Witnessing of Testimony of Historical Trauma," *Canadian Journal of Education* 22, no. 2 (1997): 175–91.

28. Elizabeth Ellsworth, *Teaching Positions: Difference, Pedagogy, and the Power of Address* (New York: Teachers College Press, 1997).

29. Rose, "Rethinking Representations of Slave Life at Historical Plantation Museums," 265–341.

30. Ibid., 421.

31. Ibid., 289.

32. Deborah P. Britzman and Alice Pitt, "Pedagogy in Transferential Time: Casting the Past of Learning in the Presence of Teaching," in *Action as a Living Practice*, ed. Terrance Carson and Dennis Sumara (New York: Peter Lang, 1997), 65–76; Robert C. Bogdan and Sari Knopp Biklen, *Qualitative Research for Education: An Introduction to Theories and Methods*, 3rd ed. (Needham Heights, MA: Allyn & Bacon, 1998); Geoffrey E. Mills, *Action Research: A Guide for the Teacher Researcher* (Upper Saddle River, NJ: Merrill Prentice Hall, 2003).

33. Bunch, "Fueled by Passion."

34. For example, Eichstedt and Small, *Representations of Slavery*.

35. Pamela Maykut and Richard Moorehouse, *Beginning Qualitative Research: A Philosophical and Practical Guide* (London: Routledge Falmer, 1994); and Gery W. Ryan and H. Russell Bernard, "Data Management and Analysis Methods," in *Collecting and Interpreting Qualitative Materials*, ed. Norman K. Denzin and Yvonna S. Lincoln (Thousand Oaks, CA: Sage, 2003), 256–309. ·

36. Rose, "Rethinking Representations of Slave Life at Historical Plantation Museums," 141.

37. Ibid., 142.

38. Ibid.

39. Ibid., 149.

40. Ibid., 153.

41. Ibid., 150.

42. Ibid., 180.

43. Britzman, *Lost Subjects*, 113.

44. Rose, "Rethinking Representations of Slave Life at Historical Plantation Museums," 180.

45. Ibid.

46. Ibid.

47. Ibid.

48. Ibid., 163.

49. Ibid., 176.

50. Ibid., 176, 223.

51. Ibid., 188.

52. Ibid.

53. Shoshana Felman, "Education and Crisis, or the Vicissitudes of Teaching," in *Testimony: Crisis of Witnessing in Literature, Psychoanalysis and History*, ed. Shoshana Felman and Dori Laub (New York: Routledge, 1992), 47–56.

54. Eppert, "Throwing Testimony against the Wall."

55. Ibid.

56. Eichstedt and Small, *Representations of Slavery*.

57. BREC's Magnolia Mound Plantation, "About Magnolia Mound Plantation," June 1, 2015, http://www.brec.org/index.cfm/park/detail/112.

58. BREC's Magnolia Mound Plantation, "Tour Training Manual" (Unpublished Notebooks, Baton Rouge, LA, 2009), 2.

59. Kane, "Institutional Change at Northern Historic Sites," 48.

CHAPTER 6

Toward a Commemorative Museum Pedagogy

Introduction

OMMEMORATIVE MUSEUM Pedagogy is a sensitive and workable approach for history workers to consider as they take on the challenges of representing and interpreting difficult histories. Based on my research on interpreting difficult histories and my current thinking, a viable CMP includes five elements:

1. Recognition of a history as a difficult history. The critical assessment of the impact the historical event(s) had on people and what the history potentially means to present-day learners.
2. Allowance for the dynamics of the 5Rs. Recognize learners' learning crises and learners' abilities to work through their losses in learning.
3. Use of the three building blocks to develop ethical representations: the Face, the Real, and the Narrative. Emphasize the personhood of the historical individuals and groups; critically research historical content to include multiple perspectives; identify an interpretation baseline from which stories and dialogs can stem.
4. Provision for safe and respectful environments in which learners can engage in learning difficult histories, conditions that allow for ongoing dialogs, learners' growing self-awareness through introspective and reflective considerations, emotional support, emotional and intellectual resources, and boundaries to protect learners from accusations, implicating rhetoric, and from excessive shock.
5. Institutional and history workers' commitments to the challenges to interpreting difficult histories. Commitments include authentic concern and interest in the

history in order to avoid voyeuristic spectacles and exploitive representations, and commitments to do social good and to be empathetic to the historical Others and present-day learners. The commitments that are needed come from the range of history workers who will support, develop, deliver, sustain, and evaluate the historical interpretation.

These five elements of CMP are needed to develop and deliver purposeful, productive, and responsible interpretations of difficult histories, and for history workers and visitors to learn about difficult histories. Becoming familiar with CMP will help to create a reflective culture within a history organization that will support the time and resources needed to sensitively interpret difficult histories. The following five sections briefly expand on these five elements and rely on the information presented in the preceding chapters. The 5Rs and the three building blocks discussed in detail in the earlier chapters are the core of CMP. These five elements along with the 5Rs and the three building blocks provide the basis for effective implementation of CMP. They form a comprehensive approach to answering the two driving questions posed at the beginning of this book: 1) What happens when learners grapple with difficult knowledge? and 2) What pedagogical strategies can history workers use to engage learners in learning difficult histories?

The finishing remarks that conclude this chapter center on a discussion about an event that unfolded while I was writing this book. In 2015, the nation was embroiled in a national conversation about the meanings of Confederate statues and symbols on display in public spaces in the nation's cities and towns. I discuss how this event illustrates well the need for CMP to interpret difficult histories and the important role historians are called upon to address difficult histories in our daily lives and for the future. Finally, I offer closing thoughts to encourage history workers to take on the challenges of interpreting difficult histories, which will continuously be needed to better understand how the lived experiences of Others are meaningful today.

Recognizing a History as a Difficult History

At the end of the millennium, culture critic Andreas Huyssen explains that the structuring of our lives was increasingly subjected to new kinds of pressures. Memories of the twentieth century, Huyssen says, confront us with a unique history of genocide and mass destruction that mars attempts to glorify the past.[1] "After experiences of World War I and the Great Depression, of Stalinism, Nazism, and genocide on an unprecedented scale, after the trials of decolonization and histories of atrocities and repression they have brought to our consciousness, the view of Western modernity and its promises has darkened considerably within the West itself."[2]

Now well into the twenty-first century, history workers' rising sense of responsibility to examine history through painful remembrances, coupled with the increasing demands of the public's interest in histories of the oppressed, has led to the need for sensitive pedagogical strategies to interpret difficult histories. Today, we more readily recognize that most histories carry with them events of tragedy, injustice, subjugation, and violence.

History workers are increasingly more aware that every effort to recall a history often carries with it ties to duplicity, forgetting, and silencing. In addition, more and more history workers realize that, for every learner of history, there stands the possibility that a history recalled will be tied to his or her conscious memory and can challenge long-held identities. Interpreting difficult history demands from history workers a highly cognizant stance. History workers' abilities to recognize difficult histories and the psychological impact those histories likely will have on learners will improve the quality of the learners' public history experiences and increase the impact the recalled history can have for social good and on society more broadly.

While many history workers today have allowed their work to help shape our society's moral concerns for memory, these efforts are increasingly supported by the public's twenty-first-century anxieties over our destabilizing identities that have been shaken and awakened, in part, by globalization and the effects of cultural technology. Our twenty-first-century sensibilities are giving rise to such concepts as "the empathetic museum" and to public history organizations such as the International Coalition of Sites of Conscience. At the close of the twentieth century, museologists, including Lois Silverman[3] and Richard Sandell,[4] demonstrated the changing role for museums from discretely cultural institutions to agents for social equity. A role for difficult histories in how history organizations do their work is helping to propel a paradigm shift in how we use history to not just singularly honor the past, but to also more inclusively and critically recall the past in order to inform how we live. For example, history organizations can influence legislative policy and inform public education.

Difficult histories can be stories of tragedy, suffering, or injustice. Because they are stories that are laced with ribbons of emotion that are intertwined with traumatic experiences that we can never fully know, history workers must allow their historical interpretations to be fluid and open to expansion and revision. Recognizing a history as a difficult history means history workers' take a position toward a history that is never dismissive or indifferent to the possibilities that Others suffered. The responsibility of interpreting history, therefore, demands that history workers approach their work with a sense of purpose and inquiry in knowing that past lives matter. This responsibility is shaped with a commitment to thoroughness, inclusiveness, and open-mindedness. As discussed in chapter 3, a learner's passion for ignorance is a form of resistance; it is a way of refusing to recognize how Others were affected by the historical events. Such resistances can and must be sensitively addressed as part of the implementation of CMP.

When the aspects of a history that can make it difficult are recognized, the work of revising interpretations or expanding historical representations is at risk of that disagreeable accusation, which is sometimes pointed at history workers, of "rewriting history." Brushing history against the grain, as discussed in earlier chapters, is necessarily a critical practice to dig more deeply into memory to discover the Real and to more inclusively develop the Faces that were part of the difficult history. Interpreting difficult histories is necessarily a critical endeavor, one that is open to new information, new perspectives, and questions. As new information and artifacts surface, history workers need to remain continually sensitive to the possibilities that the new information can revive old or trigger new, possible resistances. Learners will likely resist changes to long-held understandings, the painful memories, and the tough stories. Because difficult histories are regularly challenged and shaped by the instability of memories and are subject to the eventuality of newly found evidence and testimonials, history workers must anticipate controversy and not allow complacency or the easing of tensions to diminish the purpose of their historical interpretations.

A collection of life-size bronze figures of enslaved children face visitors inside a restored plantation church at Whitney Plantation, Gramercy, Louisiana. Photograph by author.

When is a difficult history difficult? Likely, always. While some of the stories and images related to particular difficult histories can become familiar or they can seem too distant to the learners' conscious world, the ethical responses to commemorate the suffering of others should nevertheless not diminish. It is part of the history workers' task to develop representations and interpretations that continuously demonstrate how a history is relevant and why the learner should care about the history in the present and for the future. Movements toward greater cultural understanding are avenues to broadening education and communication, which require support from local and national cultural and educational institutions. As integral members of a global society, history organizations therefore have a responsibility to interpret and represent the harmonious and the difficult, and often, controversial histories.

Interpretations of difficult histories are useful for society as well as for individual learners. Unjust social practices, including racism and sexism, can be questioned and examined through interpretations of difficult histories. Learners' resistances to difficult histories demonstrate that social change happens slowly, and rarely happens in an orderly fashion. Change unfolds with receptive starts and resistive retrenchments. There are debates and tensions. The influence difficult histories have on change occurs on the macro level through proclamations by civic leaders, and also on the micro level, through shifts in understanding by everyday people. Learning about difficult histories is almost always met with a measure of resistance, which might be passive or active, and can be mournful or even melancholic.

By commemorating and interpreting difficult histories, history organizations can contribute powerful content to the collective narrative, effectively demonstrating that difficult histories matter in the present. And to that purpose, museums and history organizations must take risks to represent difficult histories, even when the histories are uncomfortable and even painful to recall. Historical representations of difficult histories have the power to awaken a passion in learners by asking them to look at history from multiple viewpoints, viewpoints that can reveal the struggles for a more just and compassionate moral order.

Allowance for the Dynamics of the 5Rs: Loss in Learning

A second critical element for implementing CMP is the allowance for the dynamics of the 5Rs to emerge for learners, explained in detail in chapter 3. CMP recognizes that learning difficult knowledge is a kind of learning to live with internal losses. History workers and visitors who are grappling with difficult histories need to work through the difficult knowledge in a process of mourning their internal losses in a sensitive and supportive environment. When difficult history is too much to bear, learners will resist engaging with the content that is too painful to hear, read, or view. However, controversy and tension are necessary to encourage social justice. History professor James McWilliams explains, "Every major breakthrough in the history of human thought has required thinkers to risk rejecting the existing understanding of truth, grapple with doubt, and make mistakes—many of them humiliating—before finding answers."[5]

Difficult histories are admittedly uncomfortable and even shocking, which means history workers are challenged to assist their audiences to work through their resistances in order to connect learners productively to the histories. A learning objective for learners who are faced with learning a difficult history is to be empathically moved by the history in order to want to know more and to be able to envision how the history is meaningful today.

History workers prepared to interpret difficult histories recognize how learners struggle to learn difficult histories. Learners show their responses to difficult histories through spoken words and by physical actions. The environment that encourages learning through the 5Rs (reception, resistance, repetition, reflection, and reconsideration) is shaped by a respectful and perceptive culture within the history organization or museum. To allow for the learners to work through their resistances and their personal learning crises, history workers can strategically use the 5Rs to prepare and train staff, design accommodating exhibits, and plan flexible time schedules.

Staff training for CMP is needed for all the history workers in an organization, including educators, curators, administrators, exhibit designers, volunteers, and frontline workers, because everyone has a part in developing and delivering the interpretations of the difficult histories. The team of history workers who are collectively working to address the demands to ethically represent difficult histories should be trained on how the 5Rs are part of the learning process. In addition, history workers should be trained to anticipate learners' resistances in order to support the learners who need to work through those resistances.

An approach to train history workers to use CMP includes explaining the concept of difficult history and providing examples of the risks and benefits of interpreting difficult history discussed in chapter 2. CMP requires history workers to be prepared for the types of challenges and questions that likely will come from learners who are resistant to facing the tragic histories and to newer viewpoints or voices from the past. Establishing a culture for CMP to be effective demands that history workers have opportunities to practice and become competent in detecting learners' responses to difficult knowledge in order to provide learners with time, opportunities, and resources to work through any of the 5Rs. Skills to assist learners include listening and observation skills and techniques to provide suitable resources and information to answer learners' questions.

Adequately trained history workers have invested study time and have made commitments to sensitively interpret the difficult histories. Trained history workers are informed and are well read on the difficult history and related subjects. They have been given opportunities to discuss related topics and current events connected to the difficult history in order to respond to learners and community members in a timely, honest, and informed manner. Trained history workers who are well prepared to deliver a difficult history interpretation are more likely to view their contributions to the history organization with more tenancy, patience, reflection, and empathy.

Exhibit and program designs that allow for the dynamics of the 5Rs will include strategies that can accommodate the variety of responses learners might express when they are faced with difficult history interpretations. The 5Rs are gradual, nonlinear phases that require ample amounts of time in order for each learner to make sense of the difficult history. As described in more detail in chapter 3, exhibits and programs that include an orientation or introductory information that explain that the interpretation could be upsetting or even shocking will help learners shape their expectations. Subsequently, pacing the interpretation format so that learners have opportunities to repeat or revisit information and reflect on content and concepts is also an important component to CMP interpretation designs. Flexibility is another key characteristic of exhibit and program designs that allow for learners' unpredictable needs to work through the difficult knowledge. Time frames and options for interactions within galleries or discussions, for example, need to be flexible in order to allow for the multitude of ways learners can proceed through and among the 5Rs. A CMP strategy includes opportunities for learners to express their reactions and feelings about the difficult history during and after each presentation.

Front-end evaluations can be especially useful in planning the time frames needed for program and exhibit components. Such visitor research results can help history workers plan comfortable amounts of time and fitting spaces to support learners. Administrative staff and board members also need opportunities and time to become familiar with the difficult history and be made aware of the many possible controversies tied to the history. History workers need time to work through the difficult knowledge in order to fully appreciate why the history organization is interpreting the history in a particular way and to be prepared to recognize possible visitors' and communities' responses.

Interpreting difficult histories with CMP includes opportunities to involve community members and experts in planning and in implementing exhibits and programs. An excellent example of involving community leaders and experts in interpreting difficult histories comes from the Missouri History Museum. Melanie Adams, director of Community Education and Events, organizes "Talking Circles," which are public events to view and discuss films, books, and current events, and neighborhood discussion panels led by experts in the field and by community leaders to explore difficult histories and pressing social issues.

Allowing for the dynamics of the 5Rs also means history workers are open to discovering the conflicts and voids in their interpretations. History workers and visitors will notice, question, and evaluate what is it about these histories that makes them so painful to confront. History workers will be adaptable and willing to actively address ongoing developments and learners' demands to know more. CMP is a means for teaching history as stories we live with, stories that are tied to our sense of limits and possibilities, hopes and fears, and identities and differences. CMP opens up interpretations of difficult histories to compel us to confront stories within ourselves that reveal to us how we are historically and socially in the present.[6]

The Three Building Blocks

CMP provides a recursive culture within an organization that is committed to interpreting a difficult history. History workers who use CMP to recall difficult history are continually asking how the stories can be told to serve productive ends, why are we telling these stories now, and how they are relevant to today's audiences. Recursive thinking involves reflective conversations and ongoing introspective consideration about how the team of history workers are approaching and representing the difficult histories. History workers who are invested in CMP are open to reflective conversations that regularly ask, "What are we thinking now about this difficult history?" History workers who are charged with researching and developing historical interpretations for difficult histories need to be critically self-aware that the historical representations, while purposeful, are also powerful enough to move learners and have the potential to weigh heavily on audiences' emotions, and stir and even trigger controversy.

CMP is simultaneously a pedagogy that addresses how learners engage in learning difficult histories and is also an approach for developing ethical representations for difficult histories. The pedagogy and approach intersect with the three building blocks for developing ethical representations explained in chapter 4, "the Face, the Real, and the Narrative." Purposeful historical interpretations reach into the historical trove of Real evidence to describe the Faces of historical Others in order to tell stories through Narratives that, while upsetting and uncomfortable, can move learners to care about the oppression and injustices suffered.

The intersections of the 5Rs and the three building blocks become more and more apparent as learners increasingly realize what the historical traumas and horrors mean to the learners and to society. History workers should express their personal anxieties and not repress them. In a training setting or program planning meeting, for example, history workers can describe their hesitations and concerns about the risks of interpreting difficult histories in order to work through their resistances and to address their concerns about how to responsibly interpret the history.

History workers' concerns and apprehension can arise when they are collecting and identifying the Real artifacts and writing the Narratives to develop the Faces that are necessary to interpret a difficult history. The process to develop representations of suffering requires history workers to use Real content. The research process to select the Real content, for example, can involve history workers reading testimonies and bearing witness to tragedies though film, interviews, and other mediums. History workers' sensitivities, no doubt, are heightened, and their concerns about taking on the responsibilities of teaching these stories can be overwhelming, and thus workers can show resistance. In the development process and in the delivery process, history workers are continuously assessing and finding an ethical balance for the representations between respecting the present-day learners' understanding of the world and remaining respectful of the historical Others' suffering.

While historical representations use a mix of the Real, the Face, and the Narrative to inform and move learners, history workers are also contemplating how much is too much horror such that learners will shut down. Similarly, how little is so little content that learners are not moved to care about the suffering of the historical Others? History workers who are effectively using CMP will reflectively examine and identify the potential risks of developing representations that can be shocking or overwhelming by considering how the learners will respond when in each of the 5Rs. History workers are trained to reflectively ask themselves, Does this historical representation hurt someone? How will learners receive the representation, and what about the representation might arouse learners' resistance and engagement? What opportunities or tools are in place for learners to look longer and to read copy or listen for information a second or third time? Is there a venue for learners to reflect on the representation, alone or with others? Are there formats for learners to reconsider their initial resistances or to express their ideas or to find more information? History workers can use the 5Rs as a rubric to regularly reexamine the representations and interpretations.

Implementation of CMP includes sufficient time and resources to allow for recursive consideration by history workers throughout the development and implementation of historical interpretations. For example, history workers can reflect on the representations by using focus groups, and formative evaluations and later summative evaluations, to assess whether the representations support or diminish the social justice aims of the larger interpretation project. CMP can provide a culture within the history organization that allows for time and resources to readdress those representations that are otherwise not supporting learners or are not moving learners toward empathetic responses.

Examples of the Intersections of the Three Building Blocks with the 5Rs

The Face

Developing the Face is central to ethical representations of difficult histories, and yet the closer the learner approaches understanding the personhood of the historical Other who suffered, the harder the Others' stories become to learn. Learners' resistances to difficult histories are compounded by the complexity of the Others' lives and their suffering, and yet without knowing those historical relationships and suffering, the learner is less likely to be moved by the history of the Others' traumas. As illustrated by the history workers at Magnolia Mound Plantation (MMP) discussed in chapter 5, single-dimensional representations of slaves, such as the name of an enslaved individual or a job title, were more easily learned by history workers than were the stories about the enslaved families and the slaves' relationships to the plantation community, which were too much to bear. Given time to repeat the enslaved families' histories and the history of the plantation community, history workers at MMP were able to reflect on and reconsider the meanings of the slaves' lives to the historical plantation and then were able to continue to learn the more complex multidimensional representations of the plantation community.

The Real

Reception to learning difficult histories is augmented by learners' trust that the Real content used in historical representations is genuine. The Real images, artifacts, landscapes, and voices from the difficult histories encourage learners' reception to engage in learning about the difficult histories. The power and allure of authentic and genuine materials can be inviting, and can excite and motivate learners to be receptive to the historical interpretations.

The Real can also be overwhelming or intimidating when learners recognize the Real represents the pain of the historical Others that the learner cannot bear to know. The Real can then incite learners' resistance. Consider the young, teenaged student at MMP who refused to enter the slave cabin exhibit and cried out to her fellow classmates, "That's not me. I am not going in there!"[7]

A CMP culture of recursive reflection that is embedded in a history organization will support history workers' determinations about what knowledge is of most worth for developing a particular historical representation. The Real content that the history workers use to illustrate the suffering of historical Others must be defensible. The Real materials that are selected must also be relevant and deliberate in order to productively address the purpose for recalling the particular history. For example, history workers can ask experts, and relevant community members, whether the social justice aims are being addressed through a particular selection of Real content. History workers can also question and study the Real content to authenticate its ties to the difficult history and to gauge the value the Real content brings to a representation.

Brushing history against the grain includes history workers assessing the validity of a representation, and then the history workers move forward asking themselves, focus groups, experts, and even visitors questions about whose voices or what Real evidence might be missing or what tone or perspectives might be angling an argument or interpretation.

Resistance to the Real, however, is also a learning response when the difficult knowledge is too much for the learner to bear. In resistive learning moments, when learners challenge an interpretation or question the authenticity of a representation, the learner is unable, at least at first, to accept the history interpretation. Such resistance, which is often audible through learners' questions, objections, and challenges to the accuracy or authenticity of the Real, are those learning moments when the learner's internal understandings of truth are in jeopardy. Loss in learning can be detected by history workers who hear visitors' challenges to the Real content on display. History workers need to be sensitive to detecting learners' resistances to the Real content, as discussed in chapter 3. Resistance detected in response to the Real content is always significant to the history workers because, in these instances, learners are being asked to bear witness to traumatic events and are at risk of being overwhelmed. History workers who apply CMP are patient and give visitors sufficient time and support to work through their resistances to the difficult knowledge. History workers who apply CMP are also open to listening to visitors' points of view and always open to revising their historical representations with new vetted ideas and new Real evidence.

The Narrative

"No photographs allowed! You can now come in. You should know that there are 8,000 bodies in the catacombs. Remember, no photographs allowed. For three Euros you can buy the booklet of postcards. You may come in." That was the announcement yelled out to the small crowd waiting to enter the Capuchin Catacombs of Palermo, Sicily, in 2015. The visitors, who included me, were gathered at the front entrance and were not sure what to expect when they descended the stairs that led them toward the place where death was on display. Why are the corpses stored here, and why are there eight thousand? Without explanations or descriptions (i.e., narratives), the presentation was reduced to a massive spectacle of human death. The lack of information forced visitors to wonder about the corpses on display. I was in the crowd, one of many visitors who wandered about, and soon asked, "Why am I here?" Without the history of the catacombs and the stories about the entombed people, the encounter was voyeuristic.

Narratives tie together the Faces and the Real content to inform learners and to move learners to empathize with the suffering of the historical Others. The catacombs in Palermo do not tell a difficult history. The history of the Capuchin Catacombs of Palermo tells the story of a historic site where priests, monks, and wealthy Sicilians, over several centuries, paid to be interred as a respectable and privileged option for entombment. Compare the meagerness of the description of the catacombs to the narrated tour of the historical out-door courtyard in Vienna that was described in chapter 2. In 2008, as fellow tourists and I stood in the massive courtyard where once Adolf Hitler proclaimed his leadership of the Nazi Party to thousands of Austrians, we listened to the detailed narrative given by our tour guide that infused the historic space with the significance of the difficult history of fascism and genocide.

Research to identify the Real and to prepare historical Narratives should be organized with a defensible and tractable baseline history. While notions of "factual" history are al-ways open to question, history workers can effectively use an agreed-upon baseline history to build more and more complex representations. The baseline history can help learners follow the sequence of historical events and genealogies of historical individuals or groups, and then be better prepared to attempt to reconstruct the multiple relationships within a history and to the present. Difficult histories are hard, in part, because of the sorrow and pain they recall. Keeping multiple relationships within a history organized can aid learners in following the stories more clearly. A chronological record, for example, can be a useful tool to keep track of the many historical groups, individuals, and events.

The narrative shapes the learners' receptiveness to the learning encounters by provid-ing informative, well-documented, provocative, and relevant information about historical representations. Narratives can direct learners' attention and encourage learners to repeat and reflect on the difficult knowledge. Questions and facilitated and spontaneous dialogs are also part of narratives, which can guide lines of inquiry and encourage learners to work through the knowledge that is painful.

Provide Safe and Respectful Environments

A fourth element for an effective CMP approach is the provision of safe and respectful learning environments. Safety in the context of learning environments reaches beyond se-curity guards, cameras, and satchel checks. While many history organizations have security protocols to keep everyone in the facility safe from physical harm, history organizations that interpret difficult histories also should provide empathetic environments that enhance and encourage learners to work through their resistances, feelings of shock, or emotional distress. Emotionally, safe learning environments provide space, time, resources, and personnel to support learners, especially when difficult knowledge threatens the learners' psychological well-being. History workers at CMP-ready environments are prepared for learners to re-ceive, resist, repeat, reflect, and reconsider the difficult history being interpreted at their site.

History workers who develop interpretations for difficult histories must also design empathetic learning environments. The structure for CMP-ready learning environments provides conditions that will allow for ongoing dialogs and that encourage learners' growing self-awareness through introspective and reflective activities. History workers should be aware of the risks of learning a difficult history and therefore can better anticipate learners' reactions. As the learners work through their feelings of loss or express their internal learning crises, history workers should be prepared to offer emotional support, opportunities for repetition and reflection, and information resources. Empathetic learning environments are designed with socially conscientious boundaries that are respectful of varying points of view and resist righteous and implicating rhetoric.

History workers using CMP should develop ethical representations that respectfully commemorate the experiences of historically oppressed populations and their descendants who live among us today. This moral imperative is directly tied to how history workers engage learners. For example, respectful history workers are aware of how a historical representation can potentially impact learners. Perceptivity of, and sensitivity to, learners' anxieties can be well addressed by workers who allow the 5Rs to unfold for learners because the knowledge is difficult. History workers' sensitivity includes their acknowledgment of how some historical representations can offend or shame learners. The Nazi flag, unearthed human remains, and images of sacred clerics are examples of images that can be offensive. Safe and respectful learning environments do not lightly make use of such symbols. Foul language that was used in a historical event, racial slurs, or hateful sentiments buried in the Real can be offensive, and resisted not only because those terms are difficult knowledge but because those terms today are hateful, unkind, repulsive, or immoral. Sensitivity in designing safe learning environments is precautionary and requires history workers to be well informed about how the difficult history and its symbols have evolved and relate to present-day social issues.

Learning about difficult histories and being moved to care about difficult histories are ongoing experiences. History workers who use CMP appreciate the impact that difficult histories can possibly have on learners even after the history learning experience at the museum or site has ended. CMP allows for uncertainty and the unpredictable, nonlinear, and recursive nature of learning.[8] Likely after visitors leave the site where they learned about a difficult history, the learners will continue to reconsider the meanings of the exhibits and programs they experienced. The extended learning, and the possible ongoing working through of difficult knowledge, can take place over days, weeks, or months after a site visit. History workers will take into consideration ways to support learners' needs to reflect and reconsider the meanings of difficult knowledge by providing provocative questions, dialogs, and useful resources to consider after their visit.

History workers who are planning an interpretation for a difficult history or who are history-workers-in-training can organize themselves into a team, not that different from an exhibit planning team or storyboard development committee, in order to think through their own resistances and to consider how the planned representations of a difficult history will impact visitors.[9] The team approach can include curators, educators, administrators, board members, community stakeholders, and frontline workers, who will, in large part, make the decisions about how the difficult history representations are shared with the public. When history workers feel invested in the research and planning activities for the historical interpretations, their passion and enthusiasm will be reflected in the quality of their tour writing, exhibit designing, and program planning. Team members' willingness to negotiate the varied meanings of the difficult history will be central to the team's ongoing efforts for creating safe and respectful learning environments in order for the visitors' learning to productively unfold.

Education theorist William Doll contends that "through dialogue, conversation and public inquiry,"[10] learners can reflect on their tacit understandings in order to bring them to consciousness, and in the process, the learners can work through their understandings. In this light, CMP is a group dynamic in which history workers share, critique, and possibly change their personal understandings of their historical site's meanings and then recognize how their changed understandings can then inform the eventual interpretation and even the broader meanings of their site.

Safe and respectful learning environments cannot be rushed. CMP allows for both a creative group dynamic and a personally transformative learning dynamic in order to enable history workers to articulate the stories they will use to represent a difficult history. Because an effective implementation of CMP likely involves weeks and months, history workers must be resolved to stay the course. My case study described in chapter 5 shows that expanding slave life representations at a specific site required extended amounts of time.[11] Doll explains that a curriculum grows over time, and with learners' engagement, "the richer the curriculum, the more points of intersection, the more connections constructed, and the deeper the meaning."[12] CMP allows history workers and visitors time to work through the 5Rs and to go deeper into memory, multiplying the possible points of connection and potentially deepening the history workers' understandings of the historical individuals' lives.

Empathetic environments are also needed for history workers in their team meetings, outside conversations, and in group and individual research and planning efforts. CMP provides for safe and respectful spaces where history workers are able to continuously explore and reflect on ways to interpret the difficult history. Pilot tours with new content and effects, for example, need to allow for tough moments when new narratives that include language or implications that are uncomfortable or misunderstood can be critiqued and discussed. Tensions that emerge have the potential to generate productive and creative thinking to ethically represent the complexities of historical characters' lived experiences and suffering.

Commitment to Interpreting Difficult History

A fifth element for implementing CMP is composed of the commitments made by the breadth of people who make up a history organization, including board members, staff members, volunteers, partners, and community stakeholders. The decision to interpret a difficult history at first glance might look like a curatorial decision, but in actuality, the commitments that are needed come from the range of history workers who will support, develop, deliver, sustain, and evaluate the historical interpretation.

Starting on the journey to responsibly interpret difficult histories and to justly commemorate the memory of those who suffered, or taking on the challenges of expanding historical interpretation that includes a difficult history, entails commitments from history workers individually, from their institutions, and from their supporting communities. History workers committed to the challenge must recognize the sensitive and disruptive nature of the project. History workers need to recognize that interpreting difficult history can be a long, mournful, stressful, challenging, and unpredictable process.

The history organization's leadership must commit to being informed about, and sensitive to, the ties their partners and stakeholders have to the particular difficult history. Likewise, the organization's leadership needs to be aware and responsive to the ties their staff and volunteers have to the difficult history. The planning committee for the Oklahoma City Memorial and Museum, described in chapter 4, opened the planning process to a broad variety of stakeholders in Oklahoma City by asking partners and stakeholders to provide multiple perspectives of the tragedies of the 1995 Oklahoma City bombing.

The history organization's board and administration need to commit adequate time and resources in order for history workers to pursue the necessary research and planning. Scheduling and timing requires commitments from all levels of workers. Allowing time for researchers to dig into the archives and collections or to conduct interviews with survivors, descendants, or stakeholders all take considerable time. History workers who are in training (e.g., tour guides) will need time to learn the difficult history and will need time to work through their individual resistances. They will need time to practice the skills for assisting learners to repeat and reflect on the difficult history.

A history organization committed to using CMP will seek out supporters, partners, and stakeholders who are passionate and concerned about the meanings of a difficult history. Commitments also come in the form of financial investments to fund the work of interpreting difficult histories. CMP requires a commitment from history workers to be rigorous and reflective in their work in developing historical representations. The decision to interpret a difficult history should not be an isolated mandate, nor should it be a quick reaction to supporters, advocates, or critics. The history organization's decision to formally embark on the project should evolve from their mission and be based on a passion and commitment to commemorate a difficult history as an instructive opportunity for communities. The passion and commitments need to be felt throughout the range of history workers tasked with the project. Sustaining the development of the project and sustaining the life of the historical interpretation delivered through exhibits, historical sites, publications, and other public history venues require dedication to the multitude of commitments.

An institution that is committed to interpreting difficult histories is obligated to take into consideration the high risks of interpreting difficult histories. As discussed in chapter 2, the unique nature of difficult histories includes the risks of controversy, learner resistance, and the chances of overwhelming or upsetting learners. History workers who are reticent to commit to taking on the responsibility of interpreting a difficult history must eventually come to terms with, and be in support of, the history organization's decision in order to responsibly do the work of interpretation.

A history organization that adopts a CMP culture is committed to developing interpretations that are productive and meaningful to society. Institutions and their history workers who are committed to using CMP agree to take on the responsibilities to recall difficult histories with compassion, sensitivity, and dedication to social justice education. History workers who use CMP are committed to be responsive to learners' needs and to be respectful to the lives the history touches now and in the past.

Paul H. Williams contends that memorial museums, which commemorate historical events of mass trauma, oppression, and violence, invariably cherish public education, as they are geared toward foiling the future of comparable tragedies.[13] Williams asks history workers to carefully look at the mission statements of memorial museums to see how those institutions are committed to supporting moral lessons.[14] Memorial museums relate to the past remembrances as advocates for future vigilance. He explains that history workers are compelled to consider how visitors, a collective of culturally diverse learners, might respond to the call for "moral education" and how they will work through the interpretations concerning personal culpability, victimhood, and the call for visitors' responsibility to the future.[15]

An example of history workers' long-term commitment to CMP to interpret difficult histories is well illustrated at the Center for Human and Civil Rights in Atlanta, Georgia, which opened in 2014. Ambassador Andrew Young and civil rights activist Evelyn Lowery approached Atlanta mayor Shirley Franklin in 2002 with the idea to create a center that would commemorate Atlanta's unique civil rights history and use it as a foundation for dialog and learning about contemporary human rights issues. The effort gained broad-based corporate and community support to become a history organization for educating visitors on the ties between the American civil rights movement and contemporary human rights issues around the world. The difficult histories of civil rights in Atlanta served as the baseline history from which histories of oppression and social injustices from around the globe are explained and used to explore human and civil rights today.

Commitments to maintaining an atmosphere of respect among history workers and visitors within a history organization and toward the historical individuals are imperative for CMP to unfold. History workers and visitors need to be willing to look within themselves and at each other with compassion, and to openly acknowledge and respect individuals' attachments to a difficult history, historical site, or historical collection.

The Center for Human and Civil Rights purposefully created safe spaces for visitors to work through the difficult knowledge and the complexities of the social and political relationships in exhibits and live programs. Asking hard questions is encouraged and supported. The curators have created the learning experiences about difficult histories to inspire and empower visitors to participate in ongoing dialogs about human rights in their communities during and after their museum visit.

History workers' commitment to use CMP includes their willingness to experience emotional discomfort. History workers might enter the project with varying degrees of anxiety and feelings of risk they might not be able to articulate. As described in chapter 3, history workers' repressed anxieties can limit the level of engagement history workers might otherwise be willing to devote to their work. A supportive, inclusive, and respectful work environment is necessary for CMP to unfold. Anxiety and feelings of risk can contribute to history workers' resistance to learn about the history or their resistance to interpret the history in ways that the history organization had planned.

It is crucial that history workers who engage visitors in learning about a difficult history feel invested and committed to the interpretation project. CMP engages history workers in responding to historical information and visitors' resistances in ways that empower frontline history workers to feel secure speaking about the history. History workers' commitments to self-reflective study and to the institution's goal to serve the greater good can cultivate a sense of collaboration, community, and collegiality among the history organization's personnel.

History workers need to be committed to continue learning new information about the history, which might still need to become especially meaningful to them, however challenging. As new historical information surfaces, history workers must continue to ask: What do I know about the history that will further enable me to answer "Who suffered?" The depth of the question can lead to the stories not just about the victims, but also about the victims' ancestors and descendants, and those touched by the legacy of the history.

Institutional commitments to social justice education are necessary to nurture empathy among learners. Maia Szalavitz explains that inequality interferes directly with empathy: "[Inequality] creates a greater social distance between the rich and the rest—the less interaction you have with people unlike yourself, the less empathy you tend to have for them."[16] History workers using CMP are committed to pursuing and inspiring historical empathy through their interpretations of difficult histories. CMP culture is woven through with commitments to inspiring empathy to inform, to remember, and to respond.

Finishing Remarks

In the midst of writing the final pages for this book about interpreting difficult histories, the nation became engrossed in an extraordinary and highly relevant conversation. In 2015, the difficult histories of the American Civil War and American slavery were topics being debated, questioned, and explored in the media, museums, historical sites, and around kitchen tables and watercoolers. The conversation was focused on the current symbolic meanings of Confederate flags and statues placed in public spaces. The national conversation was extraordinary because for decades these debates have risen and fallen from public attention, and have been the theme of many legislative and scholarly debates without much concrete disruption to the status quo of the public history artifacts being called into question.

In the summer of 2015, however, the nation was shocked and saddened by the hate crime and murder of nine innocent black Americans gathered in a South Carolina church for bible study. A social media image was soon found of the perpetrator standing with a Confederate flag, which for the last century has represented racism for many Americans. These murders, and a rash of exposed police killings of black citizens around the nation also in 2015, further fueled the long-running debates in cities and towns throughout the nation about racism and the Civil War symbols we live with daily. History workers are trained to recognize that the meanings of historical events evolve and that the symbols from history emerge into, and recede from, collective memory. The meanings of the historical symbols that germinated from the Confederate remembrances of the American Civil War were being questioned and reconsidered. What do these statues and flags mean today, and what did they mean when they were installed in public spaces? What will they mean for the future?

What do we, as Americans, want to do with the public history artifacts from the Civil War and from the Reconstruction era? The question is difficult because it recalls memories of violence and slavery, and raises tensions by increasing attention to the perils of racism in America. History workers were being called into the local and national discussions in town halls and in the media. CMP can provide practical strategies to engage discussants in this important conversation, which can help history workers, policy makers, and citizens reconsider the meanings of the contested artifacts. The elements of CMP can help history workers contribute to a reflective and inclusive culture in which to interpret the historical artifacts—their placement and the difficult histories they stand to recall today.

That summer, the tensions and anxieties raised in the national conversations about this conflicted history, the Civil War and its memorials, reached deeply into personal and regional identities. The passion displayed by Americans who were trying to figure out how to address the call to rearrange the public history landscapes that are dotted with Confederate symbols were causing learning crises for many Americans. Some Americans view the symbols as representing a past plantation society and culture, and others view the symbols as ties to family heritage. Some of today's younger generations, who have not paid attention to the symbols, are overwhelmed by the implications of the racists roots attached to their towns and ancestors, and some older generations are pained by the implications that what they learned in school was actually ambiguous. Other citizens are pained by the reminders and the long-running national complacent responses to the symbols carved in stone and woven into flying flags that are so closely tied to racism, slavery, and violence.

This debate has highlighted further that the role of difficult history representations is accelerating at a vigorous pace. As I discuss in chapter 1, the global movement to address difficult histories is supported with the rise of a more sensitive multicultural global citizenry. A greater breadth of Americans are informed about, and empathize with, the inequalities and injustices imposed on people worldwide, and at home.

An impassioned speech to the state legislature by South Carolina representative Jenny Horne, on July 9, 2015, to remove the Confederate flag from the statehouse grounds ignited multiple calls from around the nation to reconsider the meanings of this historical symbol. One week later a call from New Orleans mayor Mitch Landrieu was broadcast in the media that New Orleans should remove statues of Confederate war heroes and a monument commemorating the White League from public circles. The next week, a call covered by the national press came from the Atlanta NAACP to remove dozens of Confederate monuments on public property and to erase the carved portraits of Confederate leaders from Stone Mountain. The conflicted conversations are reopening with veracity and with a sense of determination about how these historical artifacts matter and whether their role or symbolism has changed over the past century for many Americans. Lloyd Thompson of the New Orleans NAACP explained that readdressing the statue of Confederate general Robert E. Lee, in Lee Circle in downtown New Orleans, will not change the race issue "but at least it will start a conversation."[17]

A CMP approach involves commitments to inspiring and using empathy to inform. Civilization relies on empathy; socially, economically, and even our health depends on empathy. Szalavitz says that the term *emotional empathy* refers to people's tendency to feel moved in response to someone else's pain and distress and to care about the differences in experience. Emotional empathy is foundational for morality. The less empathy communities feel for others, the more inequality will increase in society.[18]

In the summer of 2015, we were having a national discussion about how these Civil War symbols make us feel, what the symbols teach, and how they impact our fellow citizens. The debates about the Confederate flag flown at the South Carolina statehouse were about how this symbol is painful to many Americans and to citizens of the world who are oppressed by racism or had ancestors who were oppressed by slavery and racism. While the conversations about the meanings of Civil War symbols are painful in 2015, these conversations are supported by a more empathetic population base who are able to talk about the implied racism found in the symbols and how the symbols make people feel. The interpretations of the difficult histories are precipitating competing meanings. For some Americans, the symbols prompt feelings of inherited grief, heritage, and lineage, while for other people they prompt feelings of anger, sadness, shame, and fear. The rising partisan considerations for these historical symbols have made these conversations more urgent.

While Civil War history and the history of slavery and racial oppression remain difficult, the opportunities to learn about the histories and to talk about the histories in 2015 appeared to be more accessible and more probable than in decades past. Gauging by the plethora of media reports, Americans were demonstrating that they were feeling empowered to discuss and challenge these historical symbols and other symbols. The nation's 2015 summer response to reevaluating the Confederate statues and flags has been electrifying, even though the historical artifacts, which have long been prominently displayed in public spaces, have been ignored or marginalized for decades. Awareness appears to be replacing complacency.

Many history workers, policy makers, and everyday citizens have suggested that the statues and flags from outdoor public spaces be relocated into museums. Indeed, these items are artifacts that can also be used to teach the difficult histories of war, slavery, and oppression to future generations. But what of the historical landscapes? What about the stories that are now evolving, and will new statues replace the old ones? The place where an artifact was originally installed can be important to the history and significance of the artifact. This is the history workers' project—to make sense of the changing historical landscape. The history workers' challenge is to avoid regenerating the practice of silencing or ignoring yet another history, but rather to develop Faces, find the Real, and write the Narratives to explain and use commemorations to understand the present. The skills honed by history workers are in high demand as the general public and policy makers discuss how the meanings of historical symbols, such as those from the American Civil War and Reconstruction, change.

In this way and for many more conflicted conversations, history workers are playing a major part in implementing social change. The current discussion concerning the public displays of symbols from the Civil War is one of many discussions about difficult histories and the conflicted meanings that are occurring locally, nationally, and internationally. Today's discussions are a harbinger of future discussions about difficult histories that history workers and learners can expect to face and will hopefully work through and embrace for now and for the future. I anticipate that CMP can play a role in ensuring that these difficult histories are not silenced or marginalized because they are too hard to bear. Rather, CMP is available to encourage and enable learners to work through the tough stuff of history sensitively, ethically, productively, and purposefully.

CMP guides history workers to brush history against the grain, to look for multiple perspectives, to ask whether these representations ethically recall the lived experiences of Others. CMP is the pedagogy that asks history workers to question how sharing the stories told through historical representations will change the world for the better. The process of interpreting difficult histories culminates in commemorative representations that are instructive, ethical, sensitive, and meaningful, and include unresolved tensions that reflect the proud, the conflicted, and the complex realities that call learners to care about a better society.

Notes

1. Andreas Huyssen, *Present Pasts: Urban Palimpsests and the Politics of Memory* (Redwood City, CA: Stanford University Press, 2003).
2. Ibid., 25.
3. Lois Silverman, *The Social Work of Museums* (New York: Routledge, 2009).
4. Richard Sandell, ed., *Museums, Society, Inequality* (London: Routledge, 2002).
5. James McWilliams, "The Examined Life: A Meditation on Memory," *American Scholar* (Summer 2015): 23.
6. See Roger I. Simon, *Teaching against the Grain: Texts for a Pedagogy of Possibility* (New York: Bergin & Garvey, 1992); and Julia Rose, "Collective Memories and the Changing Representations of American Slavery," *Journal of Museum Education* 29, nos. 2 & 3 (2004): 26–31.
7. Julia Rose, "Interpreting Difficult Knowledge," *History News* 66, no. 3 (2011): Technical Leaflet #255.
8. See William E. Doll Jr., *A Post-Modern Perspective on Curriculum* (New York: Teachers College Press, 1993).
9. See Timothy Ambrose and Crispin Pain, *Museum Basics* (London: Routledge, 1993).
10. Doll, *A Post-Modern Perspective on Curriculum*, 62.
11. Julia Rose, "Rethinking Representations of Slave Life at Historical Plantation Museums: Towards a Commemorative Museum Pedagogy" (PhD diss., Louisiana State University, 2006).
12. Doll, *A Post-Modern Perspective on Curriculum*, 162.
13. Paul H. Williams, *Memorial Museums: The Global Rush to Commemorate Atrocities* (New York: Berg, 2007), 128.
14. Ibid., 131.
15. Ibid.
16. Maia Szalavitz, "Empathy for the Rest of Us," *Pacific Standard* (July/August 2015): 59.
17. Lloyd Thompson, "Symbol or Statement? History in Public Spaces," Louisiana Public Broadcasting, July 22, 2015, http://lpb.org/index.php/publicsquare/topic/07_15_-_symbol_or_statement_history_in_public_spaces/.
18. Szalavitz, "Empathy," 59.

Bibliography

Abram, Ruth J. "Harnessing the Power of History." In *Museums, Society, Inequality*. Edited by Richard Sandell, 125–41. New York: Routledge, 2002.

Alexander, Jeffrey C. "Toward a Theory of Cultural Trauma." In *Cultural Trauma and Collective Identity*. Edited by Jeffrey C. Alexander, Ron Eyerman, Bernhard Giesen, Neil J. Smelser, and Piotr Sztompka, 1–30. Berkeley: University of California Press, 2004.

Allen, James. *Without Sanctuary: Lynching Photography in America*. Santa Fe, NM: Twin Palms Publishing, 2000.

Bankole, Katherine. "Plantations without Slaves: The Legacy of Louisiana Culture." In *Plantation Society and Race Relations: The Origins of Inequality*. Edited by Thomas J. Durant Jr. and J. David Knottnerus, 93–204. Westport, CT: Praeger, 1999.

Blight, David W. *Race and Reunion: The Civil War in American Memory*. Cambridge, MA: Harvard University Press, 2001.

Boler, Megan. *Feeling Power: Emotions and Education*. New York: Routledge, 1999.

Bonnell, Jennifer, and Roger I. Simon. "'Difficult' Exhibitions and Intimate Encounters." *Museum and Society* 5, no. 2 (2007): 65–85.

Britzman, Deborah P. *Lost Subjects, Contested Objects: Toward a Psychoanalytic Inquiry of Learning*. Albany: State University of New York Press, 1998.

———. "If the Story Cannot End: Deferred Action, Ambivalence, and Difficult Knowledge." In *Between Hope and Despair: Pedagogy and the Remembrance of Historical Trauma*. Edited by Roger I. Simon, Sharon Rosenberg, and Claudia Eppert, 27–58. Lanham, MD: Rowman & Littlefield, 2000.

———. *After-Education: Anna Freud, Melanie Klein, and Psychoanalytic Histories of Learning*. Albany: State University of New York Press, 2003.

Britzman, Deborah P., and Alice J. Pitt. "Pedagogy in Transferential Time: Casting the Past of Learning in the Presence of Teaching." In *Action Research as a Living Practice*. Edited by Terrance Carson and Dennis Sumara, 65–76. New York: Peter Lang, 1997.

Bunch, Lonnie G. "Fueled by Passion: The Valentine Museum and Its Richmond History Project." In *Ideas and Images: Developing Interpretive History Exhibits*. Edited by Kenneth L. Ames, Barbara Franco, and L. Thomas Frye, 283–312. Nashville, TN: American State and Local History Association, 1992.

Caruth, Cathy. *Trauma: Explorations of Memory*. Baltimore, MD: Johns Hopkins University Press, 1995.

Coates, Ta-Nehisi. "The Case for Reparations." *The Atlantic* 313, no. 5 (2014): 54–71.

Coleman Matthews, Christy. "Twenty Years Interpreting African American History: A Colonial Williamsburg Revolution." *History News* 54, no. 2 (1999): 6–11.

Crew, Spencer R., and James E. Sims. "Locating Authenticity: Fragments of a Dialogue." In *Exhibiting Cultures: The Poetics and Politics of Museum Display*. Edited by Ivan Karp and Steven D. Lavine, 159–75. Washington, DC: Smithsonian Institution Press, 1991.

Cuno, James. "What Matters Most: Museums Play a Crucial Role as Humanist Institutions." *Museum* 92, no. 6 (2013): 27–29.

DeGruy, Joy Angela. *Post Traumatic Slave Syndrome: America's Legacy of Enduring Injury and Healing.* Baltimore, MD: Uptone Press, 2005.

Doering, Zahava, Editor. "Remembering and Disremembering in Africa, also Australia, Turkey, Mexico, New York, Prague." *Curator* 55, no. 2 (2012).

———. "Special Issue on Museums and International Human Rights." *Curator* 55, no. 3 (2012).

Doll, William E., Jr. *A Post-Modern Perspective on Curriculum.* New York: Teachers College Press, 1993.

Eichstedt, Jennifer L., and Stephen Small. *Representations of Slavery: Race and Ideology in Southern Plantation Museums.* Washington, DC: Smithsonian Institution, 2002.

Ellsworth, Elizabeth. *Teaching Positions: Difference, Pedagogy, and the Power of Address.* New York: Teachers College Press, 1997.

Eppert, Claudia. "Relearning Questions: Responding to the Ethical Address of Past and Present Others." In *Between Hope and Despair: Pedagogy and the Remembrance of Historical Trauma.* Edited by Roger I. Simon, Sharon Rosenberg, and Claudia Eppert, 213–46. Lanham, MD: Rowman & Littlefield, 2000.

———. "Entertaining History: (Un)Heroic Identifications, Apt Pupils, and an Ethical Imagination." *New German Critique* 86 (Spring/Summer 2002): 71–101.

———. "Throwing Testimony against the Wall: Reading Relations, Loss and Responsible/Responsive Learning." In *Difficult Memories: Talk in a (Post) Holocaust Era.* Edited by Marla Morris and John A. Weaver, 45–65. New York: Peter Lang, 2002.

———. "Histories Re-imagined, Forgotten and Forgiven: Student Responses to Toni Morrison's *Beloved.*" *Changing English* 10, no. 2 (2003): 185–94.

Faust, Drew G. *The Creation of Confederate Nationalism: Ideology and Identity in the Civil War South.* Baton Rouge: Louisiana State University Press, 1988.

———. *Mothers of Invention: Women of the Slaveholding South in the American Civil War.* New York: Random House, 1996.

Felman, Shoshana. *Jacques Lacan and the Adventure of Insight: Psychoanalysis in Contemporary Culture.* Cambridge, MA: Harvard University Press, 1987.

Felman, Shoshana, and Dori Laub, Editors. *Testimony: Crisis of Witnessing in Literature, Psychoanalysis, and History.* New York: Routledge, 1992.

Fennelly, Lawrence. *Effective Physical Security*, 4th ed. Oxford, UK: Butterworth-Heinemann, 2013.

Ferguson, Linda. "Pushing Buttons: Controversial Topics in Museums." *Open Museum Journal* 2006. http://pandora.nla.gov.au/tep/10293.

Fleming, David. "Human Rights Museums: An Overview." *Curator* 55, no. 3 (2002): 251–56.

Foote, Kenneth E. *Shadowed Ground: America's Landscapes of Violence and Tragedy.* Austin: University of Texas Press, 2003.

Freud, Sigmund. *Beyond the Pleasure Principle.* Translated by C. J. M. Hubback. London: The International Psychoanalytical Press, 1922.

———. "Mourning and Melancholia." In *The Standard Edition of the Complete Psychological Works of Sigmund Freud*, Vol. 14. Edited and translated by James Strachey, 243–58. London: Hogarth Press, 1971; Original work published in 1917.

———. "On Narcissism: An Introduction." In *The Standard Edition of the Complete Psychological Works of Sigmund Freud*, Vol. 14. Edited by James Strachey, 73–102. London: Hogarth Press, 1971; Original work published in 1914.

———. *Beyond the Pleasure Principle*. In *The Standard Edition of the Complete Psychological Works of Sigmund Freud*, Vol. 17. Edited and translated by James Strachey, 7–64. London: Hogarth Press, 1974; Original work published in 1920.

Gable, Eric. "Maintaining Boundaries, or 'Mainstreaming' Black History in a White Museum." In *Theorizing Museums*. Edited by Sharon MacDonald and Gordon Fyfe, 177–202. Oxford, UK: Blackwell, 1996.

Gable, Eric, Richard Handler, and Anna Lawson. "On the Uses of Relativism: Fact, Conjecture and Black and White Histories at Colonial Williamsburg." *American Ethnologist* 19, no. 4 (1992): 791–805.

Giroux, Henry A. *Postmodernism, Feminism, and Cultural Politics: Redrawing Educational Boundaries*. Albany: State University of New York Press, 1991.

Gordon, Linda, and Gary Y. Okihiro, Editors. *Impounded: Dorothea Lange and the Censored Images of Japanese American Internment*. New York: W. W. Norton & Company, 2006.

Graft, Conny. "Visitors Are Ready, Are We?" In *Interpreting Slavery at Museums and Historic Sites*. Edited by Kristin Gallas and James DeWolf Perry, 71–84. Lanham, MD: Rowman & Littlefield, 2015.

Greenwald, Alice, Michael Shulan, Tom Hennes, Jake Barton, and David Layman. "The Heart of Memory: Voices from the 9/11 Memorial Museum Formation Experience." *Museum* 93, no. 3 (2014): 26–37.

Halbwachs, Maurice. *Maurice Halbwachs on Collective Memory*. Edited and translated by Lewis A. Coser. Chicago: University of Chicago Press, 1992.

Hinshelwood, R. D. *A Dictionary of Kleinian Thought*. London: Free Association Books, 1991.

Hirsch, Joanne, and Lois Silverman, Editors. *Transforming Practice*. Walnut Creek, CA: Left Coast Press, 2006.

Hobsbawm, Eric, and Terence Ranger, Editors. *The Invention of Tradition*. UK: Cambridge University Press, 1992.

Hooper-Greenhill, Eilean, Editor. *The Educational Role of the Museum*, 2nd ed. London: Routledge. 2002.

Horton, James Oliver, and Lois E. Horton, Editors. *Slavery and Public History: The Tough Stuff of American Memory*. New York: The New Press, 2006.

Huyssen, Andreas. *Twilight Memories: Marking Time in a Culture of Amnesia*. New York: Routledge, 1995.

———. *Present Pasts: Urban Palimpsests and the Politics of Memory*. Redwood City, CA: Stanford University Press, 2003.

Irwin-Zarecka, Iwona. *Frames of Remembrance: The Dynamics of Collective Memory*. New Brunswick, NJ: Transaction, 1994.

Jackson, Antoinette T. *Speaking for the Enslaved*. Walnut Creek, CA: Left Coast Press, 2012.

Jennings, Gretchen, Editor. "The Unexhibitable." *Exhibitionist* 27, no. 2 (2008).

———. "Museums, Memorials, and Sites of Conscience." *Exhibitionist* 30, no. 2 (2011).

Kammen, Michael. *Mystic Chords of Memory: The Transformation of Tradition in American Culture*. New York: Alfred A. Knopf, 1991.

Kane, Katherine D. "Institutional Change at Northern Historic Sites: Telling Slavery's Story in the Land of Abolition." In *Interpreting Slavery at Museums and Historic Sites*. Edited by Kristin Gallas and James DeWolf Perry, 47–60. Lanham, MD: Rowman & Littlefield, 2015.

Kavanagh, Gaynor. "Remembering Ourselves in the Work of Museums: Trauma and the Place of the Personal in the Public." In *Museums, Society, Inequality*. Edited by Richard Sandell, 110–24. London: Routledge 2002.

Kitwood, Tom M. *Concern for Others: A New Psychology of Conscience and Morality*. London: Routledge, 1990.

LaCapra, Dominick. *Writing History, Writing Trauma*. Baltimore, MD: Johns Hopkins University Press, 2001.

Lévinas, Emmanuel. *Ethics and Infinity: Conversations with Philippe Nemo*. Translated by Richard A. Cohen. Pittsburgh, PA: Duquesne University Press, 1985.

Linenthal, Edward T. *Preserving Memory: The Struggle to Create America's Holocaust Museum*. New York: Penguin Group, 1995.

———. *The Unfinished Bombing: Oklahoma City in American Memory*. New York: Oxford University Press, 2001.

Liss, Andrea. *Trespassing through Shadows: Memory, Photography and the Holocaust.* Minneapolis: University of Minnesota Press, 1998.

MacCannell, Dean. *The Ethics of Sightseeing*. Berkeley: University of California Press, 2011.

Maclear, Kyo. *Beclouded Visions: Hiroshima-Nagasaki and the Art of Witness*. Albany: State University of New York Press, 1999.

Mitchell, Juliet, Editor. *The Selected Melanie Klein*. New York: The Free Press, 1986.

Morris, Marla. *Curriculum and the Holocaust: Competing Sites of Memory and Representation*. Mahwah, NJ: Lawrence Erlbaum Associates, 2001.

Nora, Pierre. "Between Memory and History: *Les Lieux de Mémoire*." In *History and Memory in African-American Culture*. Edited by Geneviéve Fabre and Robert O'Meally, 284–300. New York: Oxford University Press, 1996.

Pitt, Alice. "Reading Resistance Analytically: On Making the Self in Women's Studies." In *Dangerous Territories: Struggles for Difference and Equality in Education*. Edited by Leslie G. Roman and Linda Eyre, 127–42. London: Routledge, 1997.

Rose, Julia. "Collective Memories and the Changing Representations of American Slavery." *Journal of Museum Education* 29, nos. 2 & 3 (2004): 26–31.

———. "Preserving Southern Feminism: The Veiled Nexus of Race, Class and Gender at Louisiana Historical Plantation Home Sites." *Taboo: The Journal of Culture and Education* 8, no. 1 (2004): 57–75.

———. "Melancholia to Mourning: Commemorative Representations of Slave Dwellings at South Louisiana Historical Plantations." *Journal of Curriculum Theorizing* 31, no. 3 (2005): 61–78.

———. "Rethinking Representations of Slave Life at Historical Plantation Museums: Towards a Commemorative Museum Pedagogy." PhD dissertation, Louisiana State University, 2006.

———. "Corroborating Knowledge: Curriculum Theory Can Inform Museum Education Practice." In *From Periphery to Center: Art Museum Education in the 21st Century*. Edited by Pat Villeneuve, 49–57. Reston, VA: Art Education Association, 2007.

———. "Interpreting Difficult Knowledge." Technical Leaflet #255 in *History News* 66, no. 3 (Summer 2011).

———. "Three Building Blocks for Developing Ethical Representations of Difficult Histories." Technical Leaflet #264 in *History News* 68, no. 4 (Autumn 2013).

Rothfeld, Lawrence, Editor. *Unsettling "Sensation": Arts-Policy Lessons from the Brooklyn Museum of Art Controversy*. New Brunswick, NJ: Rutgers University, 2001.

Salverson, Julie. "Anxiety and Contact in Attending to a Play about Land Mines." In *Between Hope and Despair: Pedagogy and the Remembrance of Historical Trauma*. Edited by Roger I.

Simon, Sharon Rosenberg, and Claudia Eppert, 59–74. Lanham, MD: Rowman & Little-field, 2000.

Sandell, Richard, Editor. *Museums, Society, Inequality*. London: Routledge, 2002.

Sandell, Richard, and Eithne Nightingale, Editors. *Museums, Equality and Social Justice*. London: Routledge, 2012.

Schweber, Simone. "Notes on Passing as an Insider at the US Holocaust Memorial Museum." In *Beyond Pedagogy: Reconsidering the Public Purpose of Museums*. Edited by Brenda Trofanenko and Avner Segall, 107–13. Rotterdam, The Netherlands: Sense Publishers, 2014.

Shackel, Paul A. *Memory in Black and White: Race, Commemoration, and the Post-Bellum Landscape*. Walnut Creek, CA: Altamira Press, 2003.

Silverman, Lois. "The Therapeutic Potential of Museums as Pathways of Inclusion." In *Museums, Society, Inequality*. Edited by Richard Sandell, 69–83. London: Routledge, 2002.

———. *The Social Work of Museums*. New York: Routledge, 2009.

Simon, Nina. *The Participatory Museum*. San Francisco, CA: Museum 2.0, 2010.

Simon, Roger I. *Teaching against the Grain*. New York: Bergin & Garvey, 1992.

Simon, Roger I., and Claudia Eppert. "Remembering Obligation: Pedagogy and the Witnessing of Testimony of Historical Trauma." *Canadian Journal of Education* 22, no. 2 (1997): 175–91.

Simpson, David. *9/11: The Culture of Commemoration*. Chicago: University of Chicago Press, 2006.

Sontag, Susan. *Regarding the Pain of Others*. New York: Farrar, Straus and Giroux, 2003.

Terdiman, Richard. *Present Past: Modernity and the Memory of Crisis*. Ithaca, NY: Cornell University Press, 1993.

Todd, Sharon. "Guilt, Suffering and Responsibility." *Journal of Philosophy of Education* 35, no. 4 (2001): 597–614.

Trouillot, Michel-Rolph. *Silencing the Past: Power and the Production of History*. Boston, MA: Beacon Press, 1995.

Tyson, Amy, and Azie Mira Dungey. "'Ask a Slave' and Interpreting Race on Pubic History's Front Line: Interview with Azie Mira Dungey." *The Public Historian* 36, no. 1 (2014): 36–60.

van Balgooy, Max, Editor. *Interpreting African American History and Culture at Museums and Historic Sites*. Lanham, MD: Rowman & Littlefield, 2015.

van Mensch, Léontine Meijer. "New Challenges, New Priorities: Analyzing Ethical Dilemmas from a Stakeholder's Perspective in the Netherlands." *Museum Management and Curatorship* 26, no. 2 (2011): 113–28.

Williams, Paul H. *Memorial Museums: The Global Rush to Commemorate Atrocities*. New York: Berg, 2007.

Winks, Robin. "Sites of Shame: Disgraceful Episodes from Our Past Should Be Included in the Park System to Present a Complete Picture of Our History." In *National Parks* LXVIII, no. 68 (Spring 1994): 22–23.

Young, James E. *The Texture of Memory: Holocaust Memorials and Meaning*. New Haven, CT: Yale University Press, 1993.

Zelizer, Barbie. *Remembering to Forget: Holocaust Memory through the Camera's Eye*. Chicago: University of Chicago Press, 1998.

Zolberg, Vera. "Museums as Contested Sites of Remembrance: The Enola Gay Affair." In *Theorizing Museums*. Edited by Sharon MacDonald and Gordon Fyfe, 69–82. Oxford, UK: Blackwell, 1996.

Index

war, WWI, 11, 170

war, WWII, xi, xvi, 9, 11, 14, 37, 40, 43–42, 44, 46, 57, 69, 87, 103, 105, 106, 110, 124

warning (s), 20, 60, 61, 81, 116, 124, 174

Washington, D.C., 9, 27, 43, 45, 54, 56, 57, 82, 87, 136

Washington, George, 71, 83

weapon(s), xi, 38, 44

Weil, Stephen E., 13

welcome, 127, 128, 129, 130, 158

well-being, 35, 39, 116, 179

West Africa(n), 45, 113, 114, 145

West Baton Rouge Museum, 46, 70, 80, 88, 95, 118, 127, 140

White League, 185

Whitney Plantation, 87, 110, 172

wickedness, 28, 61

Williams, Paul H., 8, 9, 14, 38, 45, 53, 54, 55, 182–183

Wilson, Fred, 112, 113

Winks, Robin, 40

wish(es), 15, 27, 73, 74, 75, 77, 124, 157

Without Sanctuary, exhibit, 115–116

witness(es), 2, 11, 13, 16, 27, 29, 30, 32, 34, 37, 38, 40, 41, 55, 57, 62, 85, 90, 94, 109, 111, 116, 121, 125, 147

witness, bear witness, 16, 29, 37, 36, 38, 50, 63, 81, 85, 162, 176, 178

witness, crisis of witnessing, 85, 94

witness, eyewitness, 36

witness, retrospective witnessing, 109

witness, secondary witness, 94

Wojnarowicz, David, 120

work(ing) through, xii, 5, 6, 34, 51, 55, 57, 72, 74–78, 79, 83, 84, 86, 87, 91, 92, 94, 95, 119, 126, 127, 129, 130, 144, 145, 154, 156, 157, 158, 160, 162, 169, 173, 174, 175, 176, 178, 179, 180, 181, 182, 183, 186

World Trade Center, ix, 11, 14, 47, 87

wound(s), emotional, 116, 144

wound(s), physical, 70

Wowereit, Klaus, 41

wrestle, 9, 11

Yerkovich, Sally, 120, 121

Young, Andrew, 183

Young, David, 128

YouTube, 83

Zelizer, Barbie 18

Zolberg, Vera 43

About the Author

Julia Rose is presently the director of the West Baton Rouge Museum. Her primary research interests focus on interpreting difficult histories and documenting historical enslaved plantation communities for museum interpretations. Currently, Rose also serves as the chairman for the Council for the American Association for State and Local History, and is a board member for the Louisiana Association of Museums. She received her PhD from Louisiana State University, a master of arts in teaching from George Washington University, and a bachelor of arts in fine art and education from State University of New York at Albany. She has held curator positions at the Columbia Historical Society in Washington, D.C.; Children's Museum of Oak Ridge; East Tennessee Historical Society; and Magnolia Mound Plantation, and was a faculty member in the master of arts in Museum Studies Program at Southern University at New Orleans. In addition, Rose is presently an adjunct faculty member at Louisiana State University, where she teaches museum studies.